MARVEL

MARVEL ENTERTAINMENT

X-MEN '92

LILAPALOOZA

**CHRIS SIMS &
CHAD BOWERS**
WRITERS

ALTI FIRMANSYAH WITH
CORY HAMSCHER [#10]
ARTISTS

MATT MILLA WITH
DONO SÁNCHEZ-ALMARA
[#6 & #10]
COLOR ARTISTS

VC's TRAVIS LANHAM
LETTERER

DAVID NAKAYAMA
COVER ART

HEATHER ANTOS & JORDAN D. WHITE
EDITORS

X-MEN CREATED BY
STAN LEE & JACK KIRBY

COLLECTION EDITOR: JENNIFER GRÜNWALD
ASSISTANT EDITOR: CAITLIN O'CONNELL
ASSOCIATE MANAGING EDITOR: KATERI WOODY
EDITOR, SPECIAL PROJECTS: MARK D. BEAZLEY
VP PRODUCTION & SPECIAL PROJECTS: JEFF YOUNGQUIST
SVP PRINT, SALES & MARKETING: DAVID GABRIEL
BOOK DESIGNER: JAY BOWEN

EDITOR IN CHIEF: AXEL ALONSO
CHIEF CREATIVE OFFICER: JOE QUESADA
PRESIDENT: DAN BUCKLEY
EXECUTIVE PRODUCER: ALAN FINE

X-MEN '92 VOL. 2: LILAPALOOZA. Contains material originally published in magazine form as X-MEN '92 #6-10. First printing 2017. ISBN# 978-1-302-90050-2. Published by MARVEL WORLDWIDE, INC., a subsidiary of MARVEL ENTERTAINMENT, LLC. OFFICE OF PUBLICATION: 135 West 50th Street, New York, NY 10020. Copyright © 2017 MARVEL No similarity between any of the names, characters, persons, and/or institutions in this magazine with those of any living or dead person or institution is intended, and any such similarity which may exist is purely coincidental. **Printed in Canada.** DAN BUCKLEY, President, Marvel Entertainment; JOE QUESADA, Chief Creative Officer; TOM BREVOORT, SVP of Publishing; DAVID BOGART, SVP of Business Affairs & Operations, Publishing & Partnership; C.B. CEBULSKI, VP of Brand Management & Development, Asia; DAVID GABRIEL, SVP of Sales & Marketing, Publishing; JEFF YOUNGQUIST, VP of Production & Special Projects; DAN CARR, Executive Director of Publishing Technology; ALEX MORALES, Director of Publishing Operations; SUSAN CRESPI, Production Manager; STAN LEE, Chairman Emeritus. For information regarding advertising in Marvel Comics or on Marvel.com, please contact Vit DeBellis, Integrated Sales Manager, at vdebellis@marvel.com. For Marvel subscription inquiries, please call 888-511-5480. **Manufactured between 2/24/2017 and 3/28/2017 by SOLISCO PRINTERS, SCOTT, QC, CANADA.**

10 9 8 7 6 5 4 3 2 1

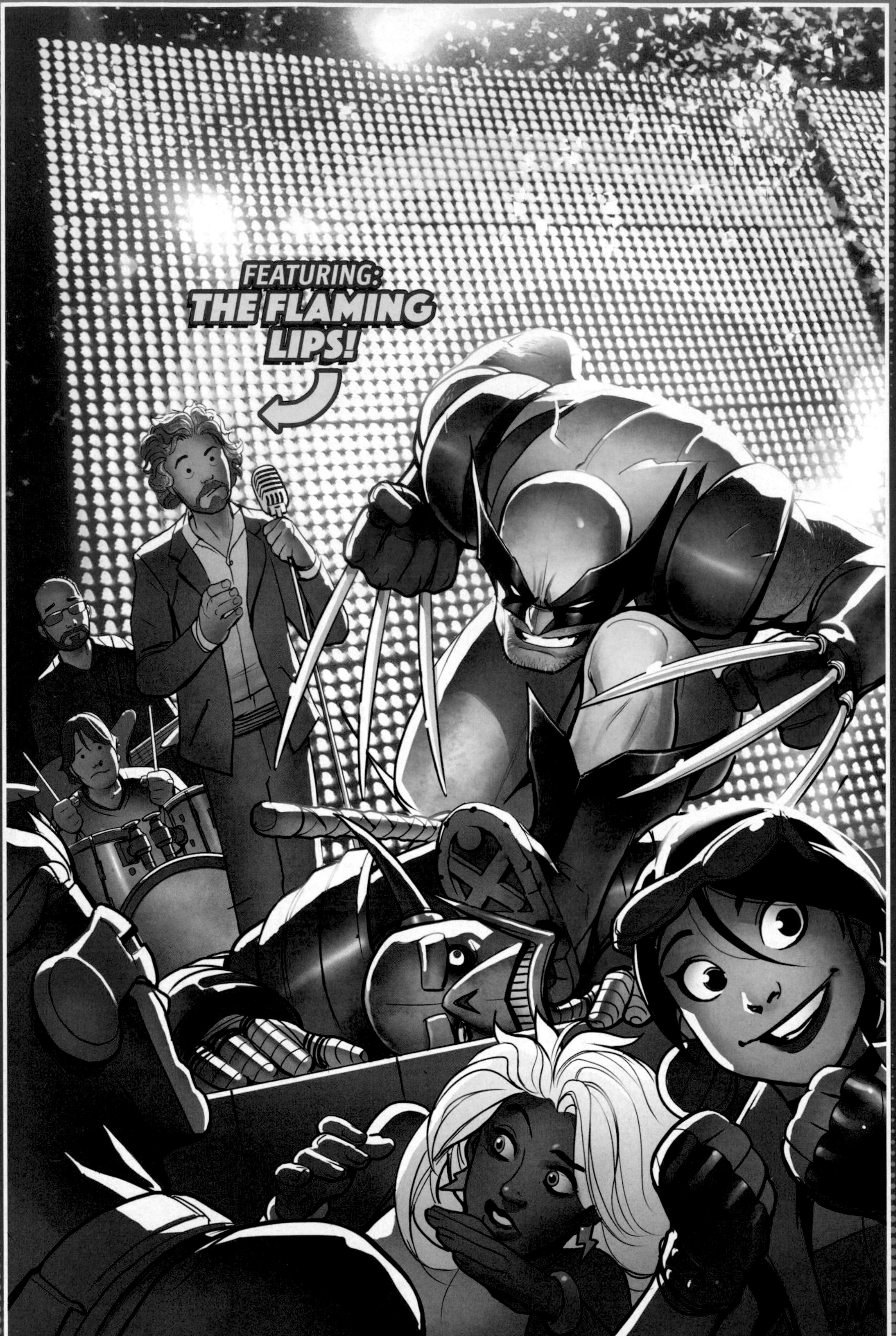
FEATURING:
THE FLAMING LIPS!

6

LILAPALOOZA

A CELEBRATION OF MUTANTS & MUSIC

Headlining Act:

LILA CHENEY

Performing With:

DAZZLER
THE FLAMING LIPS
ACE
THE TOADIES
SUGAR KANE
CATS LAUGHING
RICK JONES AND THE NEGA BAND
THE SKRULL BEATLES

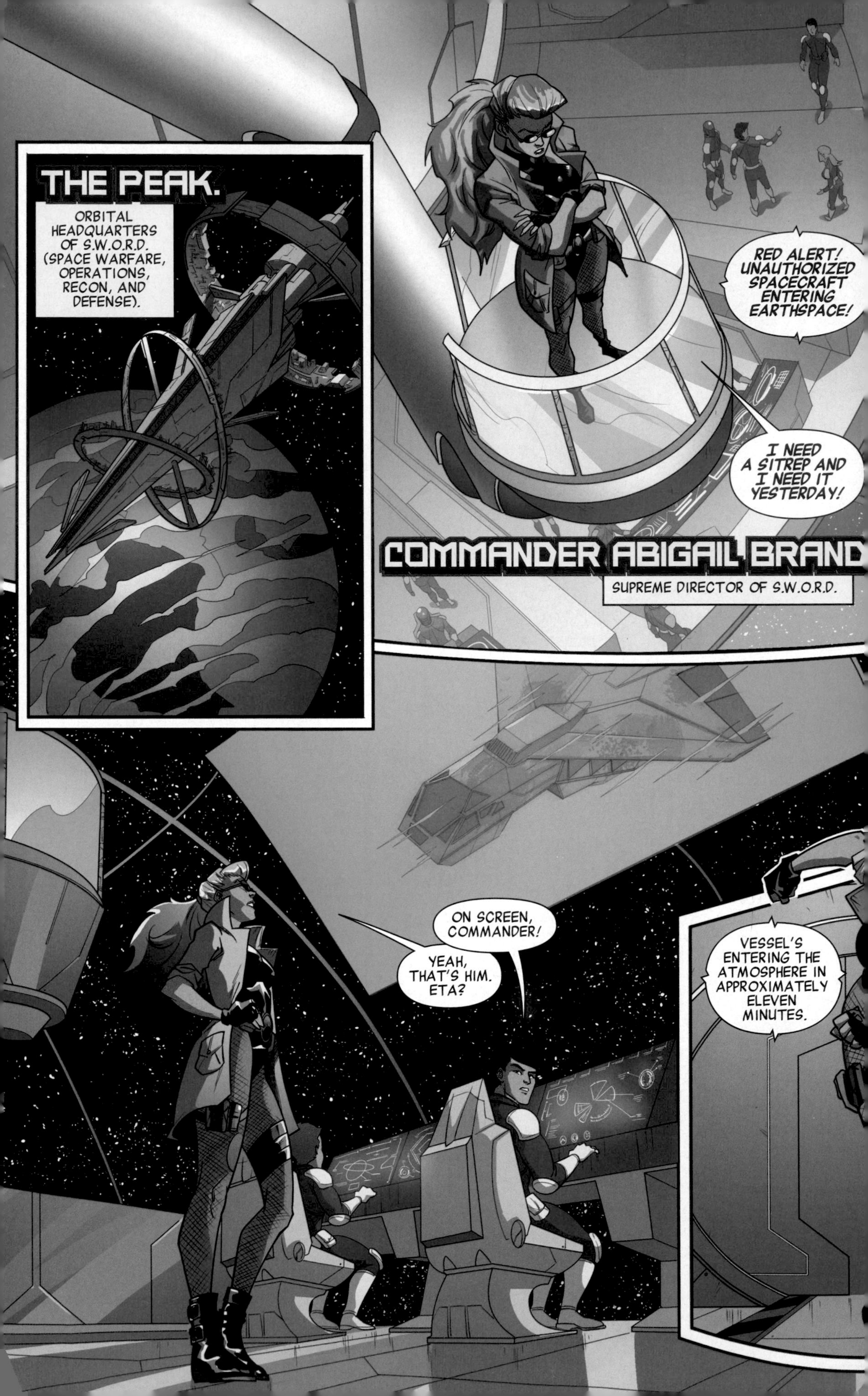
THE PEAK.
ORBITAL HEADQUARTERS OF S.W.O.R.D. (SPACE WARFARE, OPERATIONS, RECON, AND DEFENSE).
RED ALERT! UNAUTHORIZED SPACECRAFT ENTERING EARTHSPACE!
I NEED A SITREP AND I NEED IT YESTERDAY!
COMMANDER ABIGAIL BRAND
SUPREME DIRECTOR OF S.W.O.R.D.
ON SCREEN, COMMANDER!
YEAH, THAT'S HIM. ETA?
VESSEL'S ENTERING THE ATMOSPHERE IN APPROXIMATELY ELEVEN MINUTES.

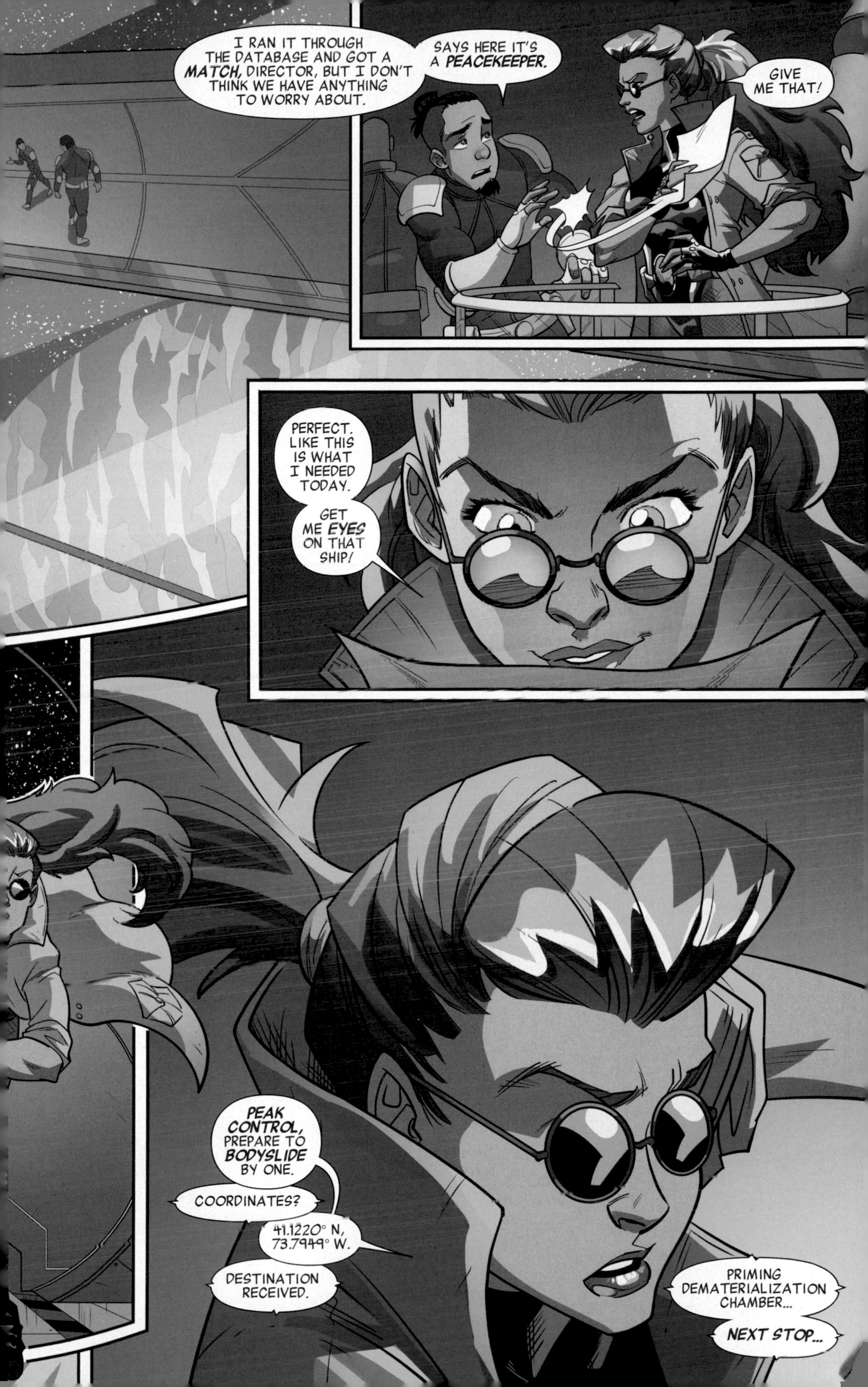
I RAN IT THROUGH THE DATABASE AND GOT A MATCH, DIRECTOR, BUT I DON'T THINK WE HAVE ANYTHING TO WORRY ABOUT.
SAYS HERE IT'S A PEACEKEEPER.
GIVE ME THAT!
PERFECT. LIKE THIS IS WHAT I NEEDED TODAY.
GET ME EYES ON THAT SHIP!
PEAK CONTROL, PREPARE TO BODYSLIDE BY ONE.
COORDINATES?
41.1220° N, 73.7949° W.
DESTINATION RECEIVED.
PRIMING DEMATERIALIZATION CHAMBER...
NEXT STOP...

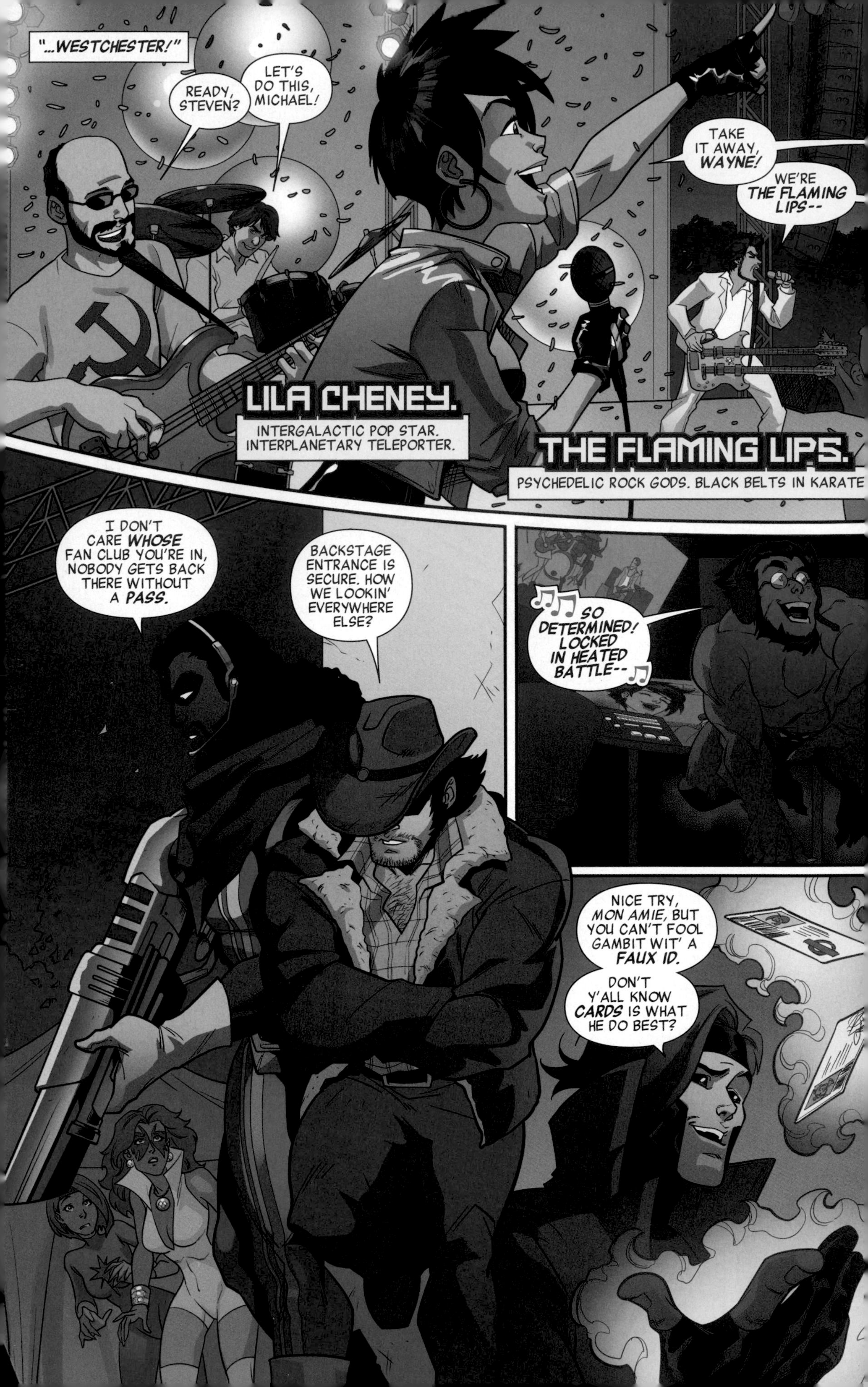
"...WESTCHESTER!"
READY, STEVEN?
LET'S DO THIS, MICHAEL!
TAKE IT AWAY, WAYNE!
WE'RE THE FLAMING LIPS--
LILA CHENEY.
INTERGALACTIC POP STAR. INTERPLANETARY TELEPORTER.
THE FLAMING LIPS.
PSYCHEDELIC ROCK GODS. BLACK BELTS IN KARATE
I DON'T CARE WHOSE FAN CLUB YOU'RE IN, NOBODY GETS BACK THERE WITHOUT A PASS.
BACKSTAGE ENTRANCE IS SECURE. HOW WE LOOKIN' EVERYWHERE ELSE?
SO DETERMINED! LOCKED IN HEATED BATTLE--
NICE TRY, MON AMIE, BUT YOU CAN'T FOOL GAMBIT WIT' A FAUX ID.
DON'T Y'ALL KNOW CARDS IS WHAT HE DO BEST?

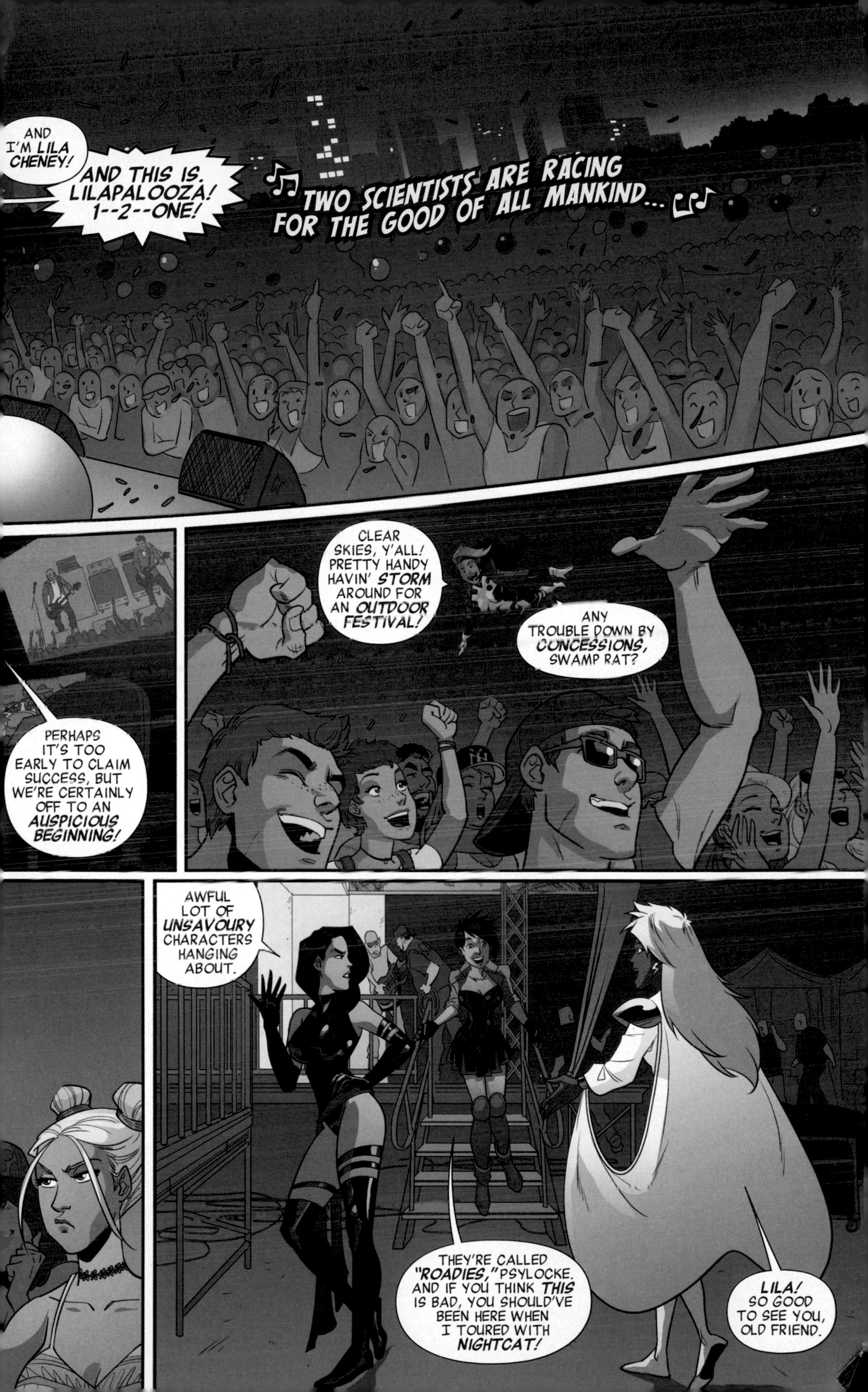

AND I'M LILA CHENEY!
AND THIS IS. LILAPALOOZA! 1--2--ONE!
TWO SCIENTISTS ARE RACING FOR THE GOOD OF ALL MANKIND...
CLEAR SKIES, Y'ALL! PRETTY HANDY HAVIN' STORM AROUND FOR AN OUTDOOR FESTIVAL!
ANY TROUBLE DOWN BY CONCESSIONS, SWAMP RAT?
PERHAPS IT'S TOO EARLY TO CLAIM SUCCESS, BUT WE'RE CERTAINLY OFF TO AN AUSPICIOUS BEGINNING!
AWFUL LOT OF UNSAVOURY CHARACTERS HANGING ABOUT.
THEY'RE CALLED "ROADIES," PSYLOCKE. AND IF YOU THINK THIS IS BAD, YOU SHOULD'VE BEEN HERE WHEN I TOURED WITH NIGHTCAT!
LILA! SO GOOD TO SEE YOU, OLD FRIEND.

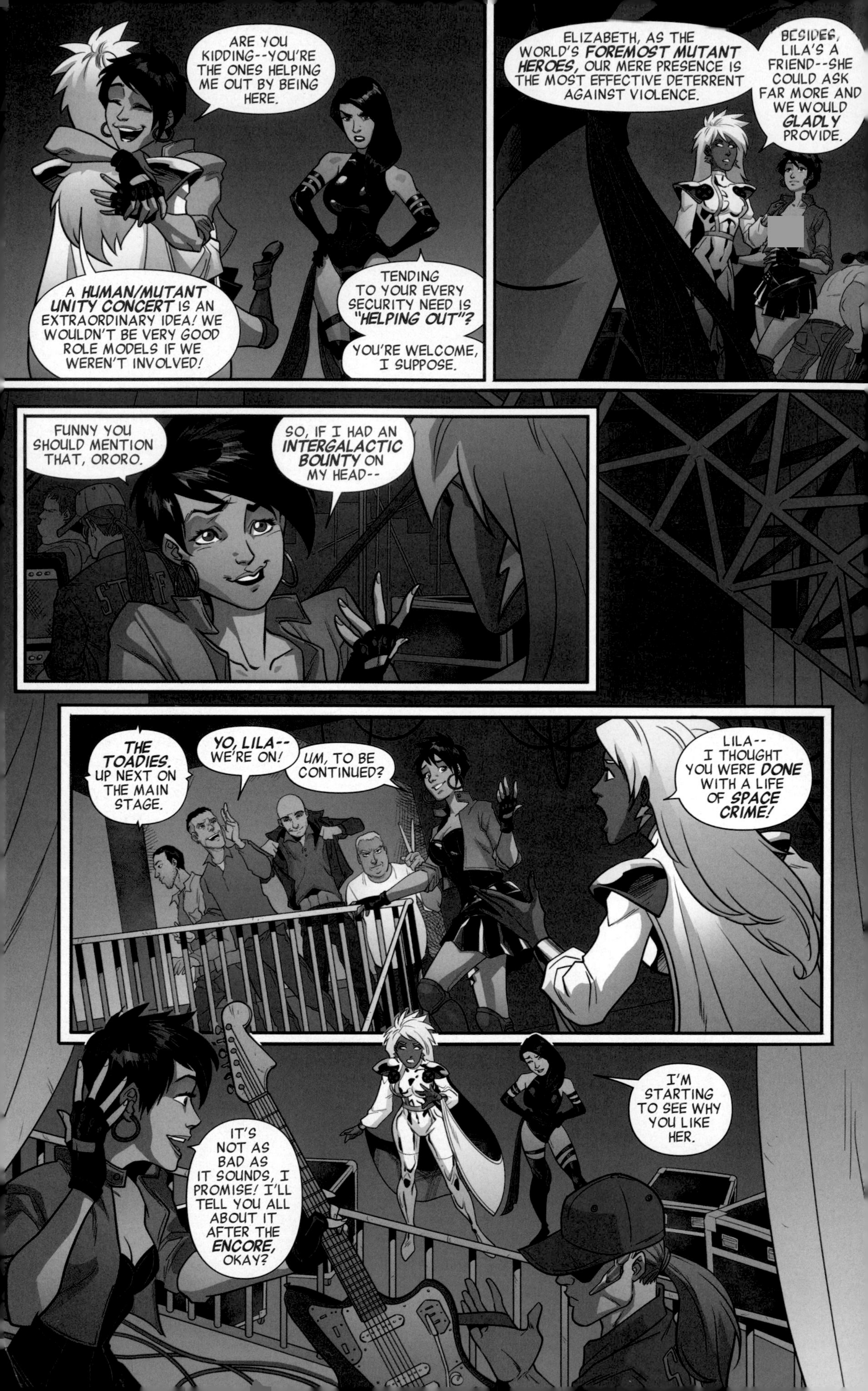
ARE YOU KIDDING--YOU'RE THE ONES HELPING ME OUT BY BEING HERE.
A HUMAN/MUTANT UNITY CONCERT IS AN EXTRAORDINARY IDEA! WE WOULDN'T BE VERY GOOD ROLE MODELS IF WE WEREN'T INVOLVED!
TENDING TO YOUR EVERY SECURITY NEED IS "HELPING OUT"?
YOU'RE WELCOME, I SUPPOSE.
ELIZABETH, AS THE WORLD'S FOREMOST MUTANT HEROES, OUR MERE PRESENCE IS THE MOST EFFECTIVE DETERRENT AGAINST VIOLENCE.
BESIDES, LILA'S A FRIEND--SHE COULD ASK FAR MORE AND WE WOULD GLADLY PROVIDE.
FUNNY YOU SHOULD MENTION THAT, ORORO.
SO, IF I HAD AN INTERGALACTIC BOUNTY ON MY HEAD--
STAFF
THE TOADIES. UP NEXT ON THE MAIN STAGE.
YO, LILA--WE'RE ON!
UM, TO BE CONTINUED?
LILA--I THOUGHT YOU WERE DONE WITH A LIFE OF SPACE CRIME!
IT'S NOT AS BAD AS IT SOUNDS, I PROMISE! I'LL TELL YOU ALL ABOUT IT AFTER THE ENCORE, OKAY?
I'M STARTING TO SEE WHY YOU LIKE HER.

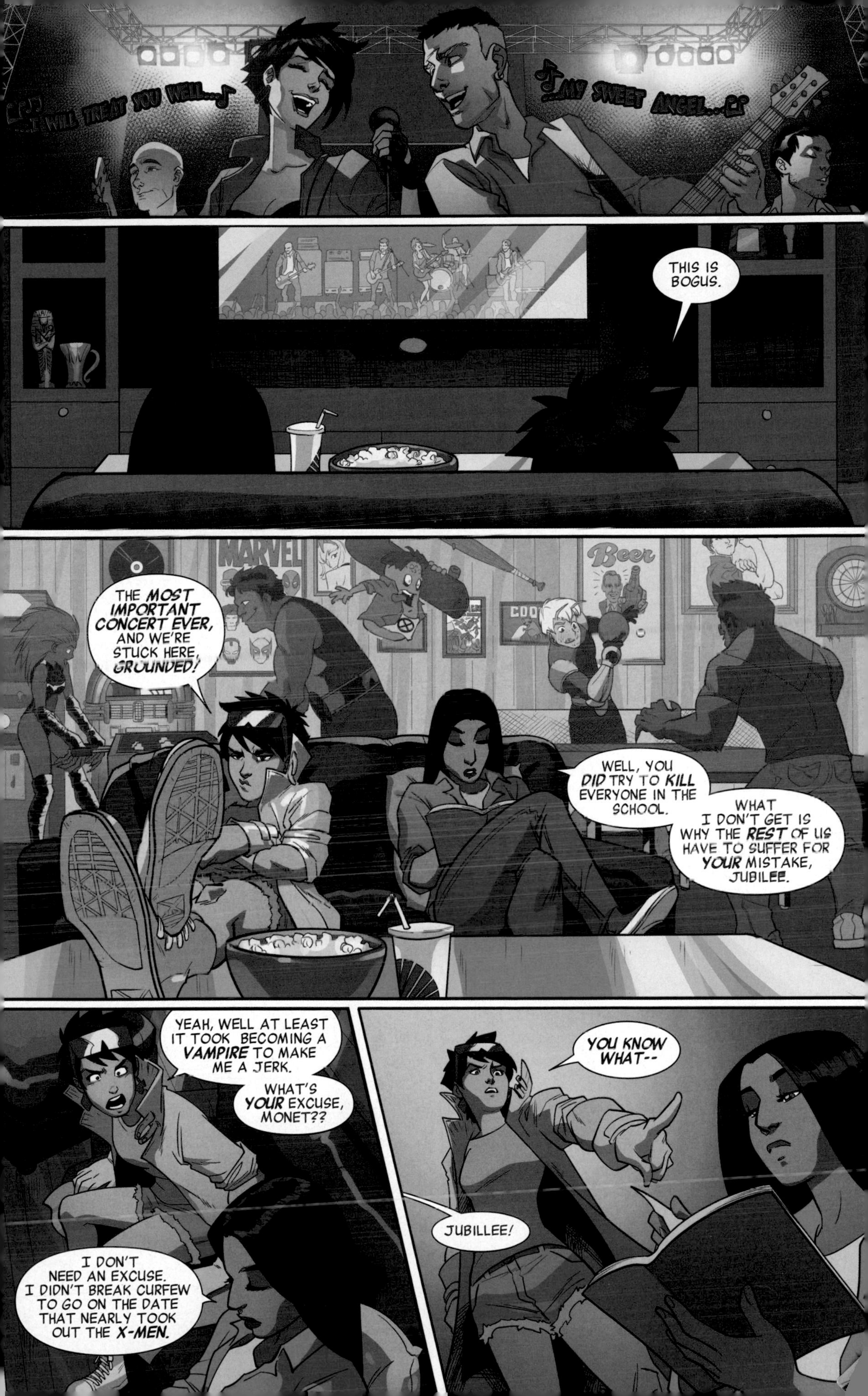

...I WILL TREAT YOU WELL...
...MY SWEET ANGEL...
THIS IS BOGUS.
THE MOST IMPORTANT CONCERT EVER, AND WE'RE STUCK HERE, GROUNDED!
WELL, YOU DID TRY TO KILL EVERYONE IN THE SCHOOL.
WHAT I DON'T GET IS WHY THE REST OF US HAVE TO SUFFER FOR YOUR MISTAKE, JUBILEE.
YEAH, WELL AT LEAST IT TOOK BECOMING A VAMPIRE TO MAKE ME A JERK.
WHAT'S YOUR EXCUSE, MONET??
I DON'T NEED AN EXCUSE. I DIDN'T BREAK CURFEW TO GO ON THE DATE THAT NEARLY TOOK OUT THE X-MEN.
YOU KNOW WHAT--
JUBILLEE!

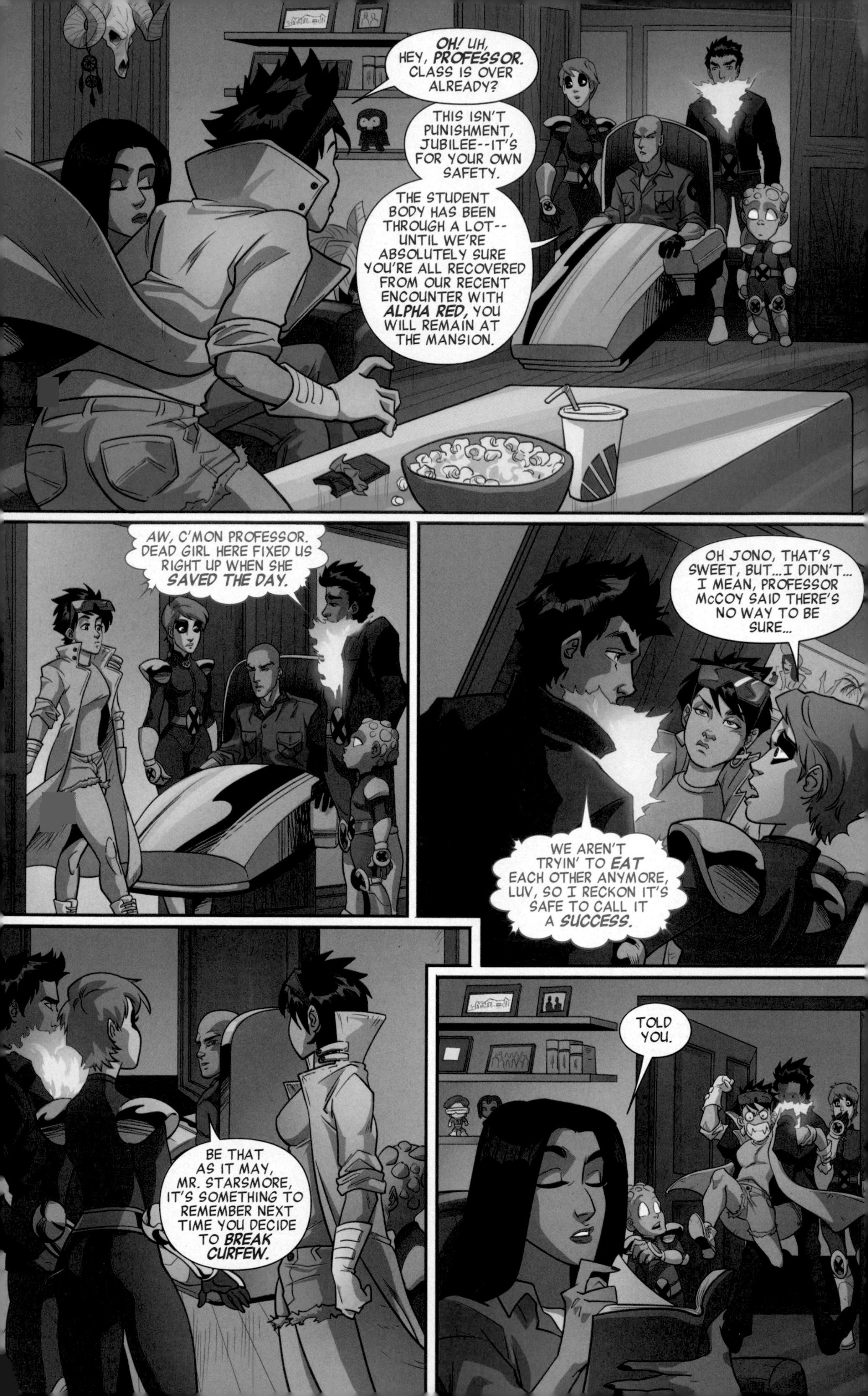
OH! UH, HEY, PROFESSOR. CLASS IS OVER ALREADY?
THIS ISN'T PUNISHMENT, JUBILEE--IT'S FOR YOUR OWN SAFETY.
THE STUDENT BODY HAS BEEN THROUGH A LOT--UNTIL WE'RE ABSOLUTELY SURE YOU'RE ALL RECOVERED FROM OUR RECENT ENCOUNTER WITH ALPHA RED, YOU WILL REMAIN AT THE MANSION.
AW, C'MON PROFESSOR. DEAD GIRL HERE FIXED US RIGHT UP WHEN SHE SAVED THE DAY.
OH JONO, THAT'S SWEET, BUT...I DIDN'T... I MEAN, PROFESSOR McCOY SAID THERE'S NO WAY TO BE SURE...
WE AREN'T TRYIN' TO EAT EACH OTHER ANYMORE, LUV, SO I RECKON IT'S SAFE TO CALL IT A SUCCESS.
BE THAT AS IT MAY, MR. STARSMORE, IT'S SOMETHING TO REMEMBER NEXT TIME YOU DECIDE TO BREAK CURFEW.
TOLD YOU.

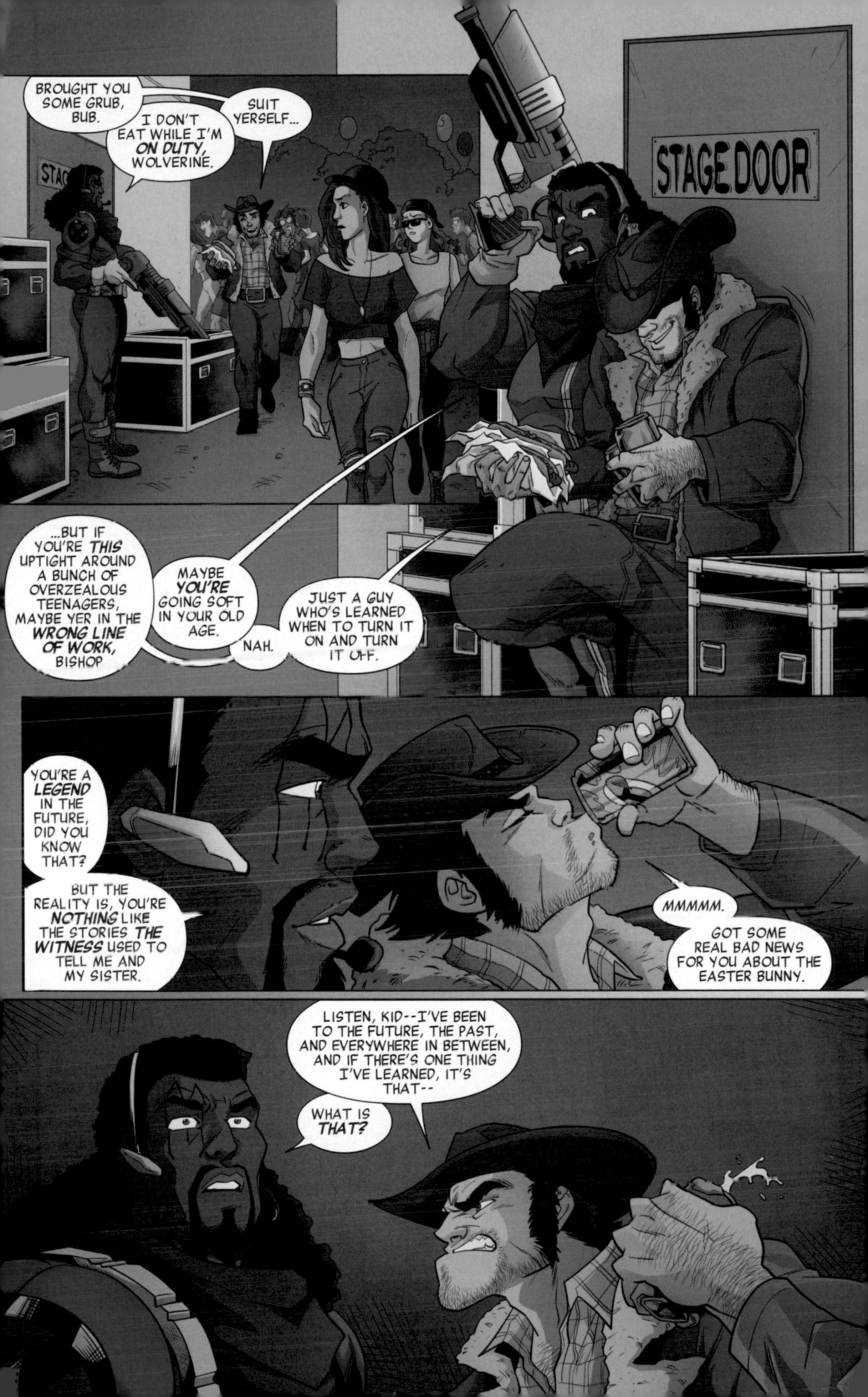
BROUGHT YOU SOME GRUB, BUB.
I DON'T EAT WHILE I'M ON DUTY, WOLVERINE.
SUIT YERSELF...
STAGE DOOR
...BUT IF YOU'RE THIS UPTIGHT AROUND A BUNCH OF OVERZEALOUS TEENAGERS, MAYBE YER IN THE WRONG LINE OF WORK, BISHOP
MAYBE YOU'RE GOING SOFT IN YOUR OLD AGE.
NAH.
JUST A GUY WHO'S LEARNED WHEN TO TURN IT ON AND TURN IT OFF.
YOU'RE A LEGEND IN THE FUTURE, DID YOU KNOW THAT?
BUT THE REALITY IS, YOU'RE NOTHING LIKE THE STORIES THE WITNESS USED TO TELL ME AND MY SISTER.
MMMMM.
GOT SOME REAL BAD NEWS FOR YOU ABOUT THE EASTER BUNNY.
LISTEN, KID--I'VE BEEN TO THE FUTURE, THE PAST, AND EVERYWHERE IN BETWEEN, AND IF THERE'S ONE THING I'VE LEARNED, IT'S THAT--
WHAT IS THAT?

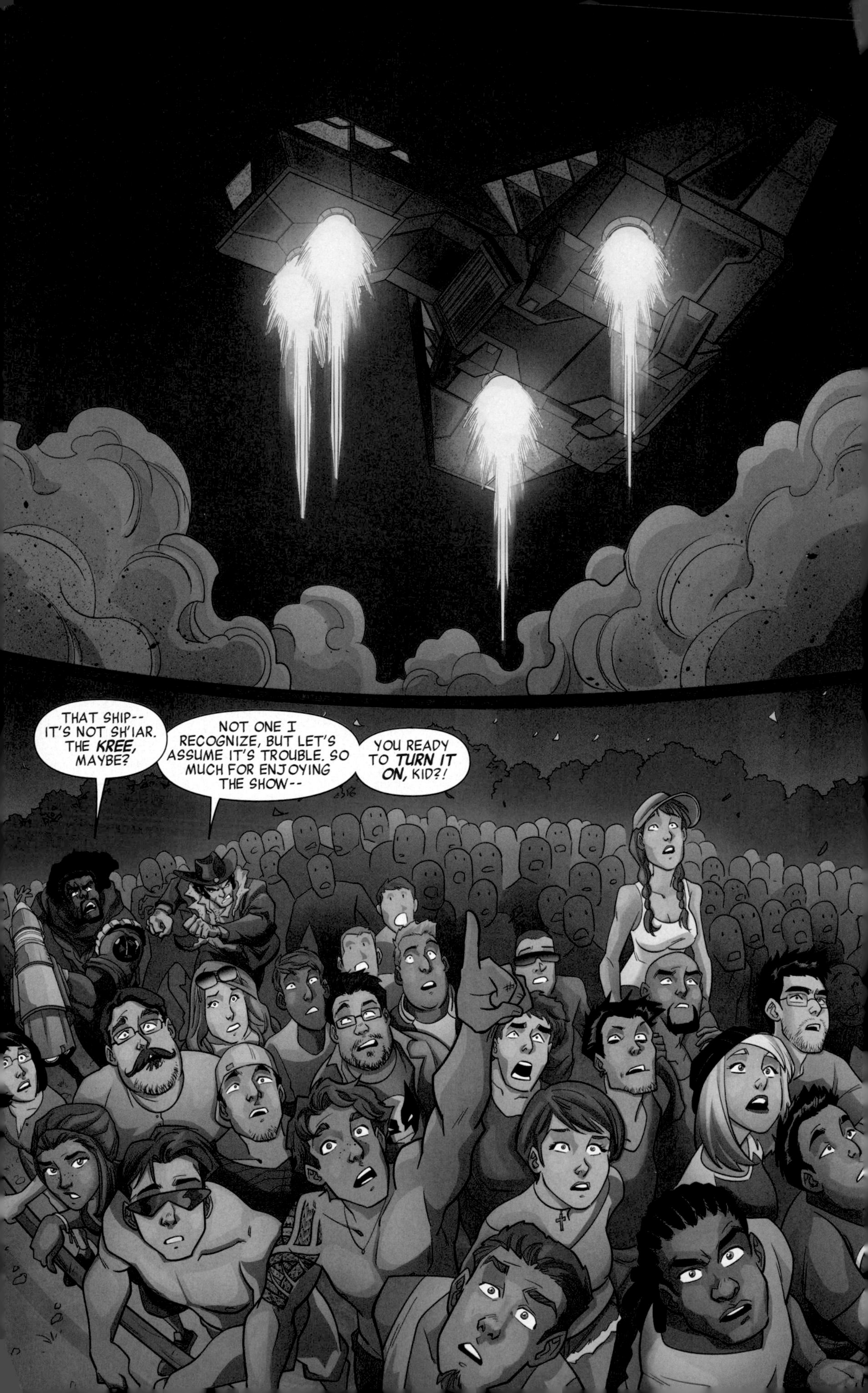
THAT SHIP-- IT'S NOT SH'IAR. THE KREE, MAYBE?
NOT ONE I RECOGNIZE, BUT LET'S ASSUME IT'S TROUBLE. SO MUCH FOR ENJOYING THE SHOW--
YOU READY TO TURN IT ON, KID?!

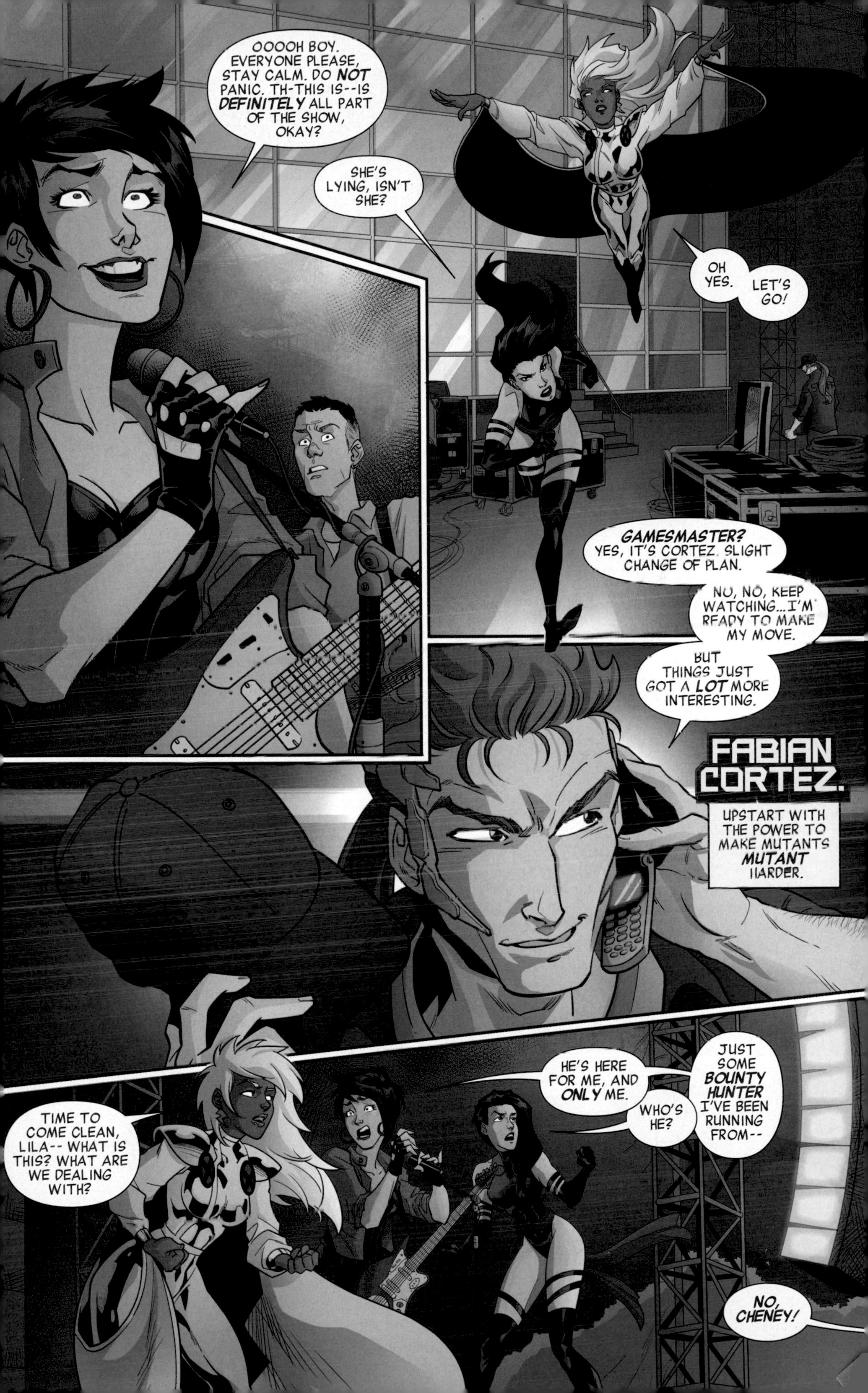

OOOOH BOY. EVERYONE PLEASE, STAY CALM. DO NOT PANIC. TH-THIS IS--IS DEFINITELY ALL PART OF THE SHOW, OKAY?
SHE'S LYING, ISN'T SHE?
OH YES.
LET'S GO!
GAMESMASTER? YES, IT'S CORTEZ. SLIGHT CHANGE OF PLAN.
NO, NO, KEEP WATCHING...I'M READY TO MAKE MY MOVE.
BUT THINGS JUST GOT A LOT MORE INTERESTING.
FABIAN CORTEZ.
UPSTART WITH THE POWER TO MAKE MUTANTS MUTANT HARDER.
TIME TO COME CLEAN, LILA-- WHAT IS THIS? WHAT ARE WE DEALING WITH?
HE'S HERE FOR ME, AND ONLY ME.
WHO'S HE?
JUST SOME BOUNTY HUNTER I'VE BEEN RUNNING FROM--
NO, CHENEY!

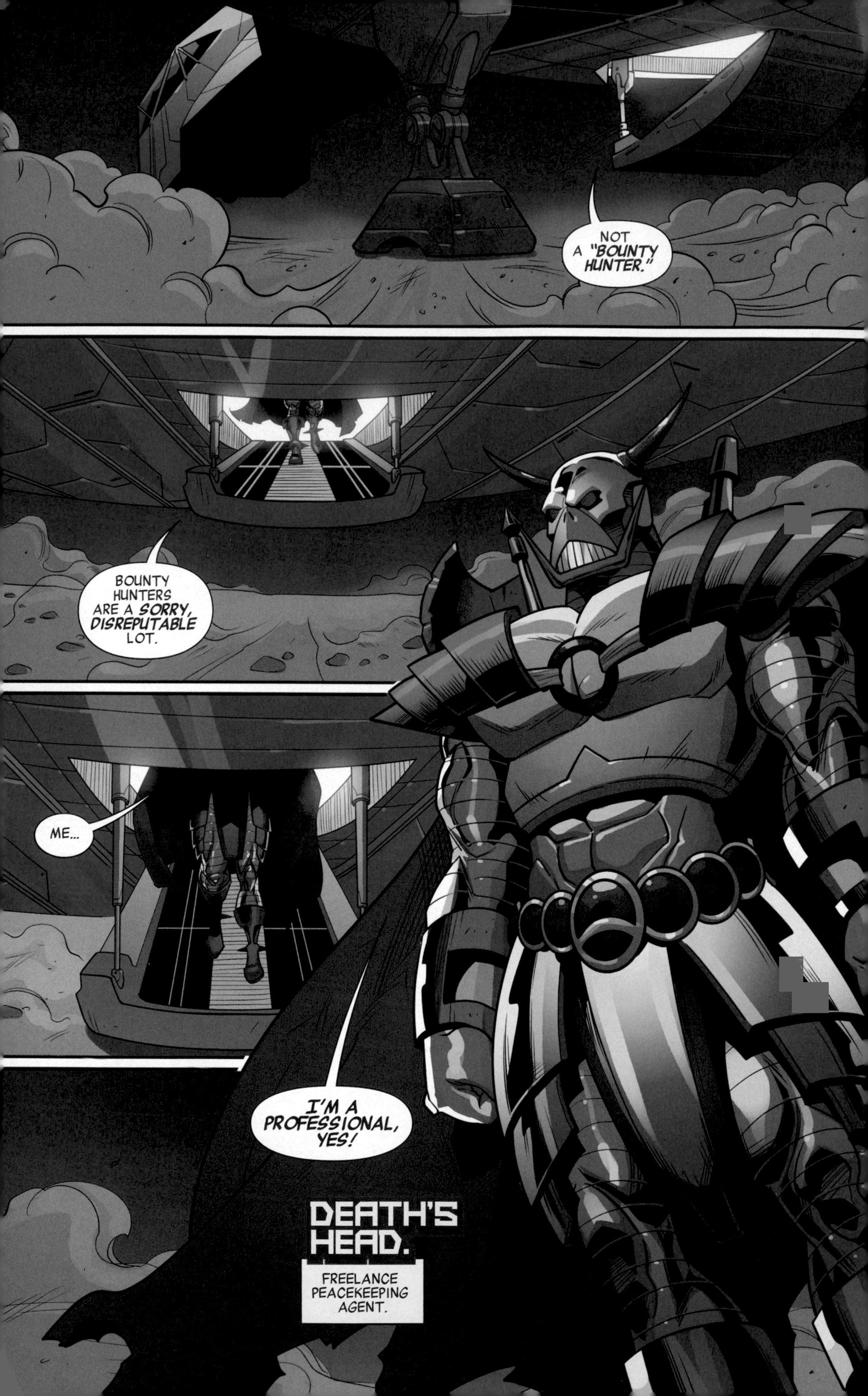
NOT A "BOUNTY HUNTER."
BOUNTY HUNTERS ARE A SORRY, DISREPUTABLE LOT.
ME...
I'M A PROFESSIONAL, YES!
DEATH'S HEAD.
FREELANCE PEACEKEEPING AGENT.

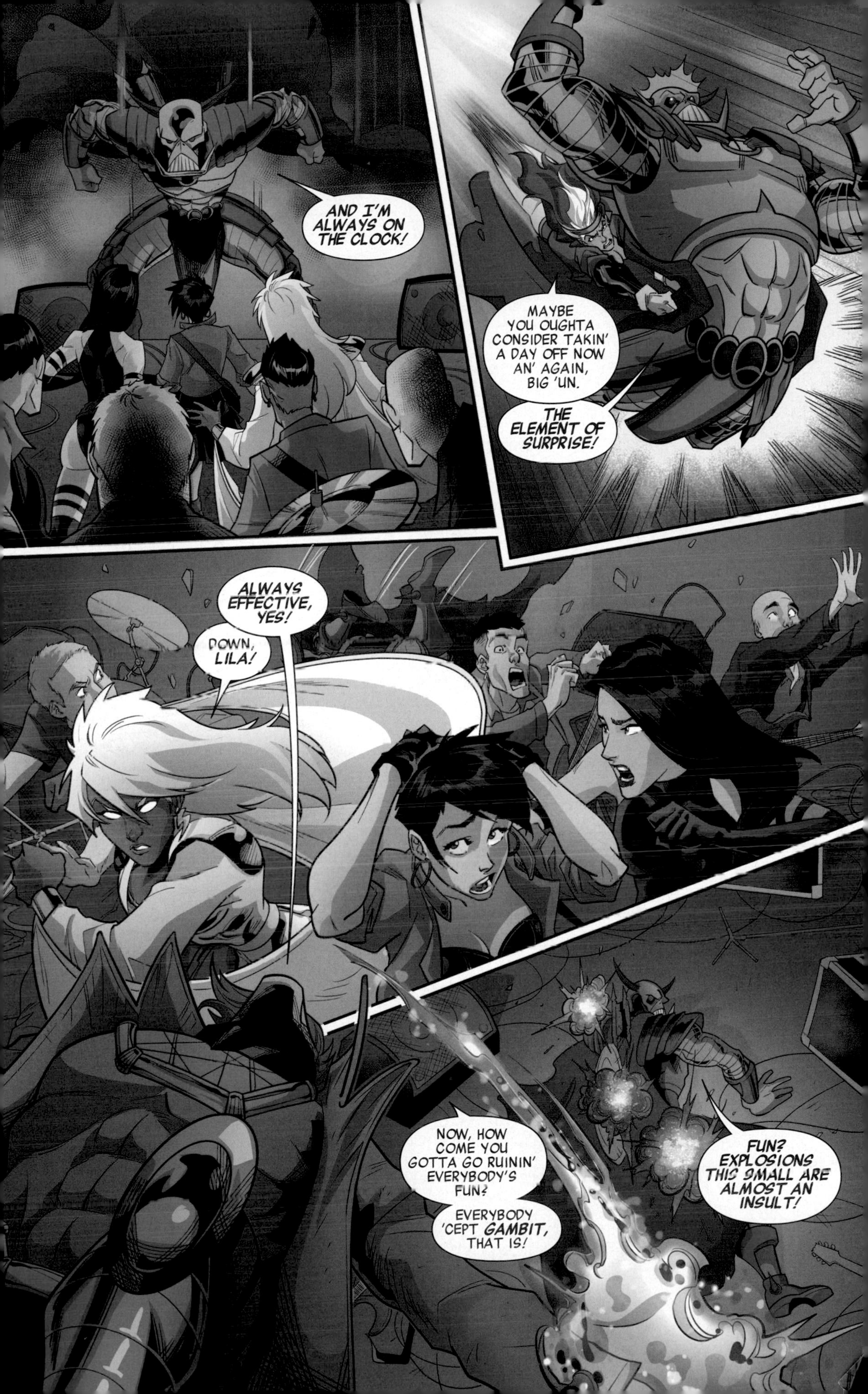
AND I'M ALWAYS ON THE CLOCK!
MAYBE YOU OUGHTA CONSIDER TAKIN' A DAY OFF NOW AN' AGAIN, BIG 'UN.
THE ELEMENT OF SURPRISE!
ALWAYS EFFECTIVE, YES!
DOWN, LILA!
NOW, HOW COME YOU GOTTA GO RUININ' EVERYBODY'S FUN?
EVERYBODY 'CEPT GAMBIT, THAT IS!
FUN? EXPLOSIONS THIS SMALL ARE ALMOST AN INSULT!

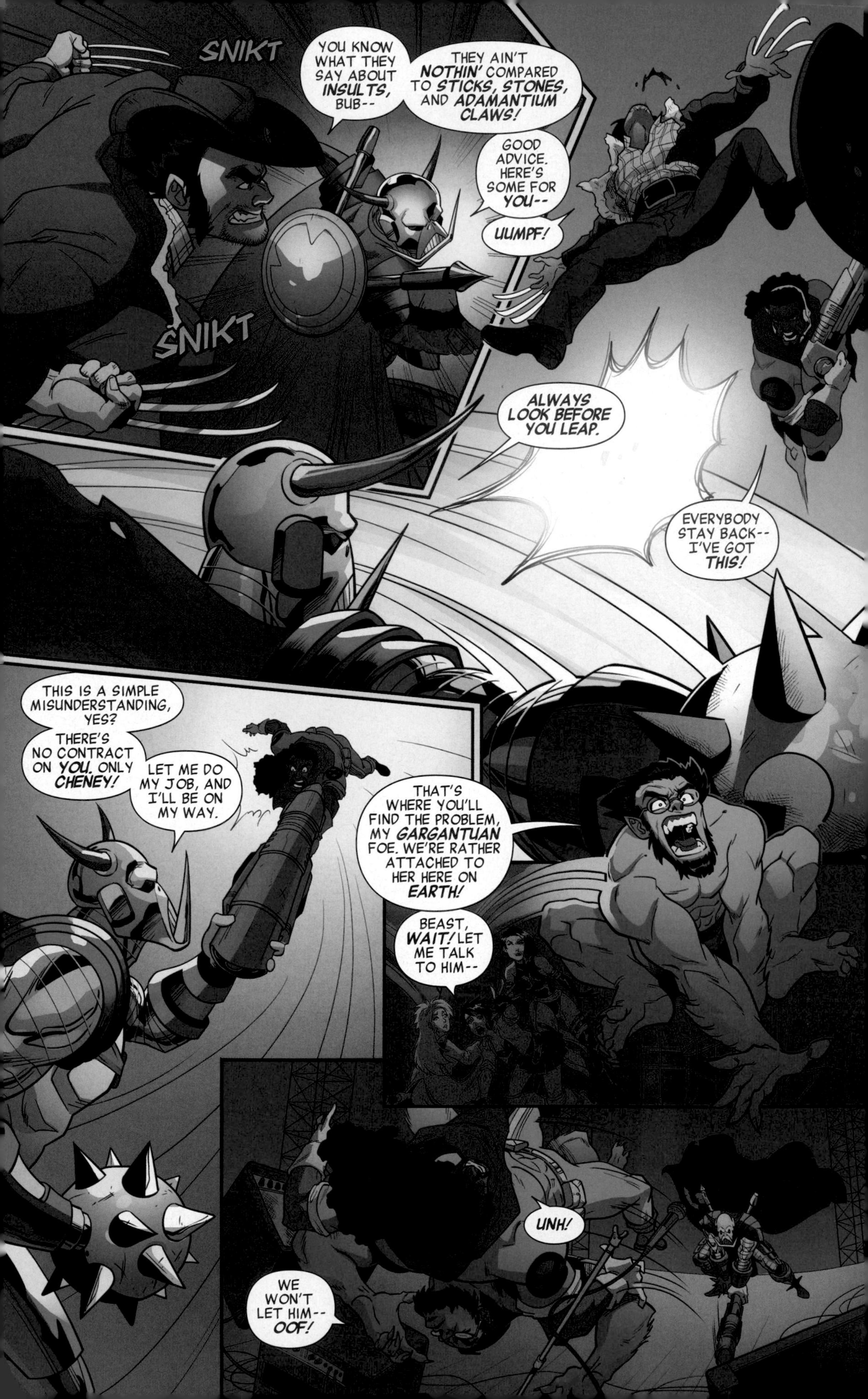
SNIKT
YOU KNOW WHAT THEY SAY ABOUT INSULTS, BUB--
THEY AIN'T NOTHIN' COMPARED TO STICKS, STONES, AND ADAMANTIUM CLAWS!
SNIKT
GOOD ADVICE. HERE'S SOME FOR YOU--
UUMPF!
ALWAYS LOOK BEFORE YOU LEAP.
EVERYBODY STAY BACK-- I'VE GOT THIS!
THIS IS A SIMPLE MISUNDERSTANDING, YES?
THERE'S NO CONTRACT ON YOU, ONLY CHENEY!
LET ME DO MY JOB, AND I'LL BE ON MY WAY.
THAT'S WHERE YOU'LL FIND THE PROBLEM, MY GARGANTUAN FOE. WE'RE RATHER ATTACHED TO HER HERE ON EARTH!
BEAST, WAIT! LET ME TALK TO HIM--
UNH!
WE WON'T LET HIM-- OOF!

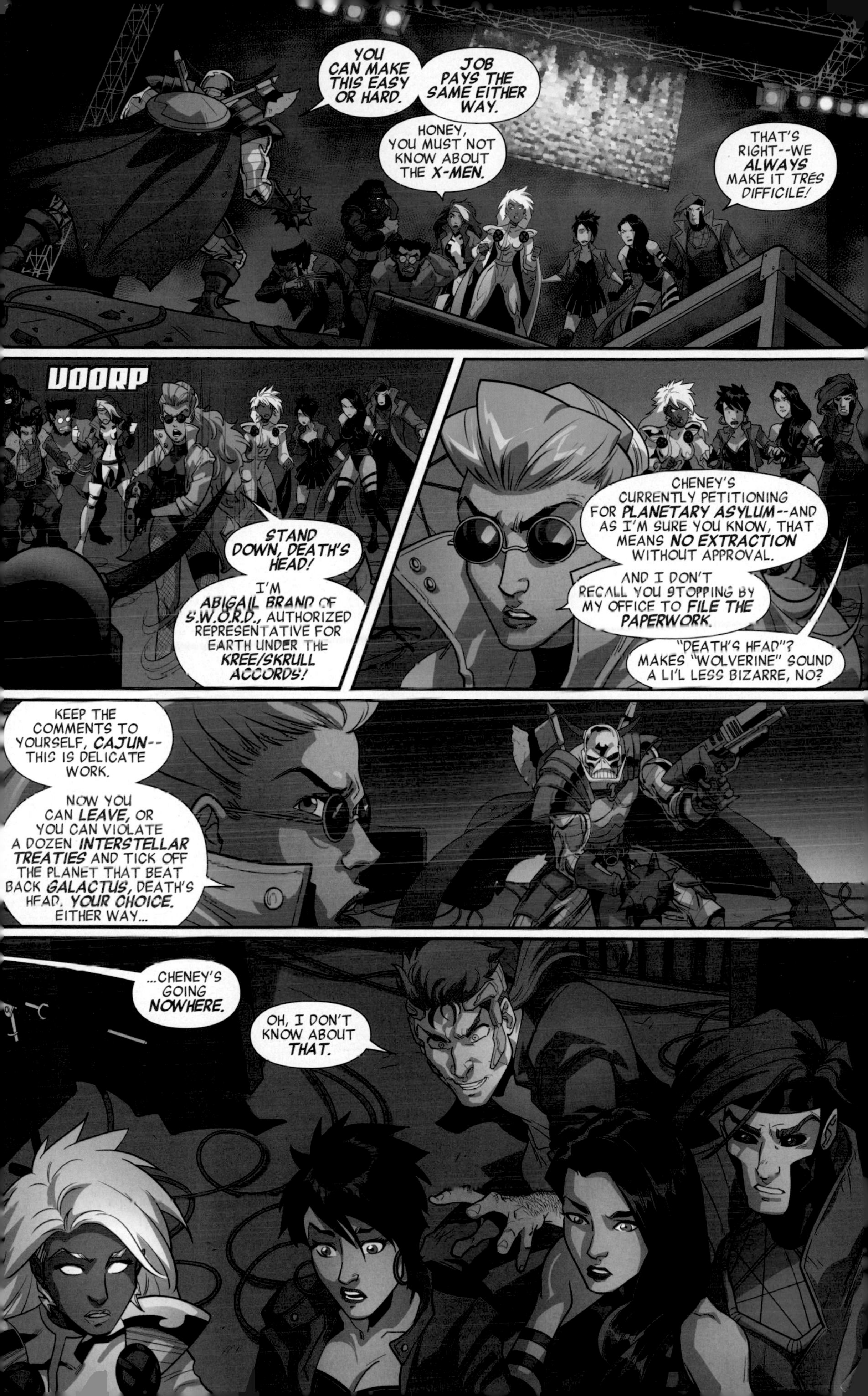
YOU CAN MAKE THIS EASY OR HARD.
JOB PAYS THE SAME EITHER WAY.
HONEY, YOU MUST NOT KNOW ABOUT THE X-MEN.
THAT'S RIGHT--WE ALWAYS MAKE IT TRÉS DIFFICILE!
VOORP
STAND DOWN, DEATH'S HEAD!
I'M ABIGAIL BRAND OF S.W.O.R.D., AUTHORIZED REPRESENTATIVE FOR EARTH UNDER THE KREE/SKRULL ACCORDS!
CHENEY'S CURRENTLY PETITIONING FOR PLANETARY ASYLUM--AND AS I'M SURE YOU KNOW, THAT MEANS NO EXTRACTION WITHOUT APPROVAL.
AND I DON'T RECALL YOU STOPPING BY MY OFFICE TO FILE THE PAPERWORK.
"DEATH'S HEAD"? MAKES "WOLVERINE" SOUND A LI'L LESS BIZARRE, NO?
KEEP THE COMMENTS TO YOURSELF, CAJUN-- THIS IS DELICATE WORK.
NOW YOU CAN LEAVE, OR YOU CAN VIOLATE A DOZEN INTERSTELLAR TREATIES AND TICK OFF THE PLANET THAT BEAT BACK GALACTUS, DEATH'S HEAD. YOUR CHOICE. EITHER WAY...
...CHENEY'S GOING NOWHERE.
OH, I DON'T KNOW ABOUT THAT.

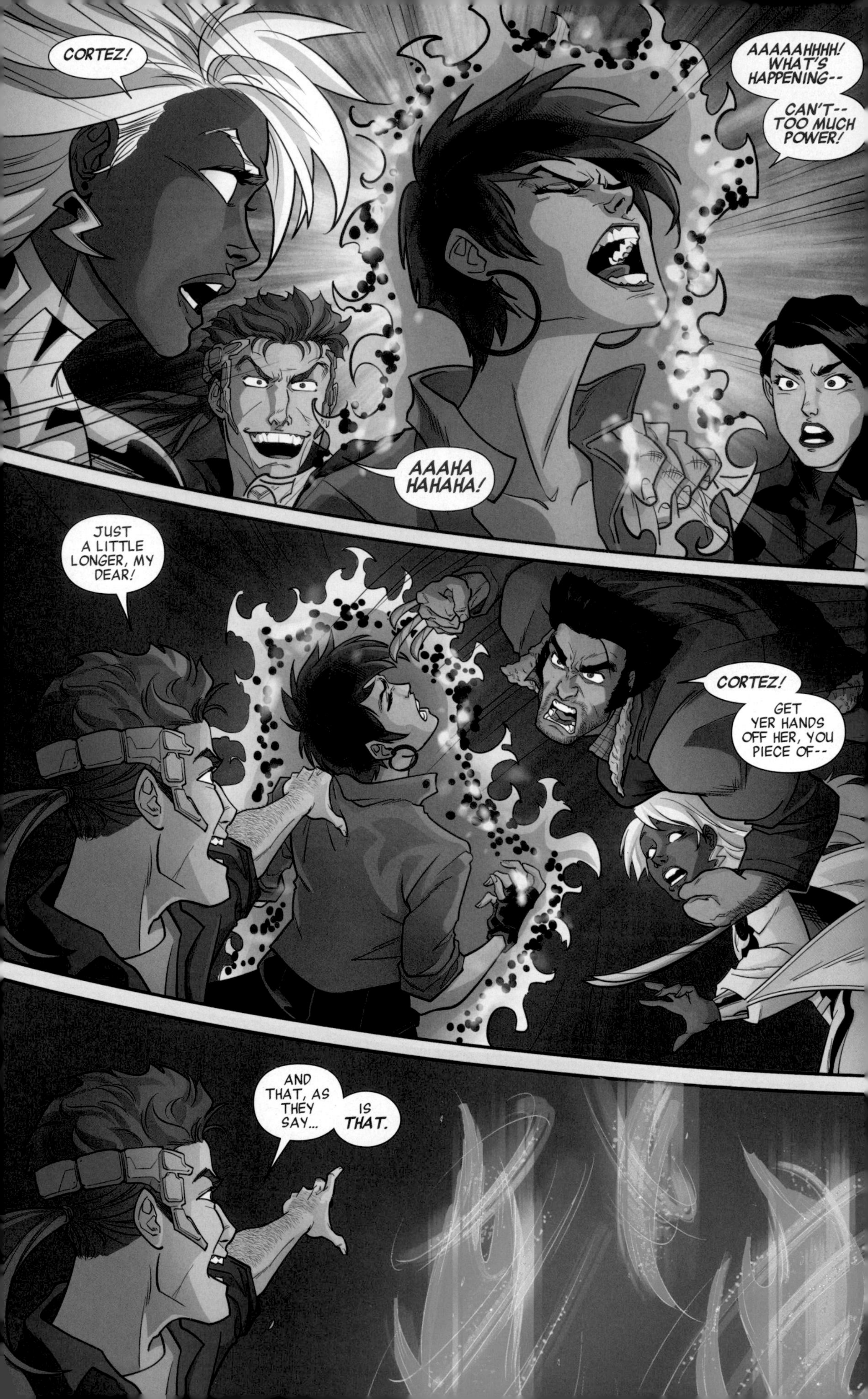
CORTEZ!
AAAAAHHH! WHAT'S HAPPENING--
CAN'T-- TOO MUCH POWER!
AAAHA HAHAHA!
JUST A LITTLE LONGER, MY DEAR!
CORTEZ!
GET YER HANDS OFF HER, YOU PIECE OF--
AND THAT, AS THEY SAY...
IS THAT.

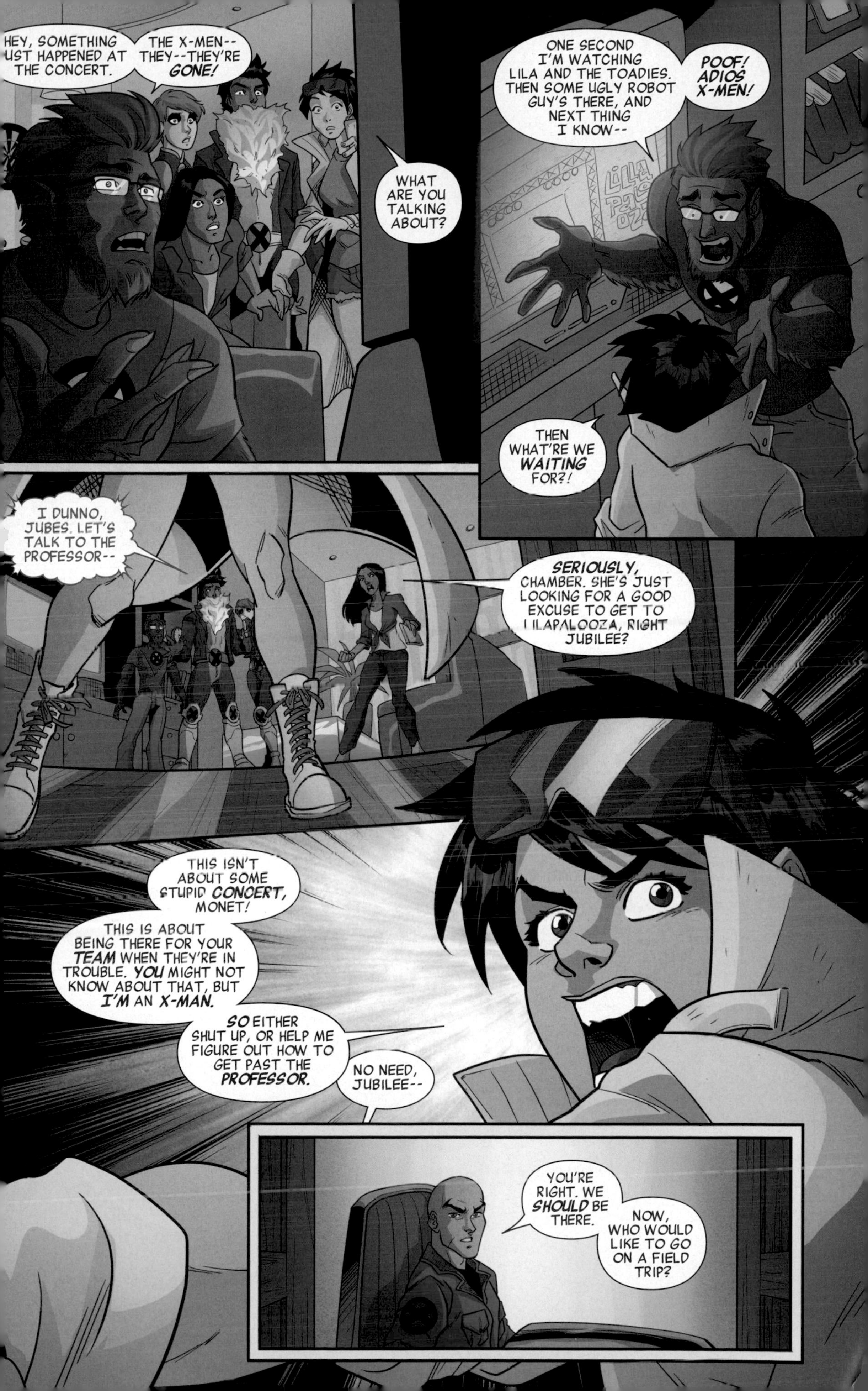

HEY, SOMETHING JUST HAPPENED AT THE CONCERT.
THE X-MEN-- THEY--THEY'RE GONE!
WHAT ARE YOU TALKING ABOUT?
ONE SECOND I'M WATCHING LILA AND THE TOADIES. THEN SOME UGLY ROBOT GUY'S THERE, AND NEXT THING I KNOW--
POOF! ADIOS X-MEN!
THEN WHAT'RE WE WAITING FOR?!
I DUNNO, JUBES. LET'S TALK TO THE PROFESSOR--
SERIOUSLY, CHAMBER. SHE'S JUST LOOKING FOR A GOOD EXCUSE TO GET TO LILAPALOOZA, RIGHT JUBILEE?
THIS ISN'T ABOUT SOME STUPID CONCERT, MONET!
THIS IS ABOUT BEING THERE FOR YOUR TEAM WHEN THEY'RE IN TROUBLE. YOU MIGHT NOT KNOW ABOUT THAT, BUT I'M AN X-MAN.
SO EITHER SHUT UP, OR HELP ME FIGURE OUT HOW TO GET PAST THE PROFESSOR.
NO NEED, JUBILEE--
YOU'RE RIGHT. WE SHOULD BE THERE.
NOW, WHO WOULD LIKE TO GO ON A FIELD TRIP?

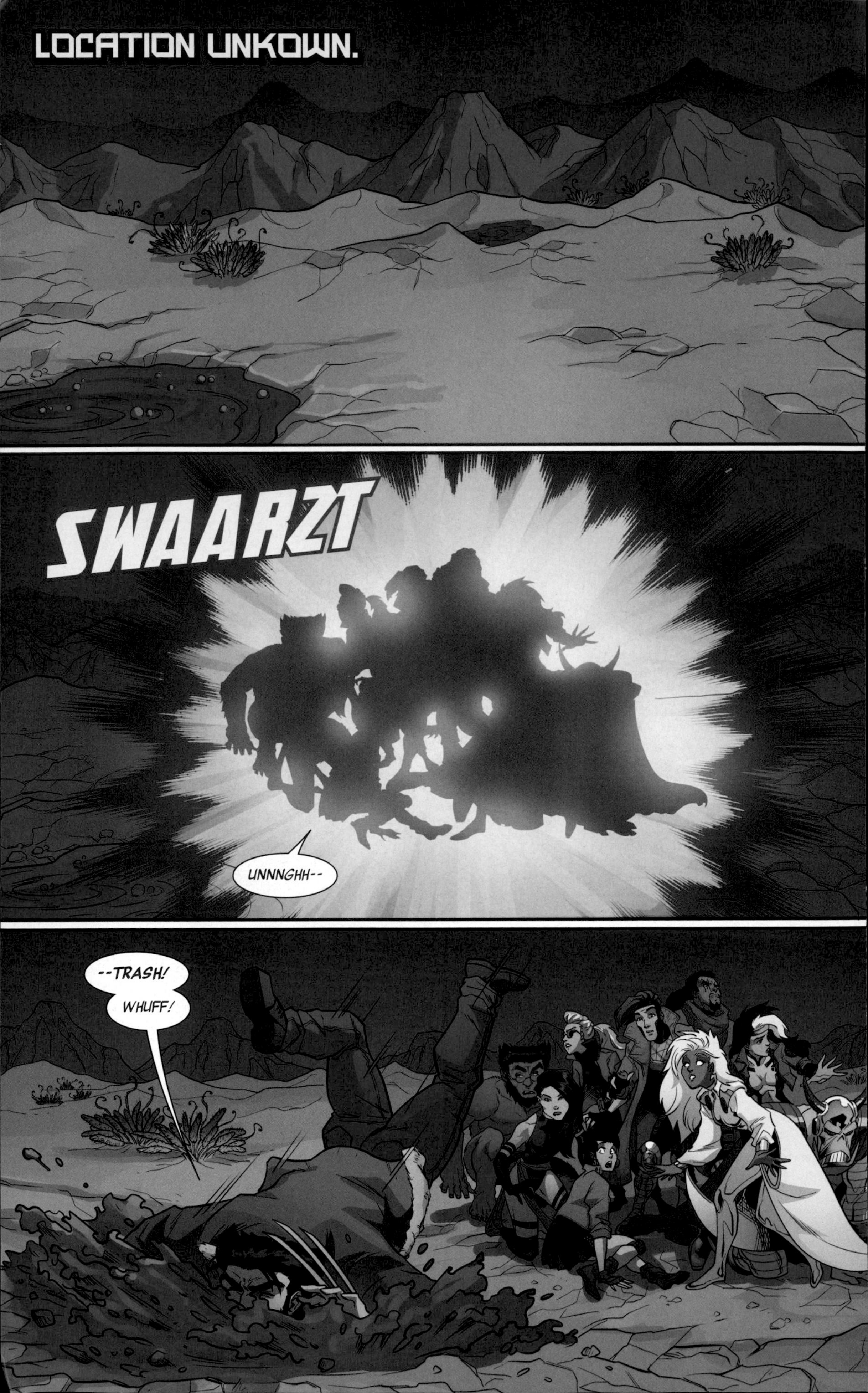
LOCATION UNKOWN.
SWAARZT
UNNNGHH--
--TRASH!
WHUFF!

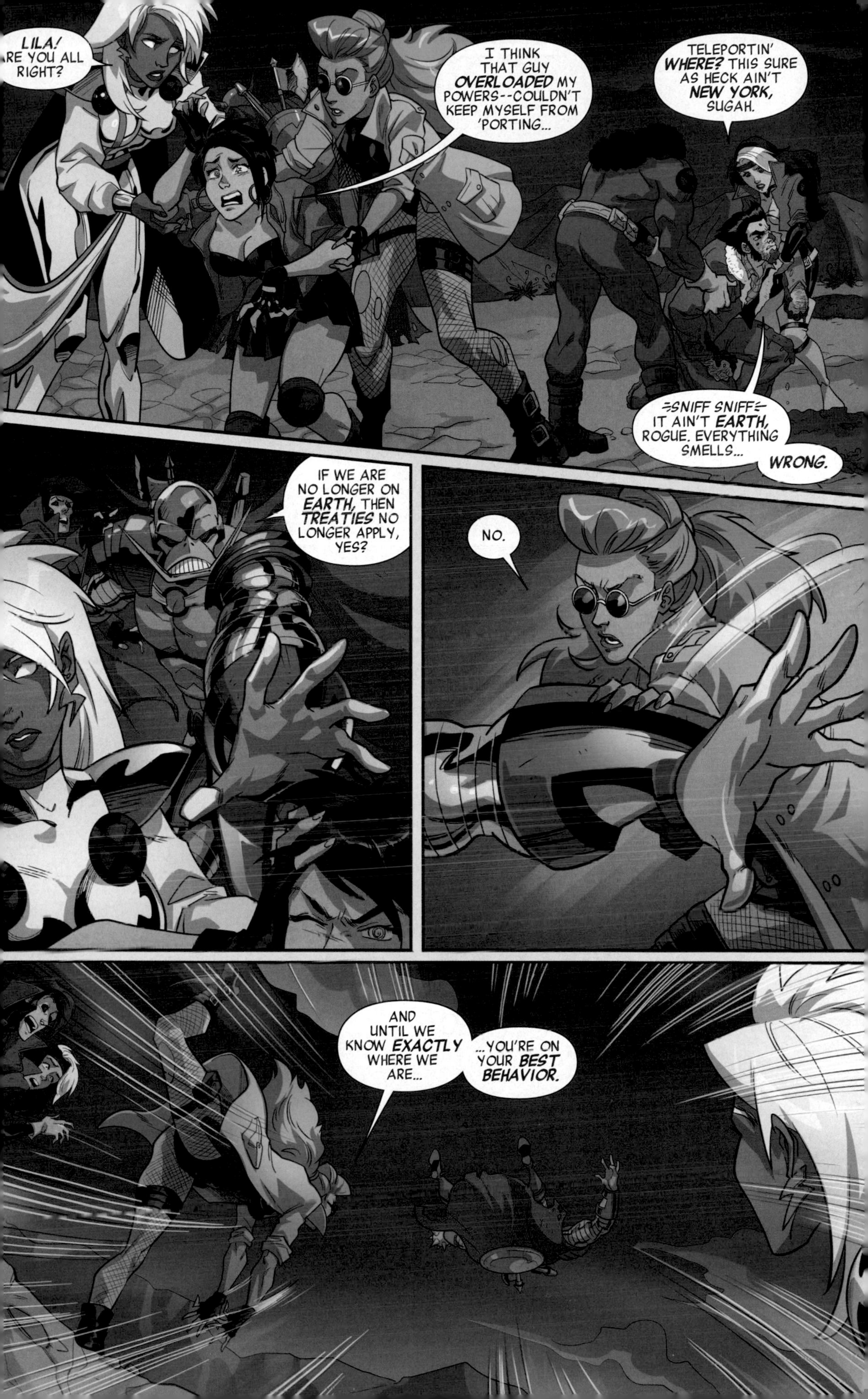
LILA! ARE YOU ALL RIGHT?
I THINK THAT GUY OVERLOADED MY POWERS--COULDN'T KEEP MYSELF FROM 'PORTING...
TELEPORTIN' WHERE? THIS SURE AS HECK AIN'T NEW YORK, SUGAH.
=SNIFF SNIFF= IT AIN'T EARTH, ROGUE. EVERYTHING SMELLS... WRONG.
IF WE ARE NO LONGER ON EARTH, THEN TREATIES NO LONGER APPLY, YES?
NO.
AND UNTIL WE KNOW EXACTLY WHERE WE ARE...
...YOU'RE ON YOUR BEST BEHAVIOR.

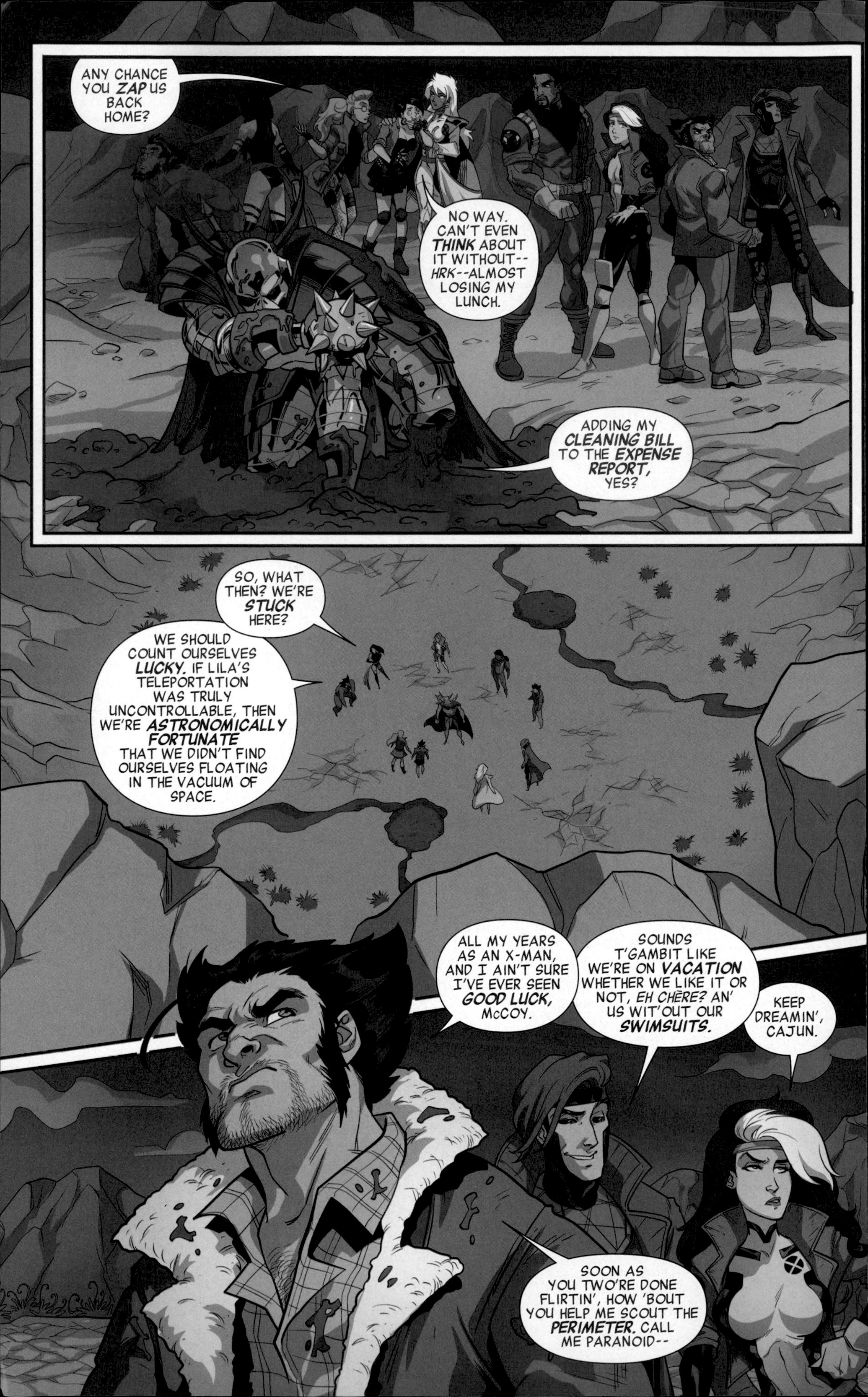
ANY CHANCE YOU ZAP US BACK HOME?
NO WAY. CAN'T EVEN THINK ABOUT IT WITHOUT-- HRK--ALMOST LOSING MY LUNCH.
ADDING MY CLEANING BILL TO THE EXPENSE REPORT, YES?
SO, WHAT THEN? WE'RE STUCK HERE?
WE SHOULD COUNT OURSELVES LUCKY. IF LILA'S TELEPORTATION WAS TRULY UNCONTROLLABLE, THEN WE'RE ASTRONOMICALLY FORTUNATE THAT WE DIDN'T FIND OURSELVES FLOATING IN THE VACUUM OF SPACE.
ALL MY YEARS AS AN X-MAN, AND I AIN'T SURE I'VE EVER SEEN GOOD LUCK, McCOY.
SOUNDS T'GAMBIT LIKE WE'RE ON VACATION WHETHER WE LIKE IT OR NOT, EH CHÈRE? AN' US WIT'OUT OUR SWIMSUITS.
KEEP DREAMIN', CAJUN.
SOON AS YOU TWO'RE DONE FLIRTIN', HOW 'BOUT YOU HELP ME SCOUT THE PERIMETER. CALL ME PARANOID--

BUT I GOT A FEELIN' WE AIN'T ALONE.
WHO IS IT, LEADER--ARE WE DISCOVERED?
NO, MY SOLIDER...
WE ARE SAVED.
X-MEN '92 PRESENTS
LILAPALOOZA

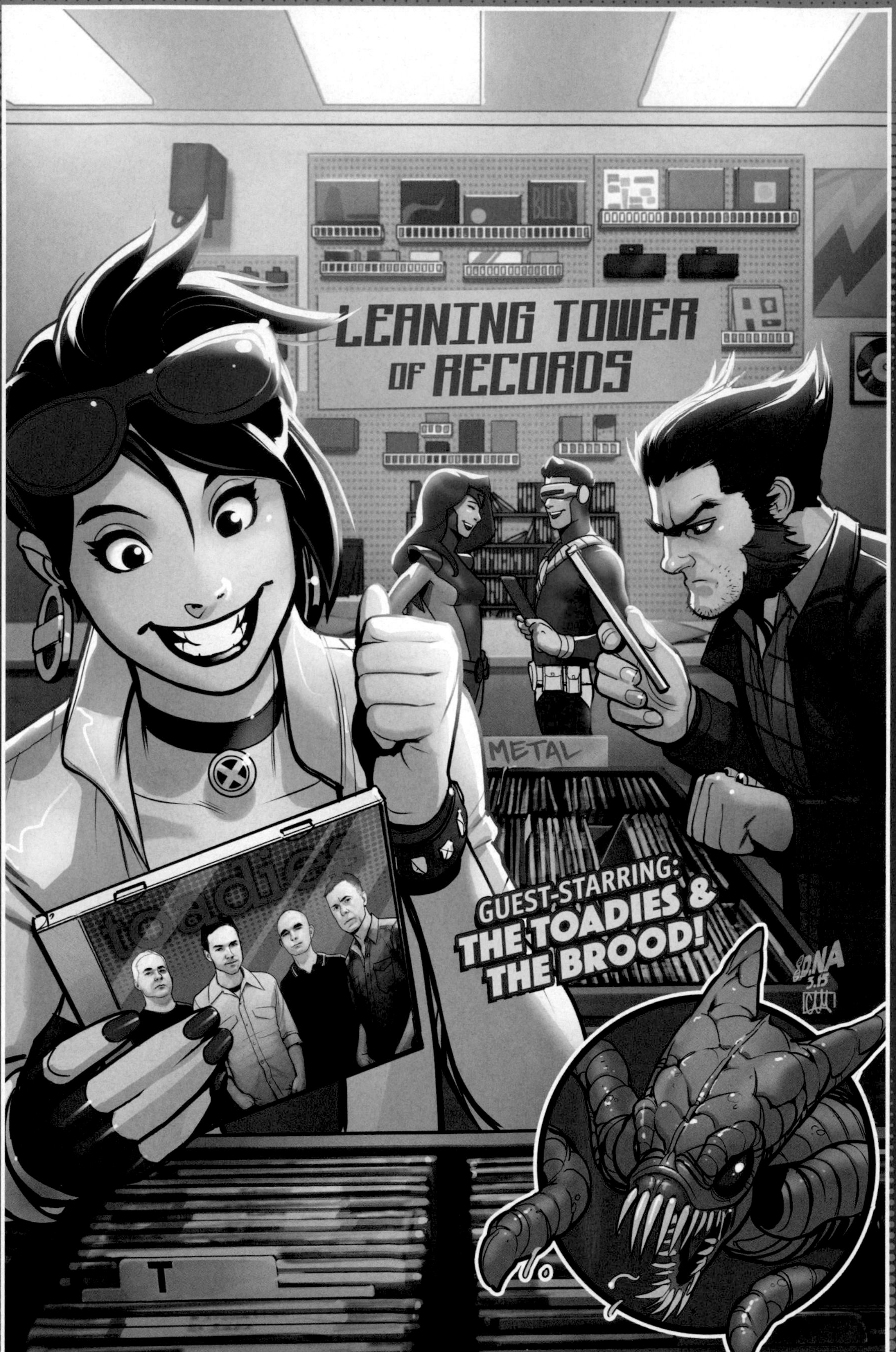
LEANING TOWER OF RECORDS
BLUES
METAL
GUEST-STARRING:
THE TOADIES &
THE BROOD!
T

7

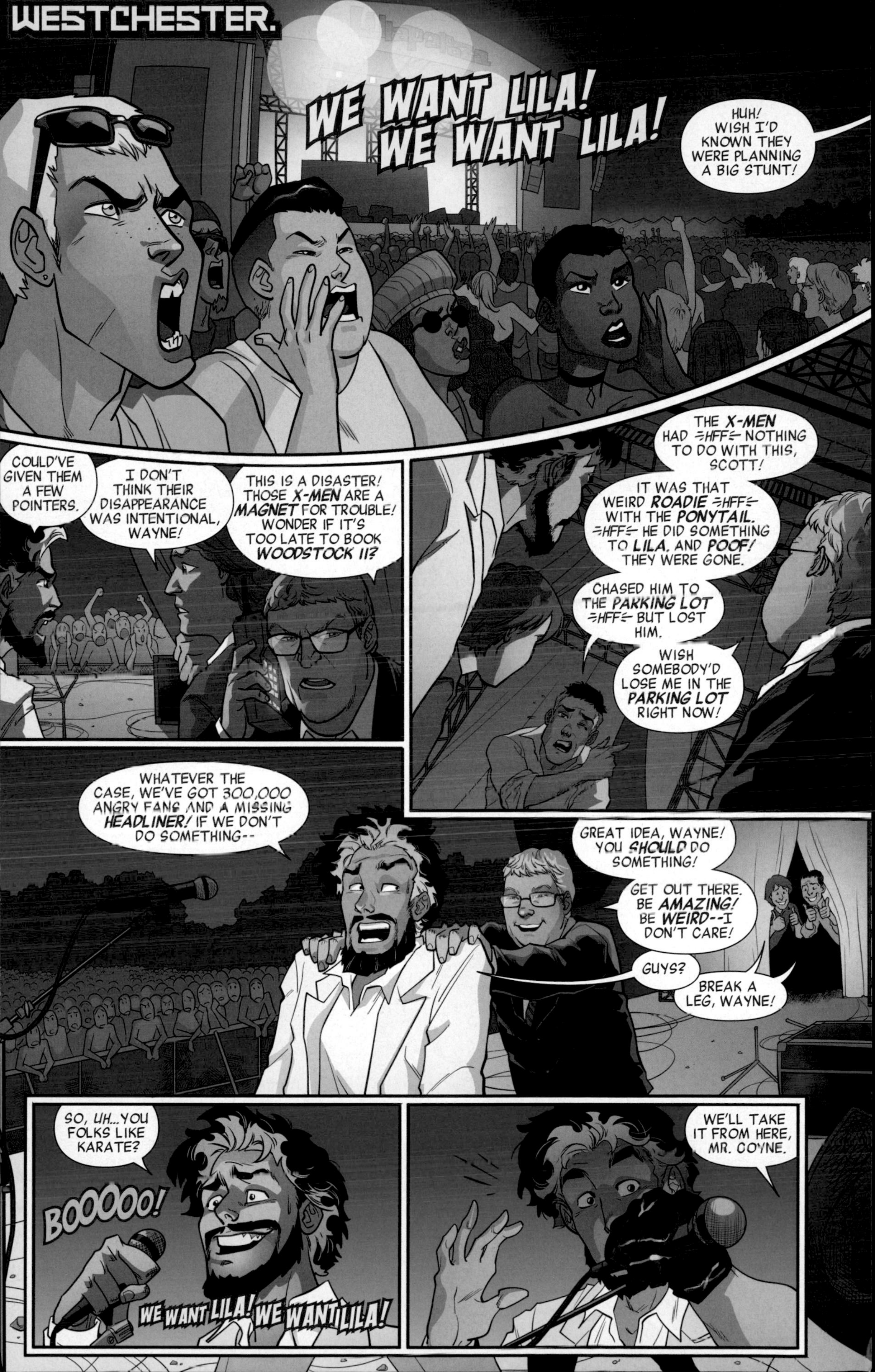
WESTCHESTER.
WE WANT LILA! WE WANT LILA!
HUH! WISH I'D KNOWN THEY WERE PLANNING A BIG STUNT!
COULD'VE GIVEN THEM A FEW POINTERS.
I DON'T THINK THEIR DISAPPEARANCE WAS INTENTIONAL, WAYNE!
THIS IS A DISASTER! THOSE X-MEN ARE A MAGNET FOR TROUBLE! WONDER IF IT'S TOO LATE TO BOOK WOODSTOCK II?
THE X-MEN HAD =HFF= NOTHING TO DO WITH THIS, SCOTT!
IT WAS THAT WEIRD ROADIE =HFF= WITH THE PONYTAIL. =HFF= HE DID SOMETHING TO LILA, AND POOF! THEY WERE GONE.
CHASED HIM TO THE PARKING LOT =HFF= BUT LOST HIM.
WISH SOMEBODY'D LOSE ME IN THE PARKING LOT RIGHT NOW!
WHATEVER THE CASE, WE'VE GOT 300,000 ANGRY FANS AND A MISSING HEADLINER! IF WE DON'T DO SOMETHING--
GREAT IDEA, WAYNE! YOU SHOULD DO SOMETHING!
GET OUT THERE. BE AMAZING! BE WEIRD--I DON'T CARE!
GUYS?
BREAK A LEG, WAYNE!
SO, UH...YOU FOLKS LIKE KARATE?
BOOOOO!
WE WANT LILA! WE WANT LILA!
WE'LL TAKE IT FROM HERE, MR. COYNE.

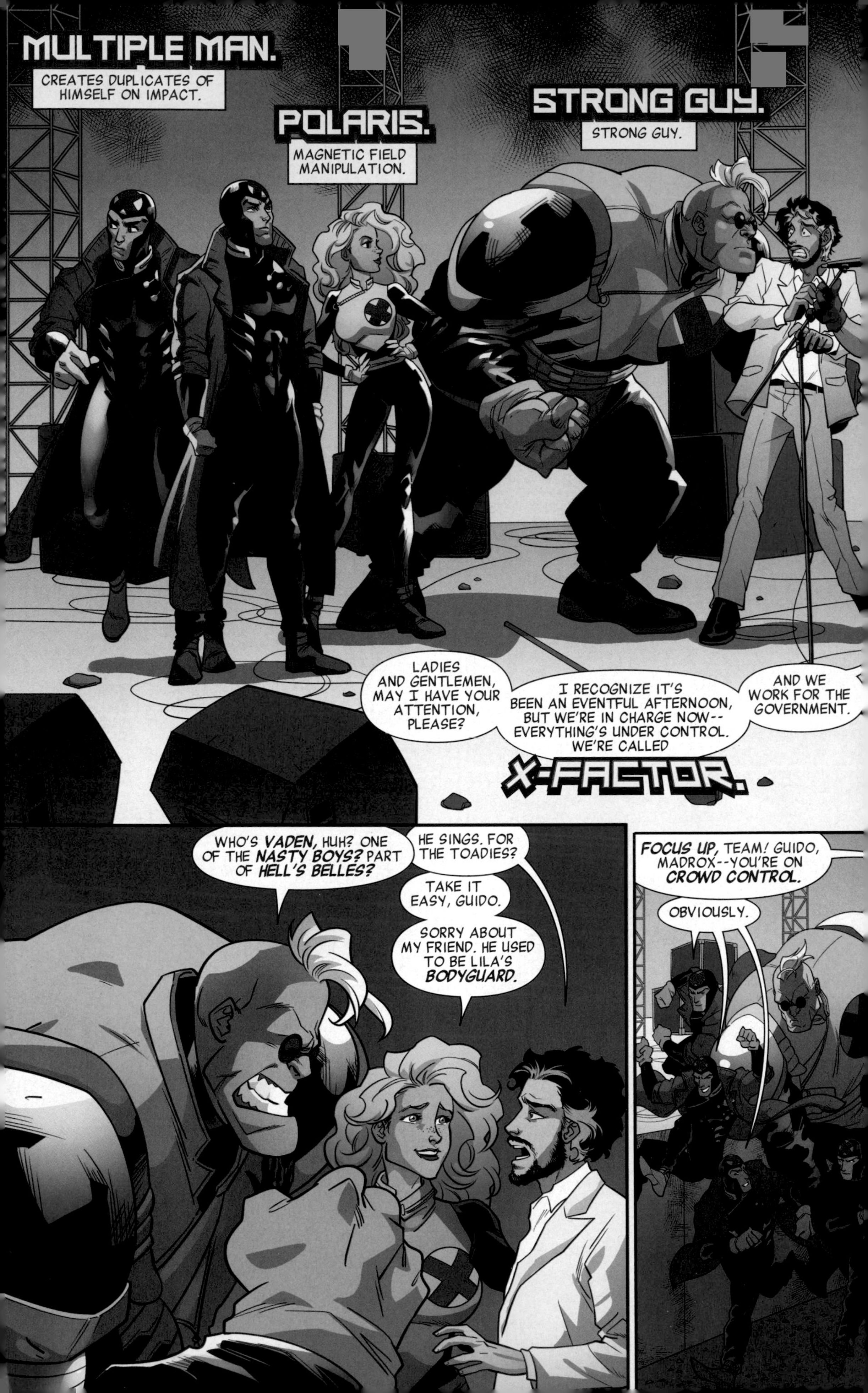
MULTIPLE MAN.
CREATES DUPLICATES OF HIMSELF ON IMPACT.
POLARIS.
MAGNETIC FIELD MANIPULATION.
STRONG GUY.
STRONG GUY.
LADIES AND GENTLEMEN, MAY I HAVE YOUR ATTENTION, PLEASE?
I RECOGNIZE IT'S BEEN AN EVENTFUL AFTERNOON, BUT WE'RE IN CHARGE NOW-- EVERYTHING'S UNDER CONTROL. WE'RE CALLED
X-FACTOR.
AND WE WORK FOR THE GOVERNMENT.
WHO'S VADEN, HUH? ONE OF THE NASTY BOYS? PART OF HELL'S BELLES?
HE SINGS. FOR THE TOADIES?
TAKE IT EASY, GUIDO.
SORRY ABOUT MY FRIEND. HE USED TO BE LILA'S BODYGUARD.
FOCUS UP, TEAM! GUIDO, MADROX--YOU'RE ON CROWD CONTROL.
OBVIOUSLY.

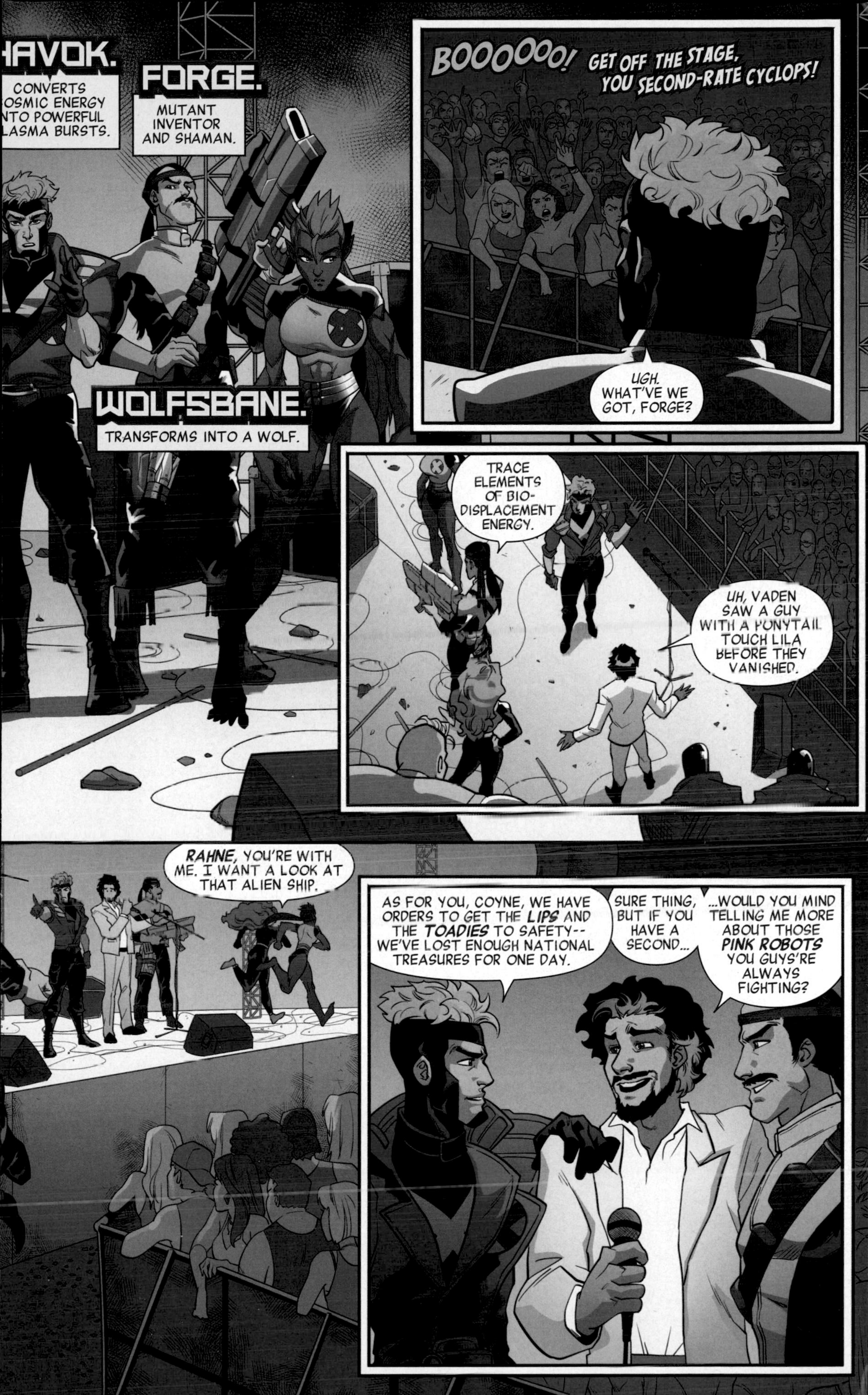
HAVOK.
CONVERTS OSMIC ENERGY NTO POWERFUL LASMA BURSTS.
FORGE.
MUTANT INVENTOR AND SHAMAN.
WOLFSBANE.
TRANSFORMS INTO A WOLF.
BOOOOOO!
GET OFF THE STAGE, YOU SECOND-RATE CYCLOPS!
UGH. WHAT'VE WE GOT, FORGE?
TRACE ELEMENTS OF BIO-DISPLACEMENT ENERGY.
UH, VADEN SAW A GUY WITH A PONYTAIL TOUCH LILA BEFORE THEY VANISHED.
RAHNE, YOU'RE WITH ME. I WANT A LOOK AT THAT ALIEN SHIP.
AS FOR YOU, COYNE, WE HAVE ORDERS TO GET THE LIPS AND THE TOADIES TO SAFETY-- WE'VE LOST ENOUGH NATIONAL TREASURES FOR ONE DAY.
SURE THING, BUT IF YOU HAVE A SECOND...
...WOULD YOU MIND TELLING ME MORE ABOUT THOSE PINK ROBOTS YOU GUYS'RE ALWAYS FIGHTING?

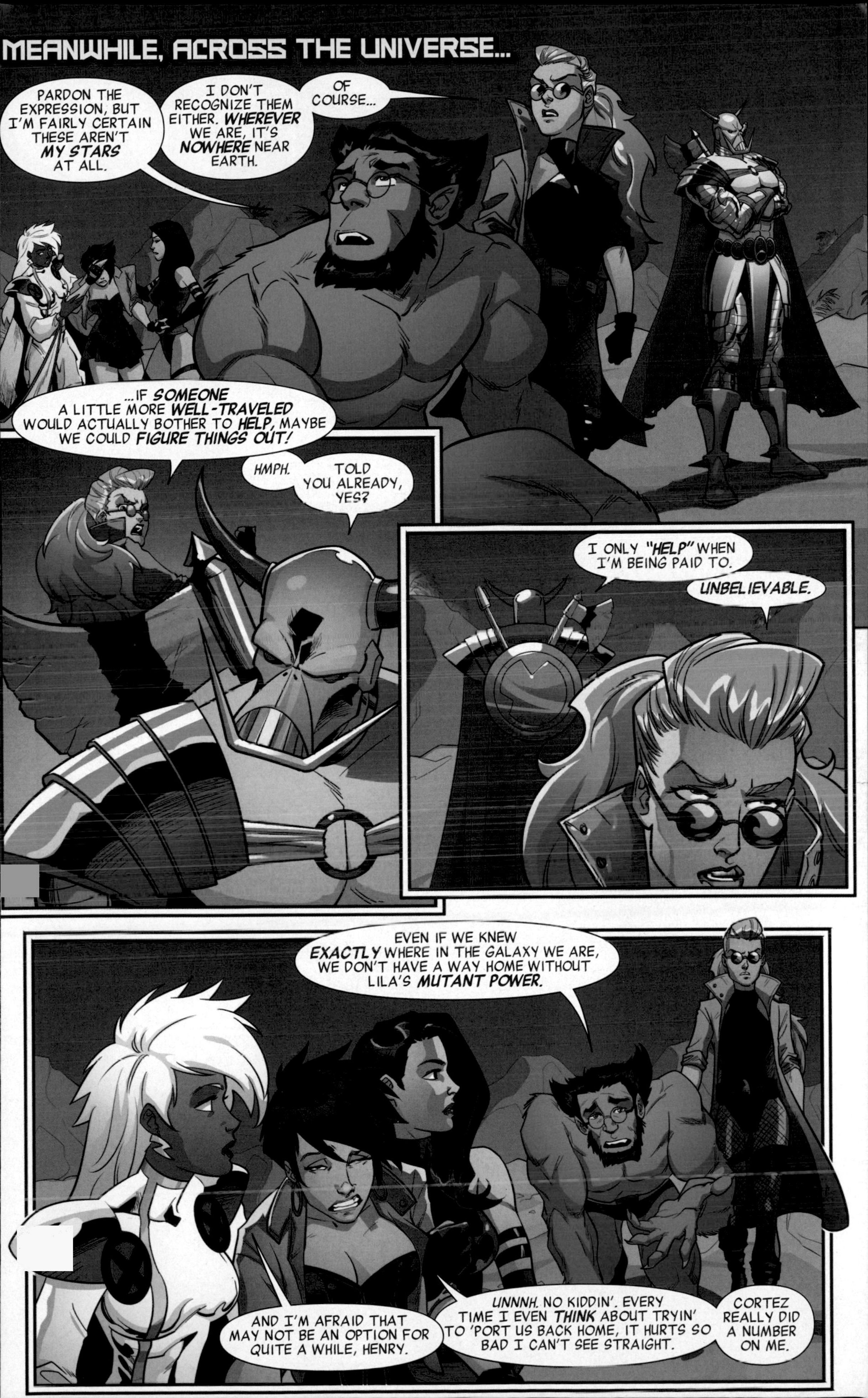
MEANWHILE, ACROSS THE UNIVERSE...
PARDON THE EXPRESSION, BUT I'M FAIRLY CERTAIN THESE AREN'T MY STARS AT ALL.
I DON'T RECOGNIZE THEM EITHER. WHEREVER WE ARE, IT'S NOWHERE NEAR EARTH.
OF COURSE...
...IF SOMEONE A LITTLE MORE WELL-TRAVELED WOULD ACTUALLY BOTHER TO HELP, MAYBE WE COULD FIGURE THINGS OUT!
HMPH.
TOLD YOU ALREADY, YES?
I ONLY "HELP" WHEN I'M BEING PAID TO.
UNBELIEVABLE.
EVEN IF WE KNEW EXACTLY WHERE IN THE GALAXY WE ARE, WE DON'T HAVE A WAY HOME WITHOUT LILA'S MUTANT POWER.
AND I'M AFRAID THAT MAY NOT BE AN OPTION FOR QUITE A WHILE, HENRY.
UNNNH. NO KIDDIN'. EVERY TIME I EVEN THINK ABOUT TRYIN' TO 'PORT US BACK HOME, IT HURTS SO BAD I CAN'T SEE STRAIGHT.
CORTEZ REALLY DID A NUMBER ON ME.

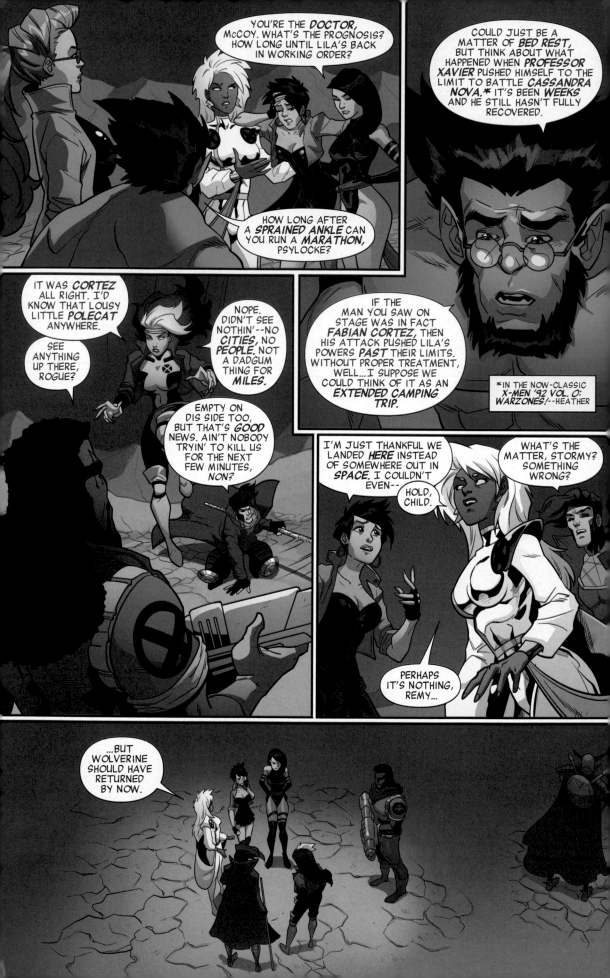

YOU'RE THE **DOCTOR**, McCOY. WHAT'S THE PROGNOSIS? HOW LONG UNTIL LILA'S BACK IN WORKING ORDER?

COULD JUST BE A MATTER OF **BED REST**, BUT THINK ABOUT WHAT HAPPENED WHEN **PROFESSOR XAVIER** PUSHED HIMSELF TO THE LIMIT TO BATTLE **CASSANDRA NOVA.** * IT'S BEEN **WEEKS** AND HE STILL HASN'T FULLY RECOVERED.

HOW LONG AFTER A **SPRAINED ANKLE** CAN YOU RUN A **MARATHON**, PSYLOCKE?

IT WAS **CORTEZ** ALL RIGHT. I'D KNOW THAT LOUSY LITTLE **POLECAT** ANYWHERE.

SEE ANYTHING UP THERE, ROGUE?

NOPE. DIDN'T SEE NOTHIN'--NO **CITIES**, NO **PEOPLE**. NOT A DADGUM THING FOR **MILES**.

EMPTY ON DIS SIDE TOO, BUT THAT'S **GOOD** NEWS. AIN'T NOBODY TRYIN' TO KILL US FOR THE NEXT FEW MINUTES, NON?

IF THE MAN YOU SAW ON STAGE WAS IN FACT **FABIAN CORTEZ**, THEN HIS ATTACK PUSHED LILA'S POWERS **PAST** THEIR LIMITS. WITHOUT PROPER TREATMENT, WELL...I SUPPOSE WE COULD THINK OF IT AS AN **EXTENDED CAMPING TRIP.**

*IN THE NOW-CLASSIC X-MEN '92 VOL. 0: WARZONES!--HEATHER

I'M JUST THANKFUL WE LANDED **HERE** INSTEAD OF SOMEWHERE OUT IN **SPACE**. I COULDN'T EVEN--

HOLD, CHILD.

WHAT'S THE MATTER, STORMY? SOMETHING WRONG?

PERHAPS IT'S NOTHING, REMY...

...BUT **WOLVERINE** SHOULD HAVE RETURNED BY NOW.

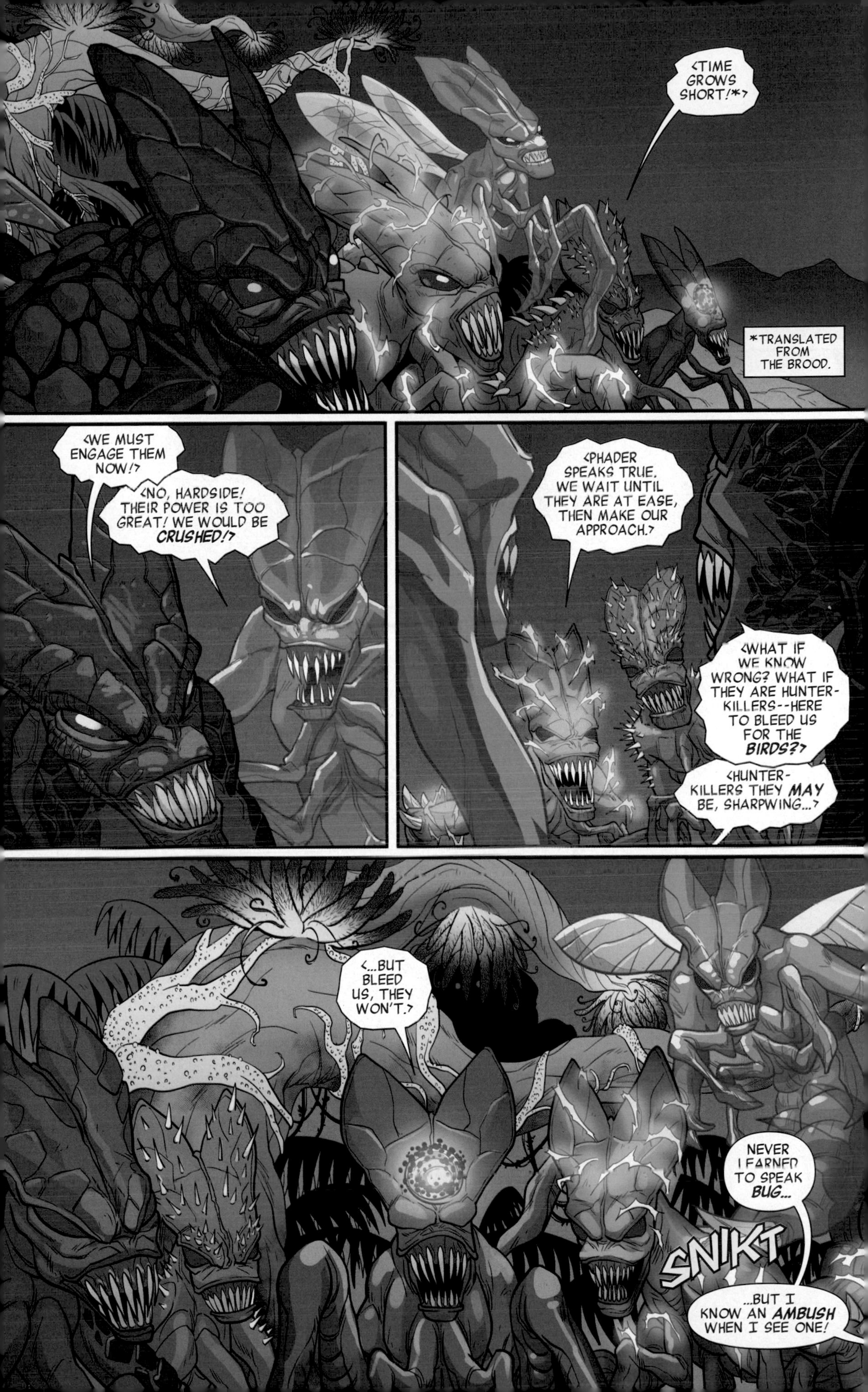

<TIME GROWS SHORT!*>
*TRANSLATED FROM THE BROOD.
<WE MUST ENGAGE THEM NOW!>
<NO, HARDSIDE! THEIR POWER IS TOO GREAT! WE WOULD BE ***CRUSHED!***>
<PHADER SPEAKS TRUE. WE WAIT UNTIL THEY ARE AT EASE, THEN MAKE OUR APPROACH.>
<WHAT IF WE KNOW WRONG? WHAT IF THEY ARE HUNTER-KILLERS--HERE TO BLEED US FOR THE ***BIRDS?***>
<HUNTER-KILLERS THEY ***MAY*** BE, SHARPWING...>
<...BUT BLEED US, THEY WON'T.>
NEVER I LEARNED TO SPEAK ***BUG...***
SNIKT
...BUT I KNOW AN ***AMBUSH*** WHEN I SEE ONE!

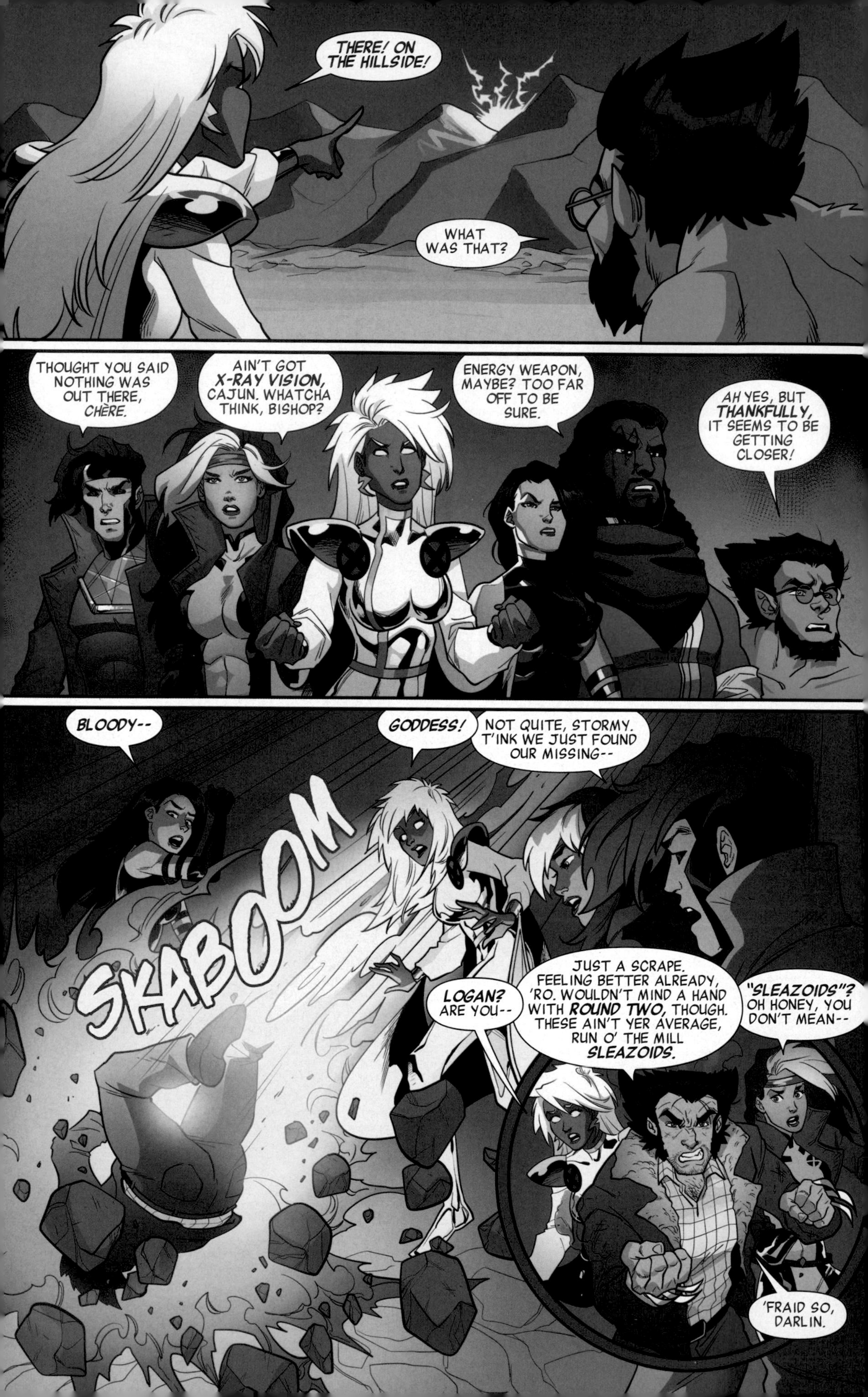
THERE! ON THE HILLSIDE!
WHAT WAS THAT?
THOUGHT YOU SAID NOTHING WAS OUT THERE, CHÈRE.
AIN'T GOT X-RAY VISION, CAJUN. WHATCHA THINK, BISHOP?
ENERGY WEAPON, MAYBE? TOO FAR OFF TO BE SURE.
AH YES, BUT THANKFULLY, IT SEEMS TO BE GETTING CLOSER!
BLOODY--
GODDESS!
NOT QUITE, STORMY. T'INK WE JUST FOUND OUR MISSING--
SKABOOM
LOGAN? ARE YOU--
JUST A SCRAPE. FEELING BETTER ALREADY, 'RO. WOULDN'T MIND A HAND WITH ROUND TWO, THOUGH. THESE AIN'T YER AVERAGE, RUN O' THE MILL SLEAZOIDS.
"SLEAZOIDS"? OH HONEY, YOU DON'T MEAN--
'FRAID SO, DARLIN.

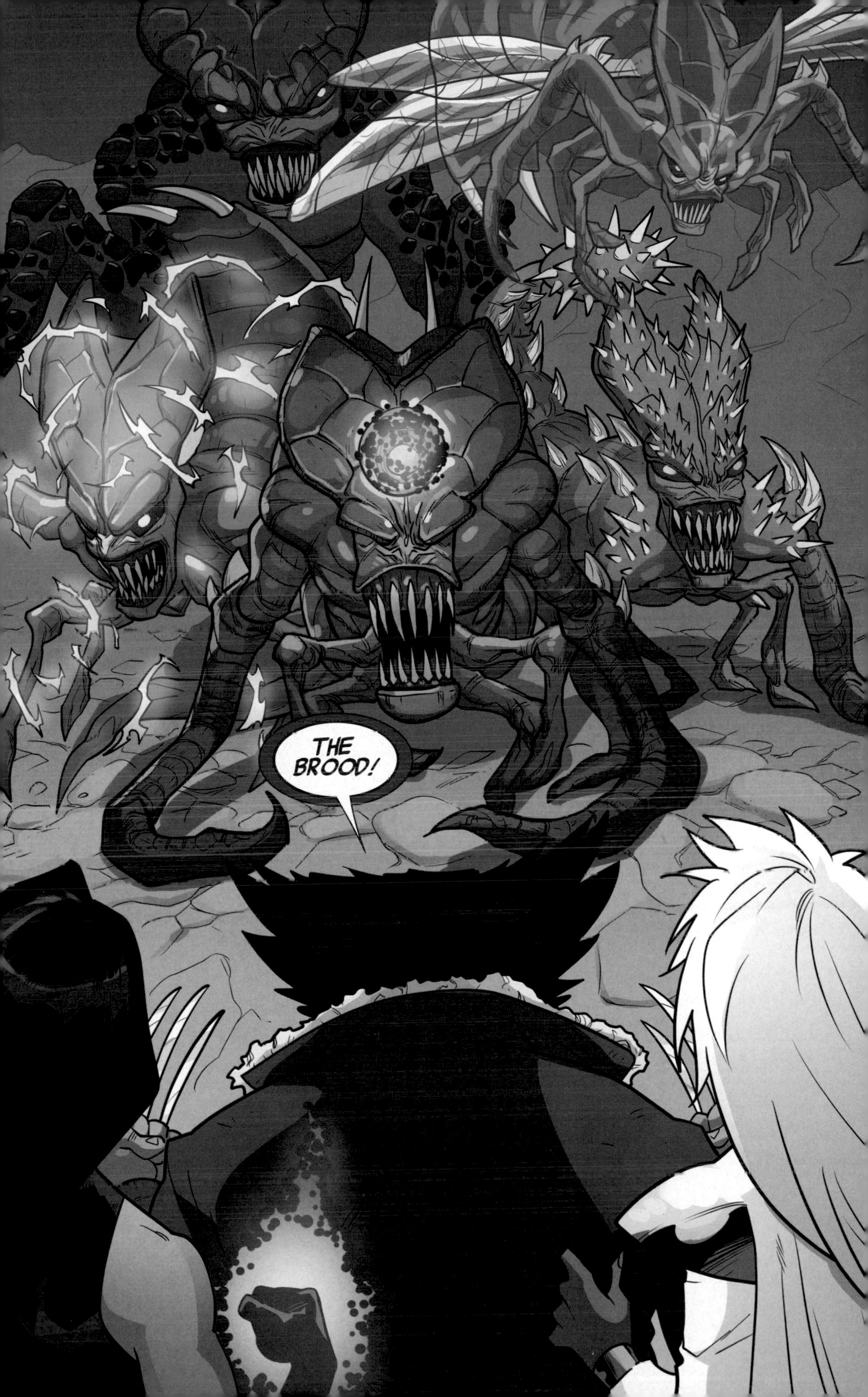
THE BROOD!

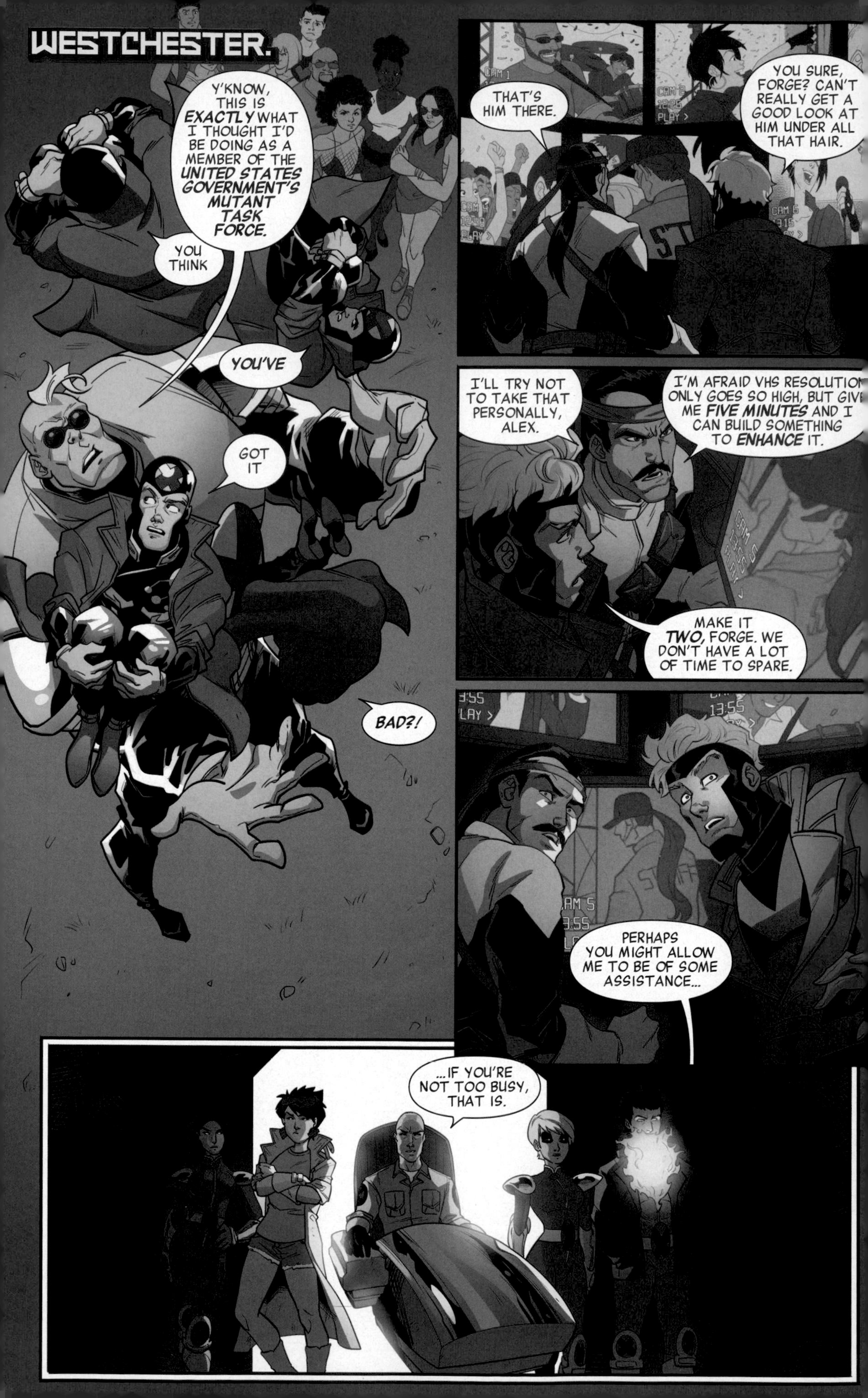
WESTCHESTER.
Y'KNOW, THIS IS EXACTLY WHAT I THOUGHT I'D BE DOING AS A MEMBER OF THE UNITED STATES GOVERNMENT'S MUTANT TASK FORCE.
YOU THINK
YOU'VE
GOT IT
BAD?!
THAT'S HIM THERE.
YOU SURE, FORGE? CAN'T REALLY GET A GOOD LOOK AT HIM UNDER ALL THAT HAIR.
I'LL TRY NOT TO TAKE THAT PERSONALLY, ALEX.
I'M AFRAID VHS RESOLUTION ONLY GOES SO HIGH, BUT GIVE ME FIVE MINUTES AND I CAN BUILD SOMETHING TO ENHANCE IT.
MAKE IT TWO, FORGE. WE DON'T HAVE A LOT OF TIME TO SPARE.
PERHAPS YOU MIGHT ALLOW ME TO BE OF SOME ASSISTANCE...
...IF YOU'RE NOT TOO BUSY, THAT IS.

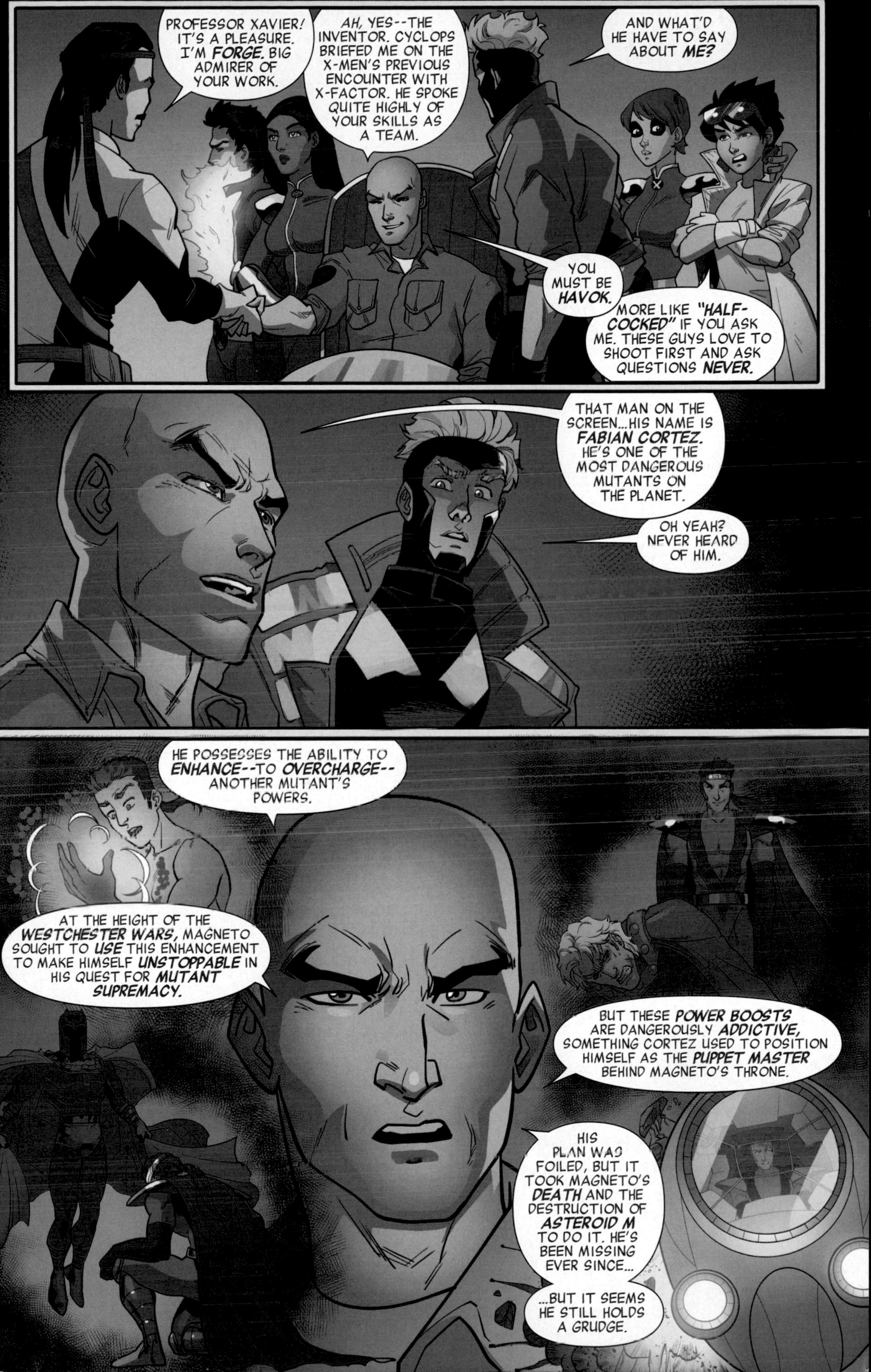
PROFESSOR XAVIER! IT'S A PLEASURE. I'M FORGE. BIG ADMIRER OF YOUR WORK.
AH, YES--THE INVENTOR. CYCLOPS BRIEFED ME ON THE X-MEN'S PREVIOUS ENCOUNTER WITH X-FACTOR. HE SPOKE QUITE HIGHLY OF YOUR SKILLS AS A TEAM.
AND WHAT'D HE HAVE TO SAY ABOUT ME?
YOU MUST BE HAVOK.
MORE LIKE "HALF-COCKED" IF YOU ASK ME. THESE GUYS LOVE TO SHOOT FIRST AND ASK QUESTIONS NEVER.
THAT MAN ON THE SCREEN...HIS NAME IS FABIAN CORTEZ. HE'S ONE OF THE MOST DANGEROUS MUTANTS ON THE PLANET.
OH YEAH? NEVER HEARD OF HIM.
HE POSSESSES THE ABILITY TO ENHANCE--TO OVERCHARGE--ANOTHER MUTANT'S POWERS.
AT THE HEIGHT OF THE WESTCHESTER WARS, MAGNETO SOUGHT TO USE THIS ENHANCEMENT TO MAKE HIMSELF UNSTOPPABLE IN HIS QUEST FOR MUTANT SUPREMACY.
BUT THESE POWER BOOSTS ARE DANGEROUSLY ADDICTIVE, SOMETHING CORTEZ USED TO POSITION HIMSELF AS THE PUPPET MASTER BEHIND MAGNETO'S THRONE.
HIS PLAN WAS FOILED, BUT IT TOOK MAGNETO'S DEATH AND THE DESTRUCTION OF ASTEROID M TO DO IT. HE'S BEEN MISSING EVER SINCE...
...BUT IT SEEMS HE STILL HOLDS A GRUDGE.

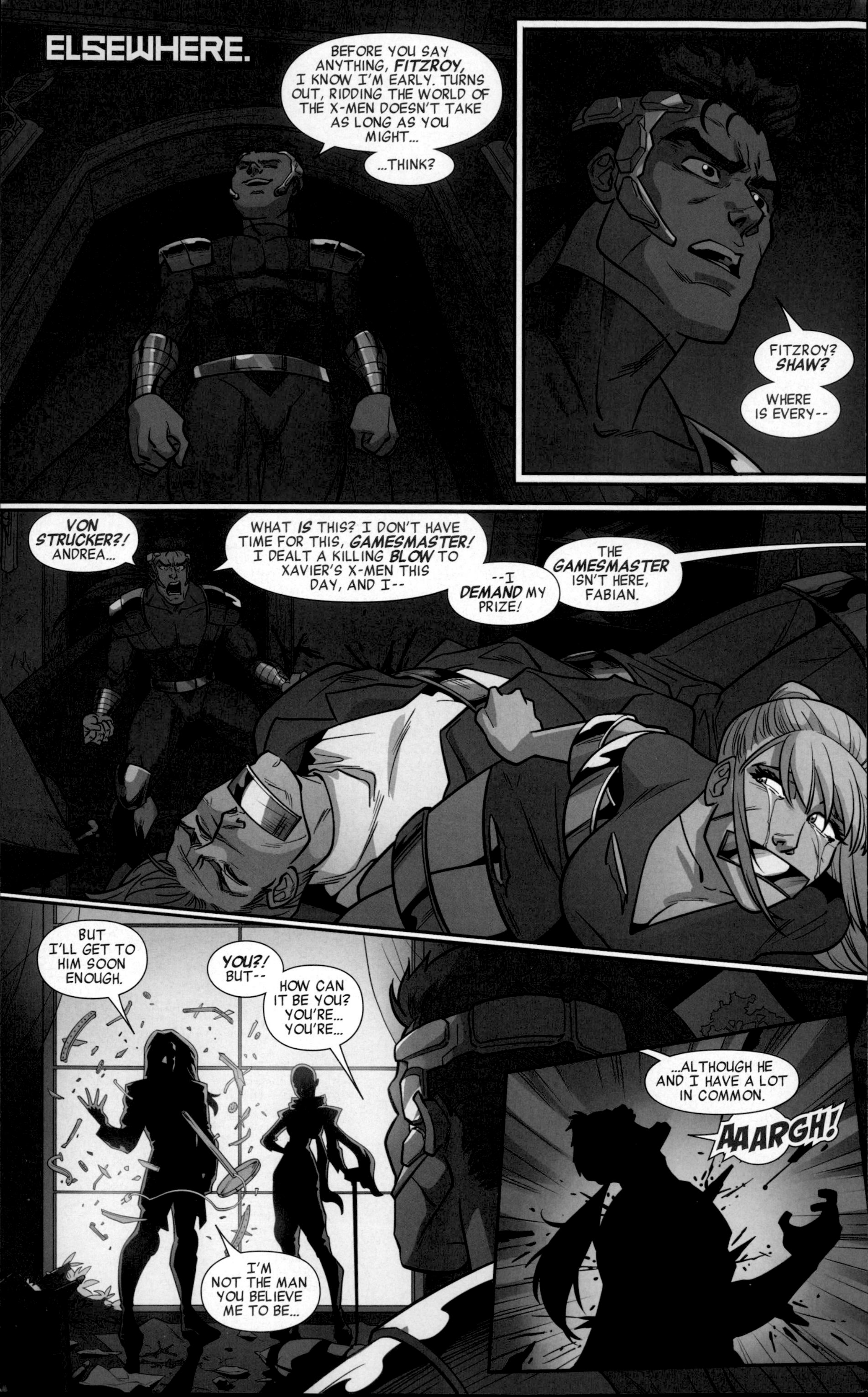
ELSEWHERE.
BEFORE YOU SAY ANYTHING, FITZROY, I KNOW I'M EARLY. TURNS OUT, RIDDING THE WORLD OF THE X-MEN DOESN'T TAKE AS LONG AS YOU MIGHT...
...THINK?
FITZROY? SHAW?
WHERE IS EVERY--
VON STRUCKER?! ANDREA...
WHAT IS THIS? I DON'T HAVE TIME FOR THIS, GAMESMASTER! I DEALT A KILLING BLOW TO XAVIER'S X-MEN THIS DAY, AND I--
--I DEMAND MY PRIZE!
THE GAMESMASTER ISN'T HERE, FABIAN.
BUT I'LL GET TO HIM SOON ENOUGH.
YOU?! BUT--
HOW CAN IT BE YOU? YOU'RE... YOU'RE...
I'M NOT THE MAN YOU BELIEVE ME TO BE...
...ALTHOUGH HE AND I HAVE A LOT IN COMMON.
AAARGH!

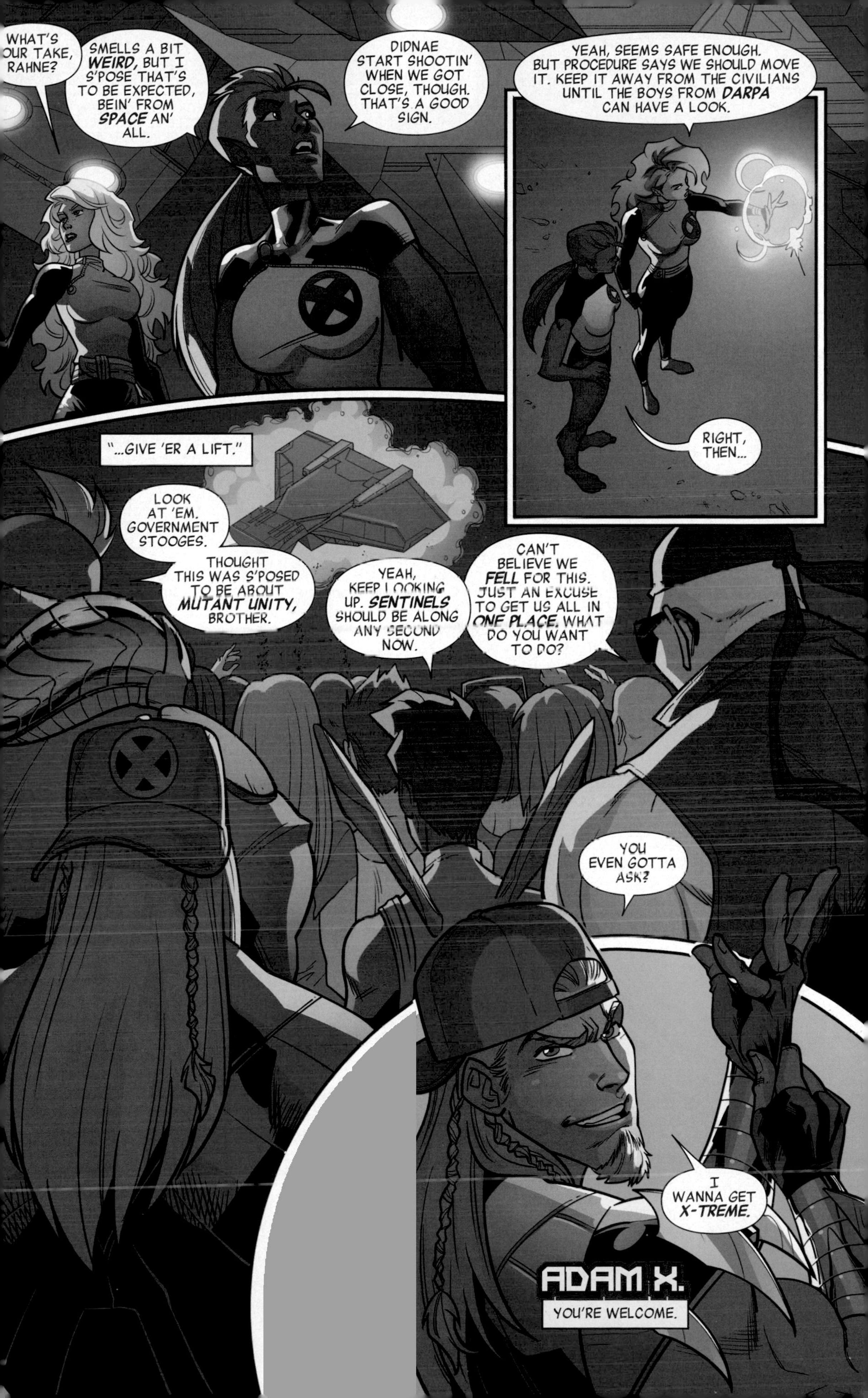
WHAT'S YOUR TAKE, RAHNE?
SMELLS A BIT WEIRD, BUT I S'POSE THAT'S TO BE EXPECTED, BEIN' FROM SPACE AN' ALL.
DIDNAE START SHOOTIN' WHEN WE GOT CLOSE, THOUGH. THAT'S A GOOD SIGN.
YEAH, SEEMS SAFE ENOUGH. BUT PROCEDURE SAYS WE SHOULD MOVE IT. KEEP IT AWAY FROM THE CIVILIANS UNTIL THE BOYS FROM DARPA CAN HAVE A LOOK.
RIGHT, THEN...
"...GIVE 'ER A LIFT."
LOOK AT 'EM. GOVERNMENT STOOGES.
THOUGHT THIS WAS S'POSED TO BE ABOUT MUTANT UNITY, BROTHER.
YEAH, KEEP LOOKING UP. SENTINELS SHOULD BE ALONG ANY SECOND NOW.
CAN'T BELIEVE WE FELL FOR THIS. JUST AN EXCUSE TO GET US ALL IN ONE PLACE. WHAT DO YOU WANT TO DO?
YOU EVEN GOTTA ASK?
I WANNA GET X-TREME.
ADAM X.
YOU'RE WELCOME.

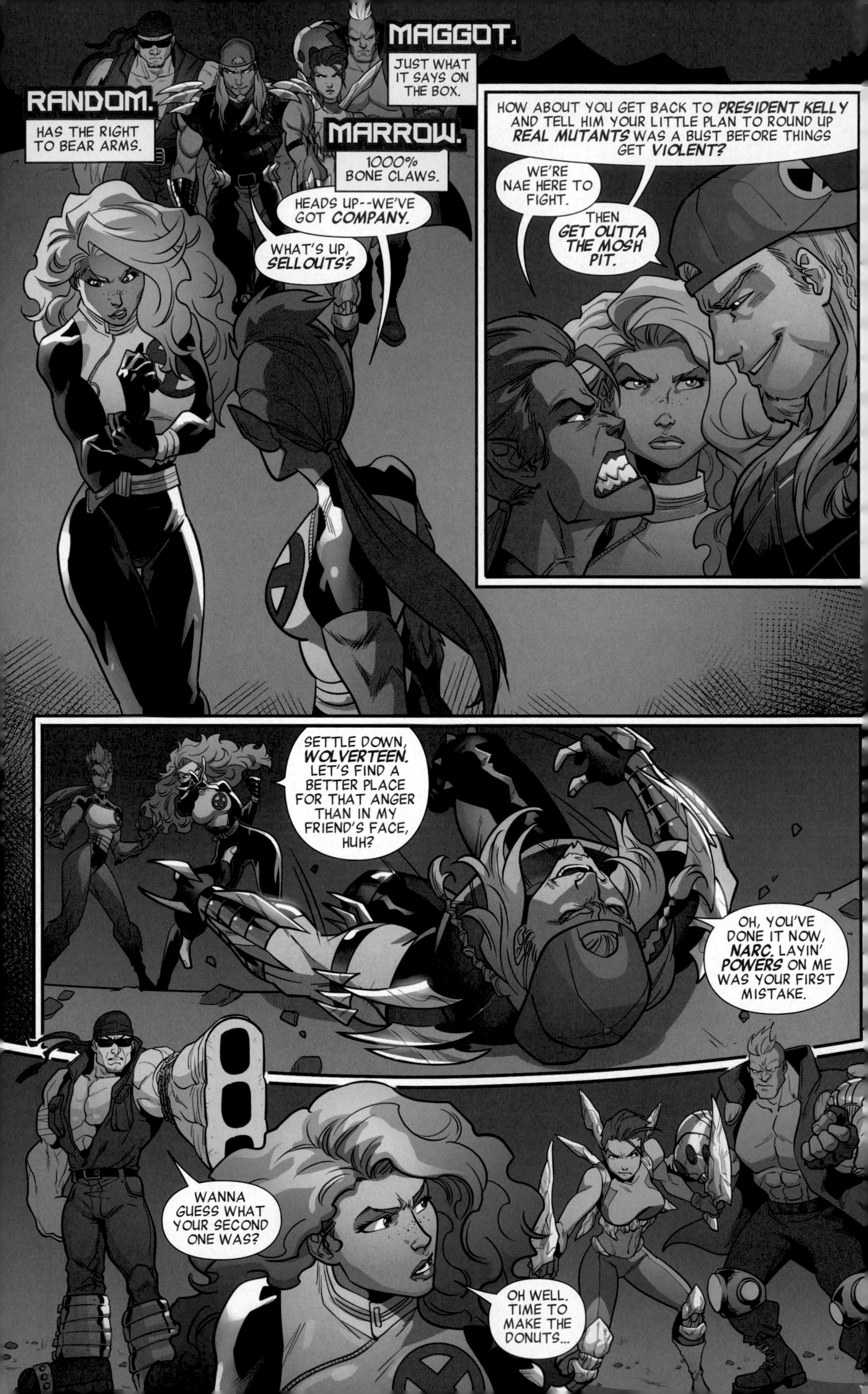

RANDOM.
HAS THE RIGHT TO BEAR ARMS.
MAGGOT.
JUST WHAT IT SAYS ON THE BOX.
MARROW.
1000% BONE CLAWS.
HEADS UP--WE'VE GOT COMPANY.
WHAT'S UP, SELLOUTS?
HOW ABOUT YOU GET BACK TO PRESIDENT KELLY AND TELL HIM YOUR LITTLE PLAN TO ROUND UP REAL MUTANTS WAS A BUST BEFORE THINGS GET VIOLENT?
WE'RE NAE HERE TO FIGHT.
THEN GET OUTTA THE MOSH PIT.
SETTLE DOWN, WOLVERTEEN. LET'S FIND A BETTER PLACE FOR THAT ANGER THAN IN MY FRIEND'S FACE, HUH?
OH, YOU'VE DONE IT NOW, NARC. LAYIN' POWERS ON ME WAS YOUR FIRST MISTAKE.
WANNA GUESS WHAT YOUR SECOND ONE WAS?
OH WELL. TIME TO MAKE THE DONUTS...

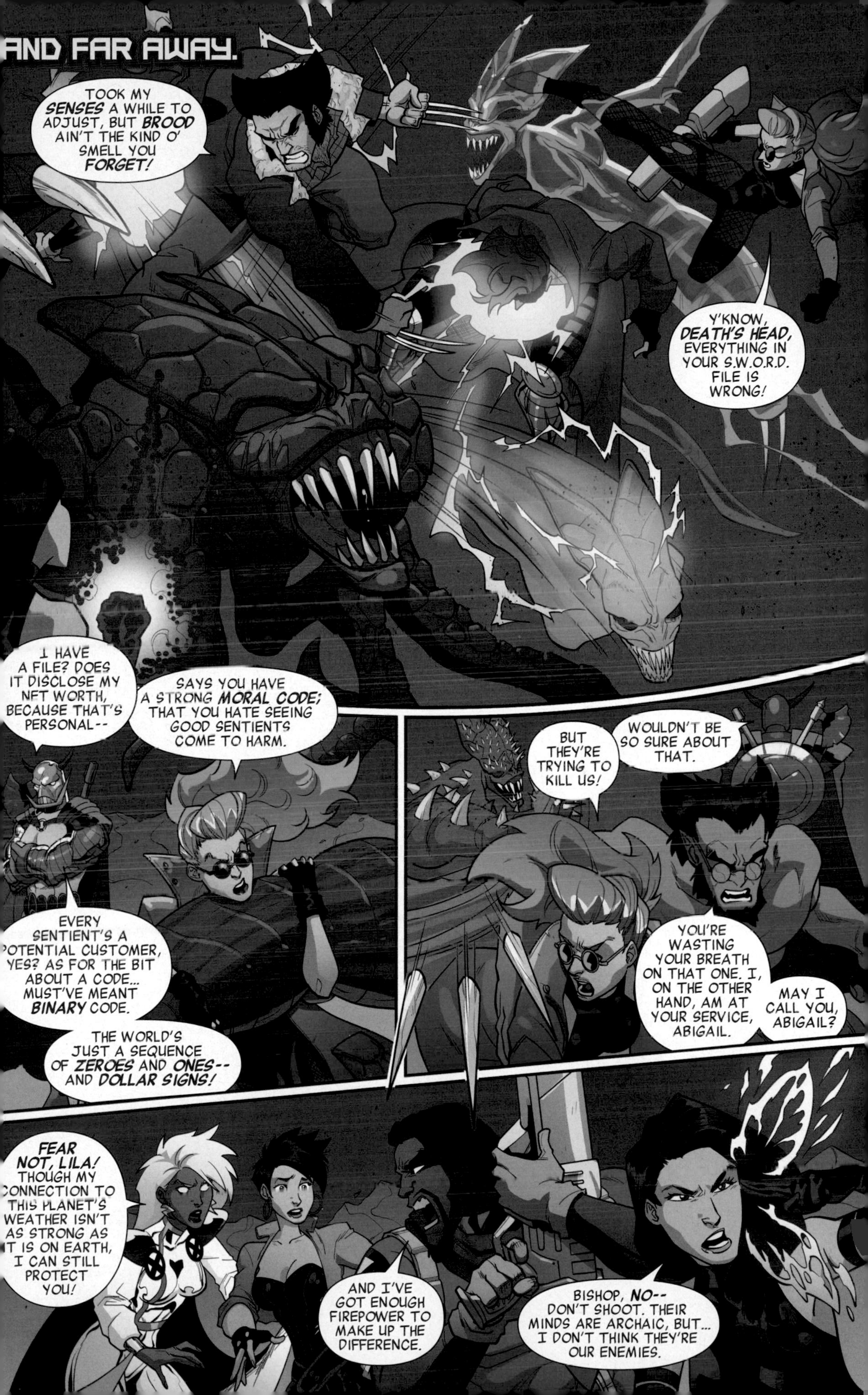
AND FAR AWAY.
TOOK MY SENSES A WHILE TO ADJUST, BUT BROOD AIN'T THE KIND O' SMELL YOU FORGET!
Y'KNOW, DEATH'S HEAD, EVERYTHING IN YOUR S.W.O.R.D. FILE IS WRONG!
I HAVE A FILE? DOES IT DISCLOSE MY NET WORTH, BECAUSE THAT'S PERSONAL--
SAYS YOU HAVE A STRONG MORAL CODE; THAT YOU HATE SEEING GOOD SENTIENTS COME TO HARM.
EVERY SENTIENT'S A POTENTIAL CUSTOMER, YES? AS FOR THE BIT ABOUT A CODE... MUST'VE MEANT BINARY CODE.
THE WORLD'S JUST A SEQUENCE OF ZEROES AND ONES-- AND DOLLAR SIGNS!
BUT THEY'RE TRYING TO KILL US!
WOULDN'T BE SO SURE ABOUT THAT.
YOU'RE WASTING YOUR BREATH ON THAT ONE. I, ON THE OTHER HAND, AM AT YOUR SERVICE, ABIGAIL.
MAY I CALL YOU, ABIGAIL?
FEAR NOT, LILA! THOUGH MY CONNECTION TO THIS PLANET'S WEATHER ISN'T AS STRONG AS IT IS ON EARTH, I CAN STILL PROTECT YOU!
AND I'VE GOT ENOUGH FIREPOWER TO MAKE UP THE DIFFERENCE.
BISHOP, NO-- DON'T SHOOT. THEIR MINDS ARE ARCHAIC, BUT... I DON'T THINK THEY'RE OUR ENEMIES.

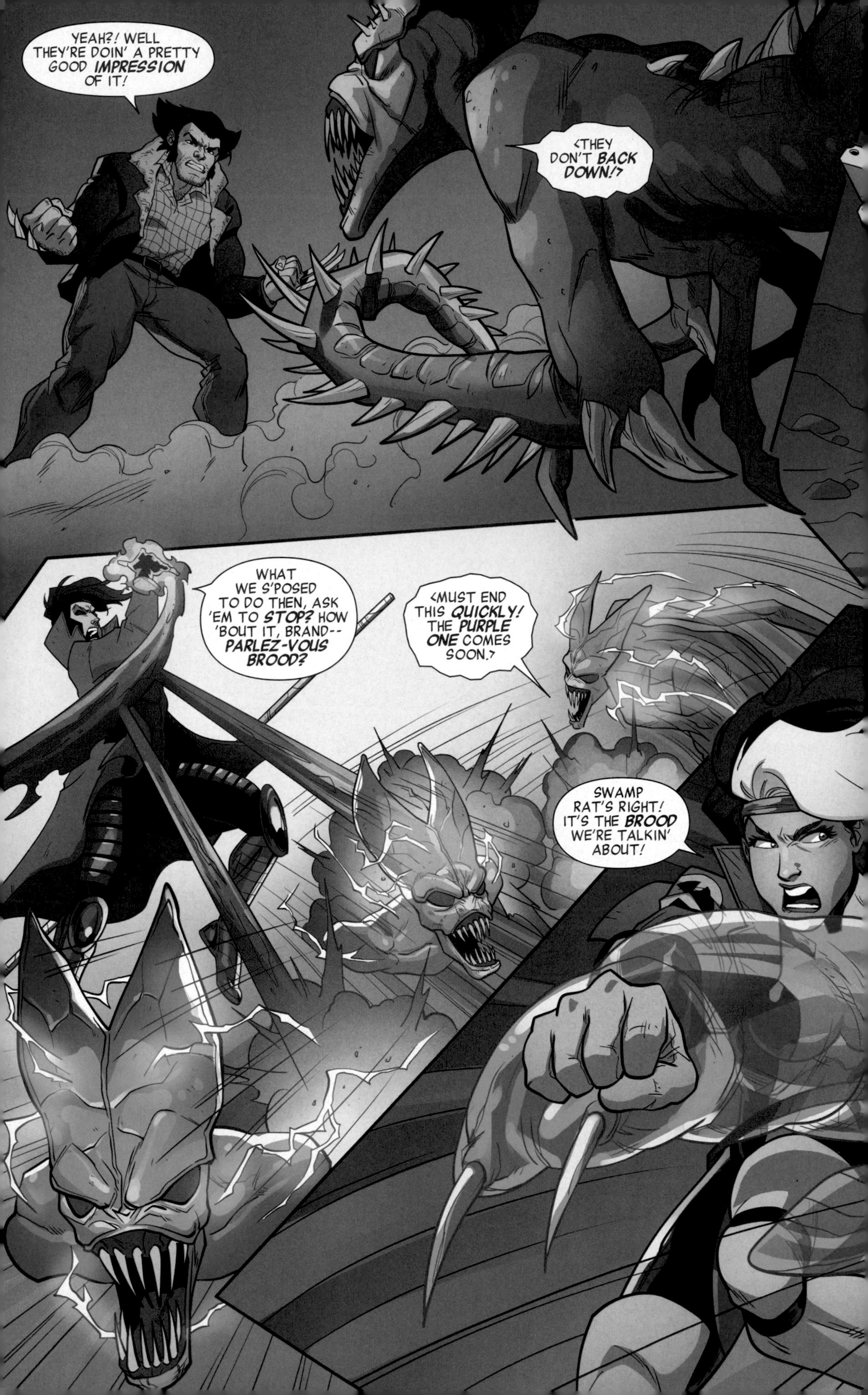
YEAH?! WELL THEY'RE DOIN' A PRETTY GOOD IMPRESSION OF IT!
<THEY DON'T BACK DOWN!>
WHAT WE S'POSED TO DO THEN, ASK 'EM TO STOP? HOW 'BOUT IT, BRAND-- PARLEZ-VOUS BROOD?
<MUST END THIS QUICKLY! THE PURPLE ONE COMES SOON.>
SWAMP RAT'S RIGHT! IT'S THE BROOD WE'RE TALKIN' ABOUT!

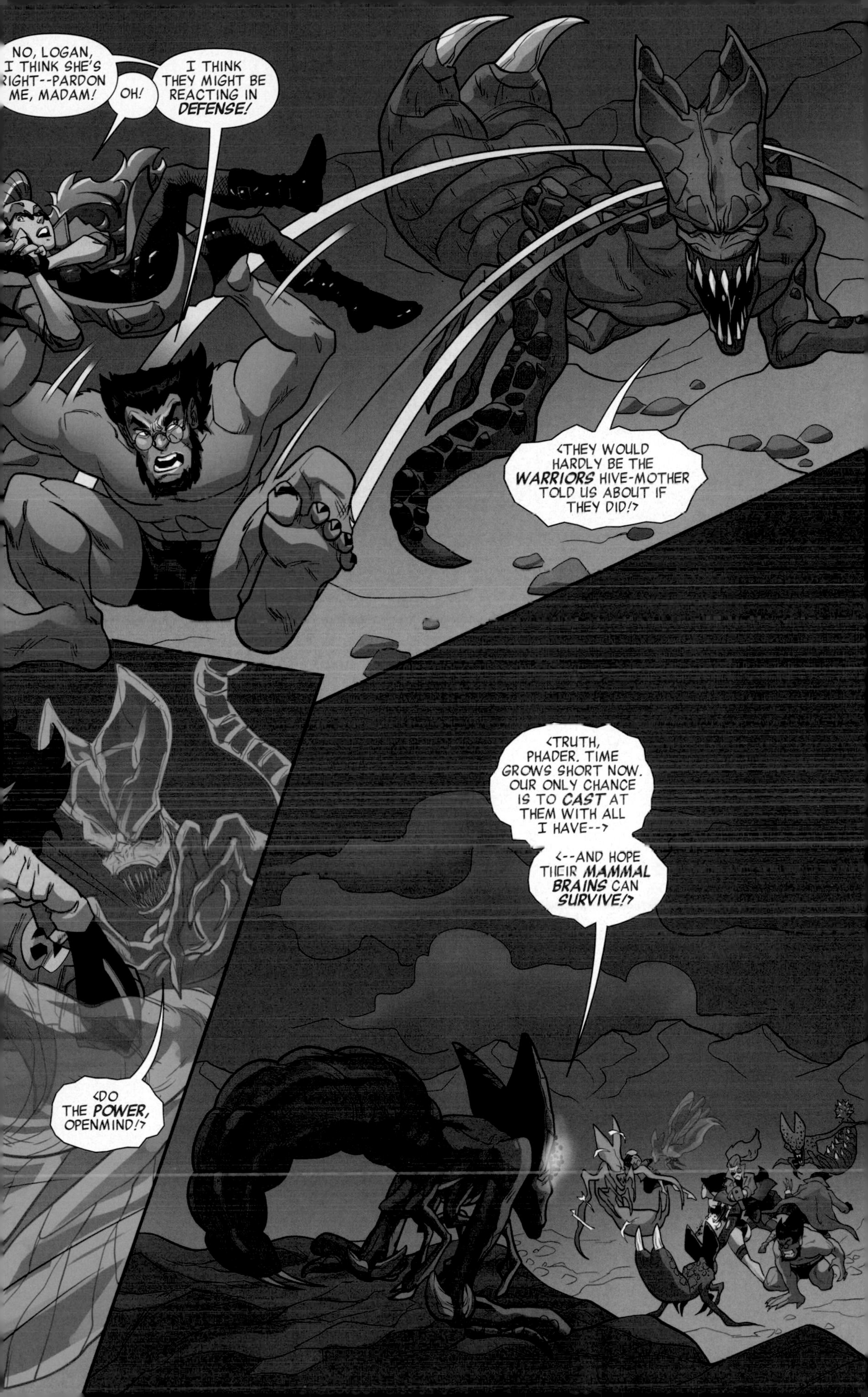
NO, LOGAN, I THINK SHE'S RIGHT--PARDON ME, MADAM!
OH!
I THINK THEY MIGHT BE REACTING IN DEFENSE!
<THEY WOULD HARDLY BE THE WARRIORS HIVE-MOTHER TOLD US ABOUT IF THEY DID!>
<TRUTH, PHADER. TIME GROWS SHORT NOW. OUR ONLY CHANCE IS TO CAST AT THEM WITH ALL I HAVE-->
<--AND HOPE THEIR MAMMAL BRAINS CAN SURVIVE!>
<DO THE POWER, OPENMIND!>

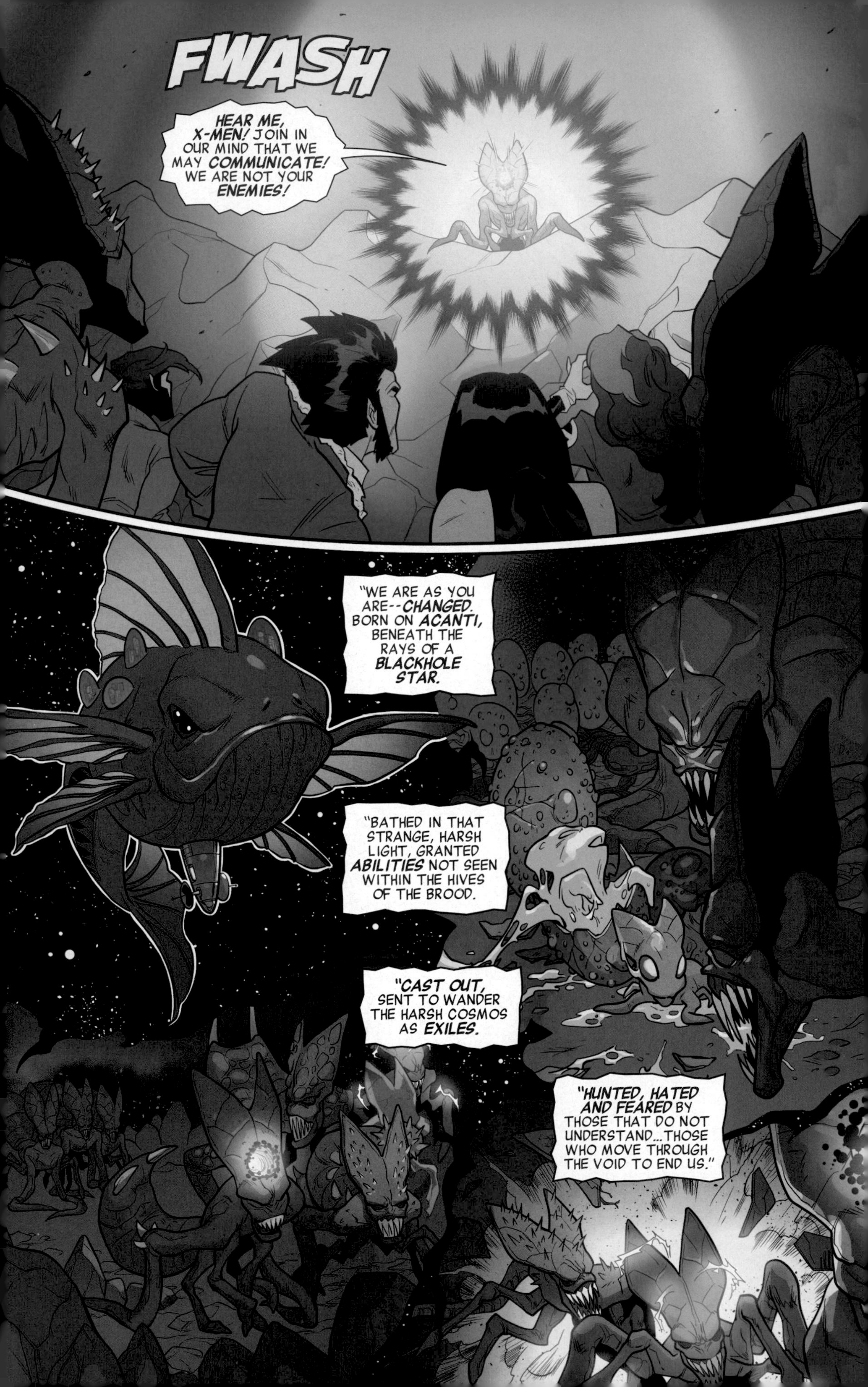
FWASH
HEAR ME, X-MEN! JOIN IN OUR MIND THAT WE MAY COMMUNICATE! WE ARE NOT YOUR ENEMIES!
"WE ARE AS YOU ARE--CHANGED. BORN ON ACANTI, BENEATH THE RAYS OF A BLACKHOLE STAR.
"BATHED IN THAT STRANGE, HARSH LIGHT, GRANTED ABILITIES NOT SEEN WITHIN THE HIVES OF THE BROOD.
"CAST OUT, SENT TO WANDER THE HARSH COSMOS AS EXILES.
"HUNTED, HATED AND FEARED BY THOSE THAT DO NOT UNDERSTAND...THOSE WHO MOVE THROUGH THE VOID TO END US."

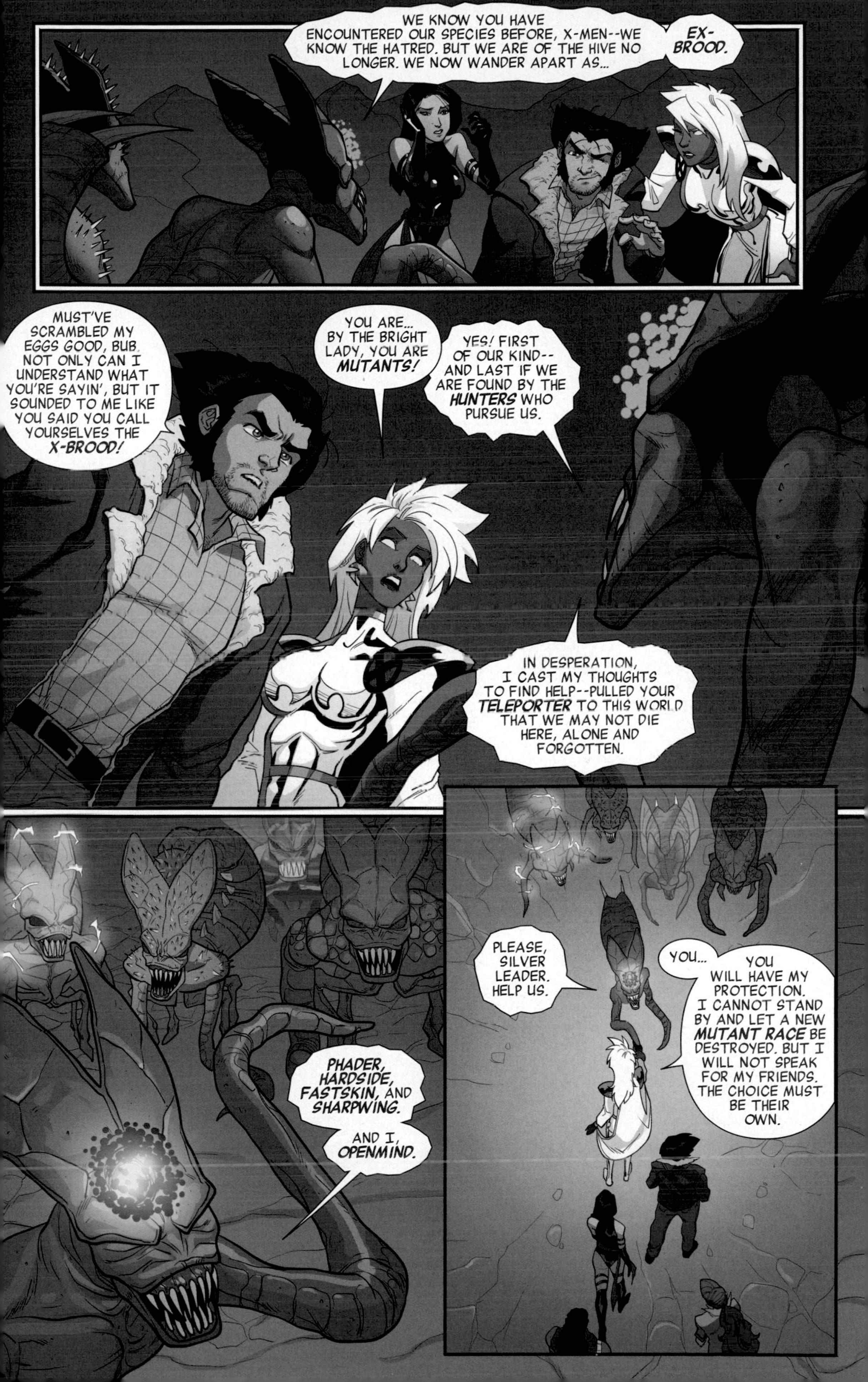

WE KNOW YOU HAVE ENCOUNTERED OUR SPECIES BEFORE, X-MEN--WE KNOW THE HATRED. BUT WE ARE OF THE HIVE NO LONGER. WE NOW WANDER APART AS...
EX-BROOD.
MUST'VE SCRAMBLED MY EGGS GOOD, BUB. NOT ONLY CAN I UNDERSTAND WHAT YOU'RE SAYIN', BUT IT SOUNDED TO ME LIKE YOU SAID YOU CALL YOURSELVES THE X-BROOD!
YOU ARE... BY THE BRIGHT LADY, YOU ARE MUTANTS!
YES! FIRST OF OUR KIND--AND LAST IF WE ARE FOUND BY THE HUNTERS WHO PURSUE US.
IN DESPERATION, I CAST MY THOUGHTS TO FIND HELP--PULLED YOUR TELEPORTER TO THIS WORLD THAT WE MAY NOT DIE HERE, ALONE AND FORGOTTEN.
PHADER, HARDSIDE, FASTSKIN, AND SHARPWING.
AND I, OPENMIND.
PLEASE, SILVER LEADER. HELP US.
YOU...
YOU WILL HAVE MY PROTECTION. I CANNOT STAND BY AND LET A NEW MUTANT RACE BE DESTROYED. BUT I WILL NOT SPEAK FOR MY FRIENDS. THE CHOICE MUST BE THEIR OWN.

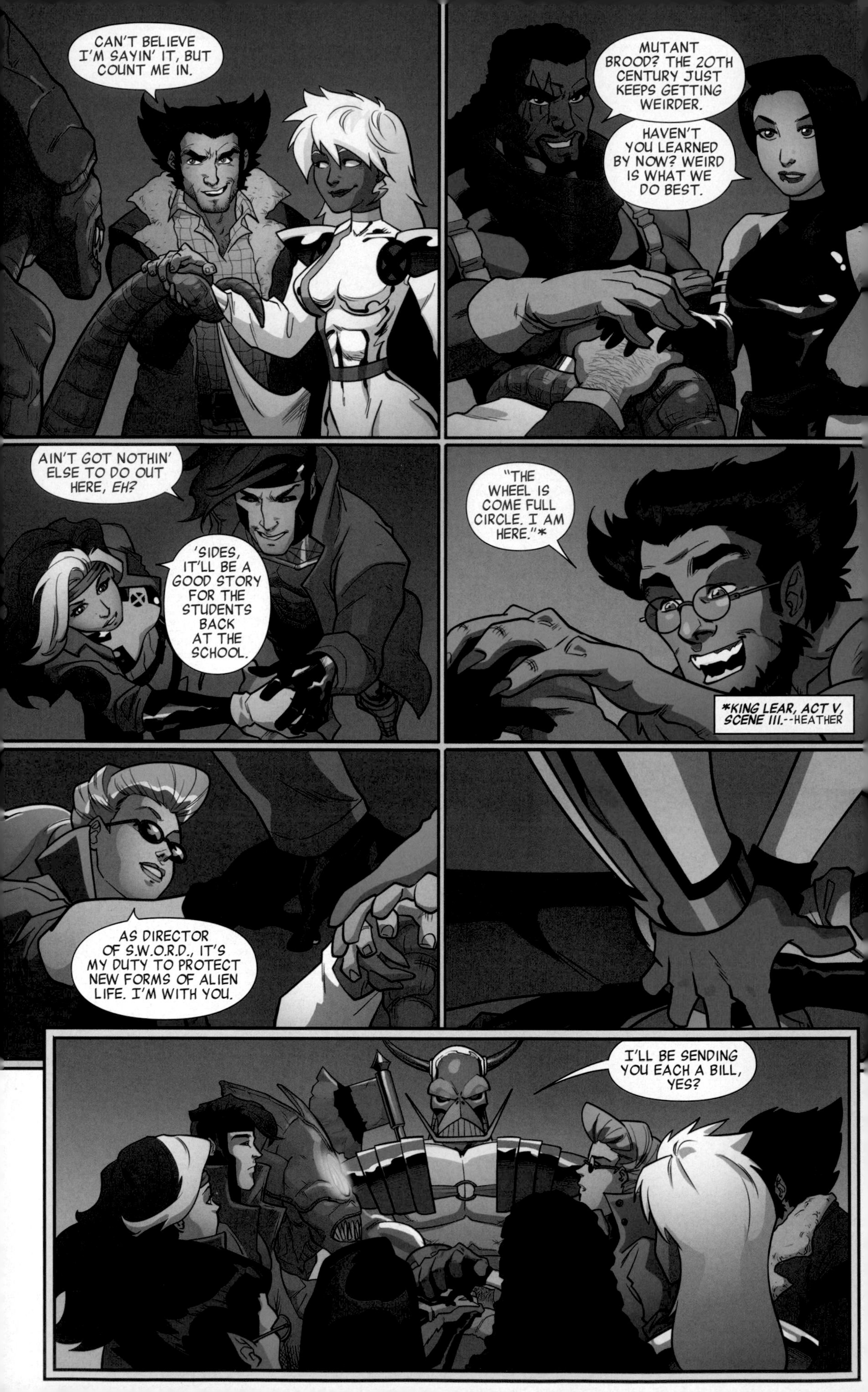

CAN'T BELIEVE I'M SAYIN' IT, BUT COUNT ME IN.
MUTANT BROOD? THE 20TH CENTURY JUST KEEPS GETTING WEIRDER.
HAVEN'T YOU LEARNED BY NOW? WEIRD IS WHAT WE DO BEST.
AIN'T GOT NOTHIN' ELSE TO DO OUT HERE, EH?
'SIDES, IT'LL BE A GOOD STORY FOR THE STUDENTS BACK AT THE SCHOOL.
"THE WHEEL IS COME FULL CIRCLE. I AM HERE."*
*KING LEAR, ACT V, SCENE III.--HEATHER
AS DIRECTOR OF S.W.O.R.D., IT'S MY DUTY TO PROTECT NEW FORMS OF ALIEN LIFE. I'M WITH YOU.
I'LL BE SENDING YOU EACH A BILL, YES?

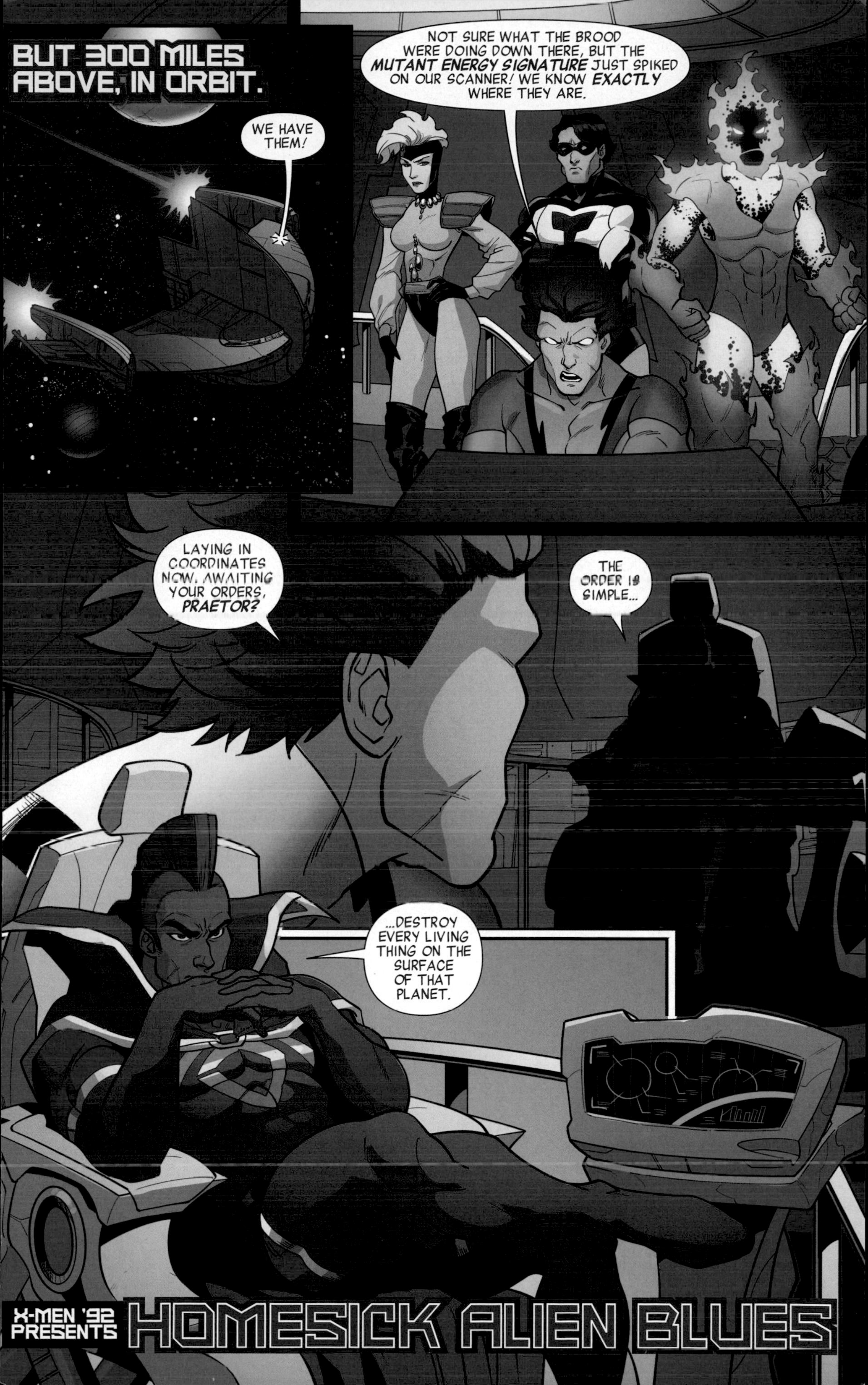
BUT 300 MILES ABOVE, IN ORBIT.
WE HAVE THEM!
NOT SURE WHAT THE BROOD WERE DOING DOWN THERE, BUT THE MUTANT ENERGY SIGNATURE JUST SPIKED ON OUR SCANNER! WE KNOW EXACTLY WHERE THEY ARE.
LAYING IN COORDINATES NOW. AWAITING YOUR ORDERS, PRAETOR?
THE ORDER IS SIMPLE...
...DESTROY EVERY LIVING THING ON THE SURFACE OF THAT PLANET.
X-MEN '92 PRESENTS
HOMESICK ALIEN BLUES

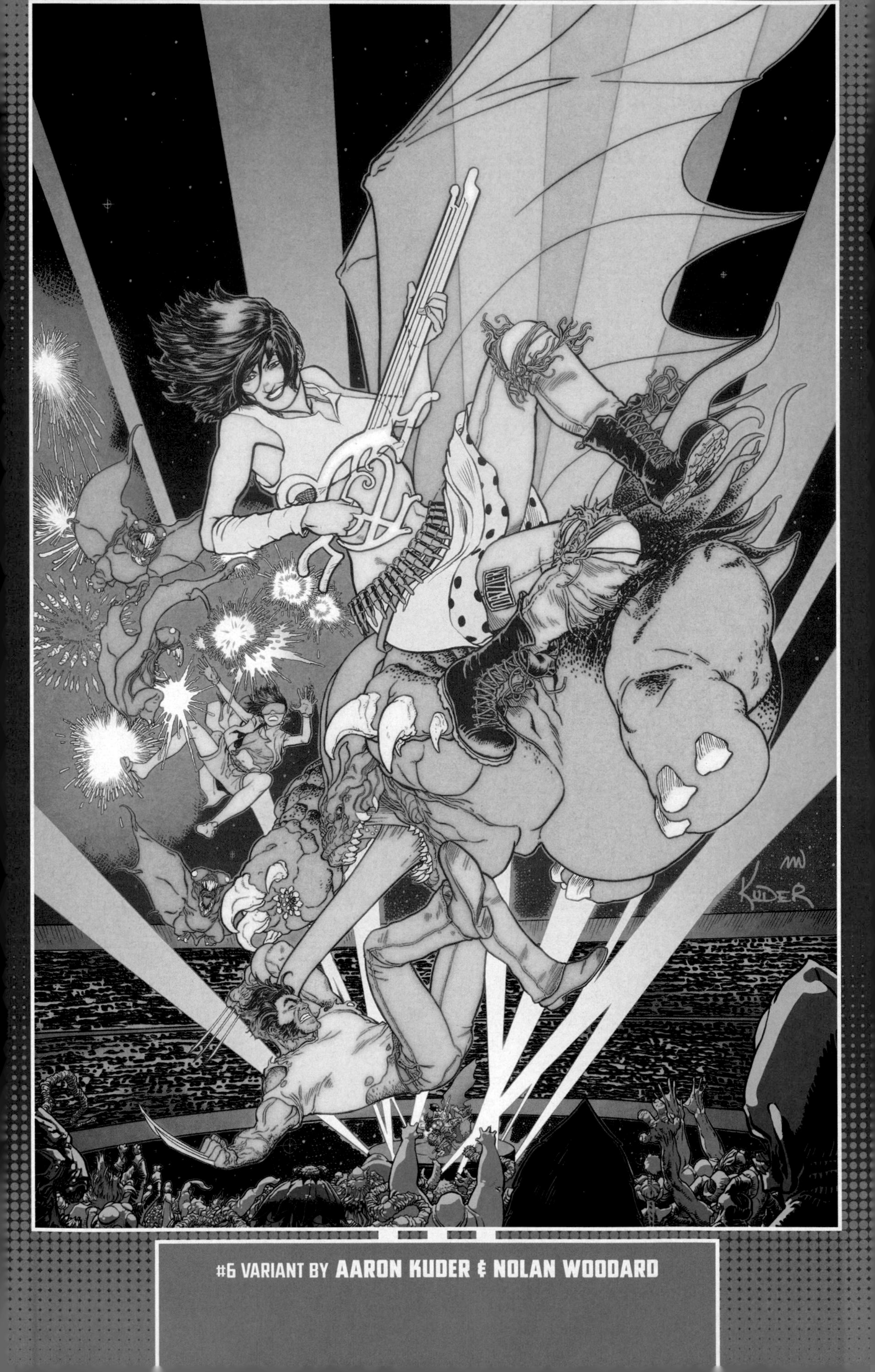
KUDER

#6 VARIANT BY **AARON KUDER & NOLAN WOODARD**

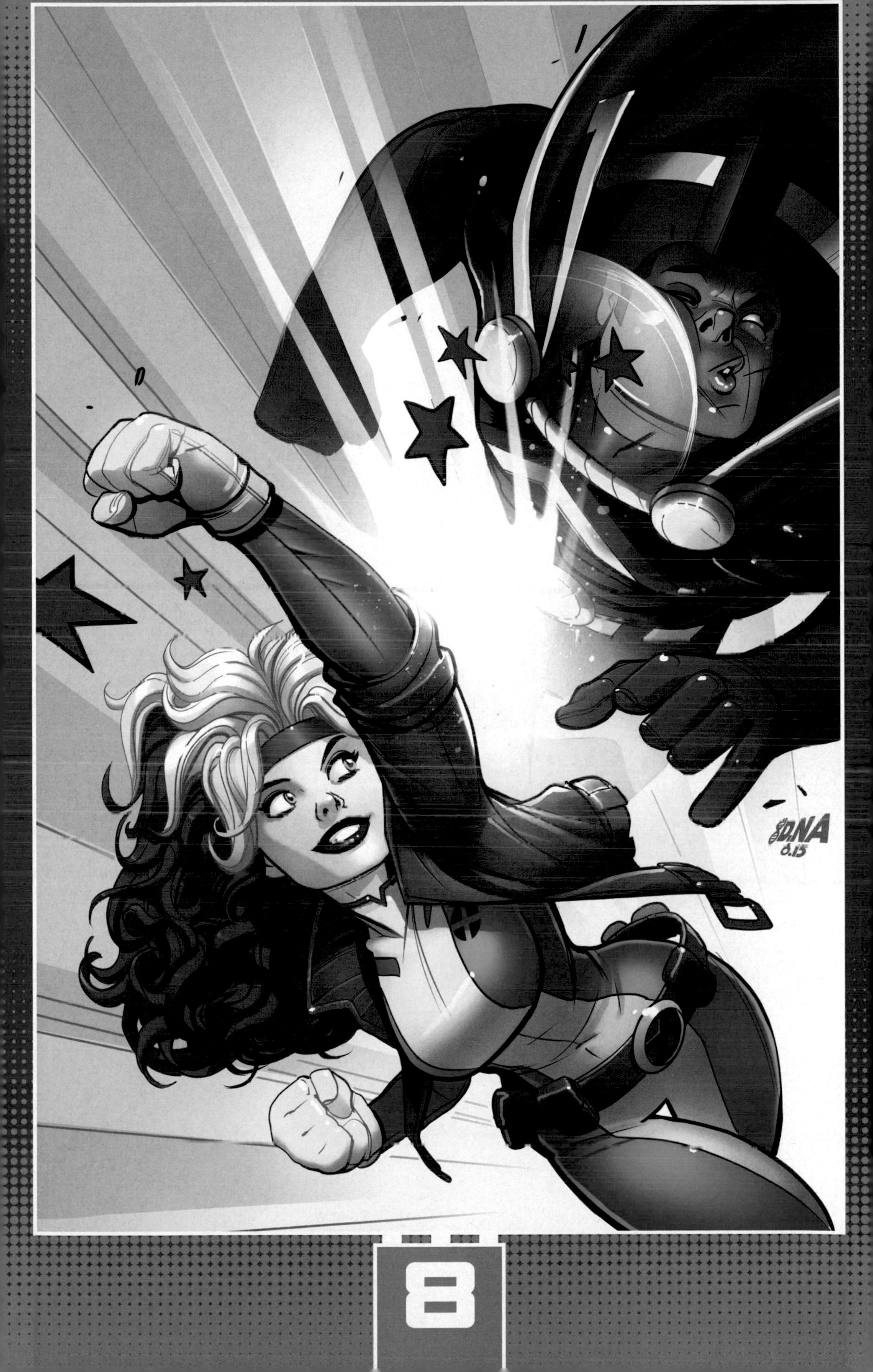

8

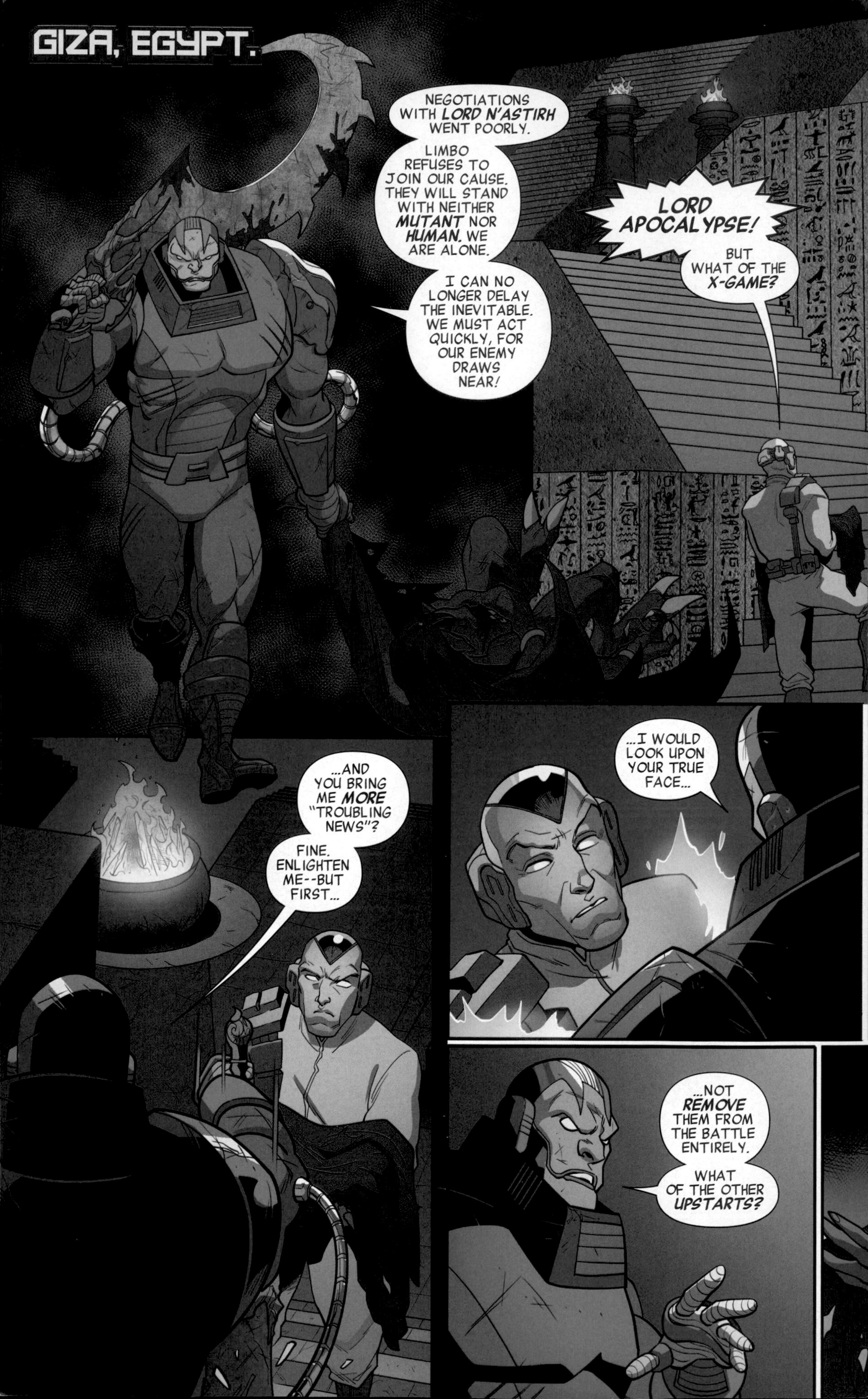
GIZA, EGYPT.
NEGOTIATIONS WITH LORD N'ASTIRH WENT POORLY.
LIMBO REFUSES TO JOIN OUR CAUSE. THEY WILL STAND WITH NEITHER MUTANT NOR HUMAN. WE ARE ALONE.
I CAN NO LONGER DELAY THE INEVITABLE. WE MUST ACT QUICKLY, FOR OUR ENEMY DRAWS NEAR!
LORD APOCALYPSE!
BUT WHAT OF THE X-GAME?
...AND YOU BRING ME MORE "TROUBLING NEWS"?
FINE. ENLIGHTEN ME--BUT FIRST...
...I WOULD LOOK UPON YOUR TRUE FACE...
...NOT REMOVE THEM FROM THE BATTLE ENTIRELY.
WHAT OF THE OTHER UPSTARTS?

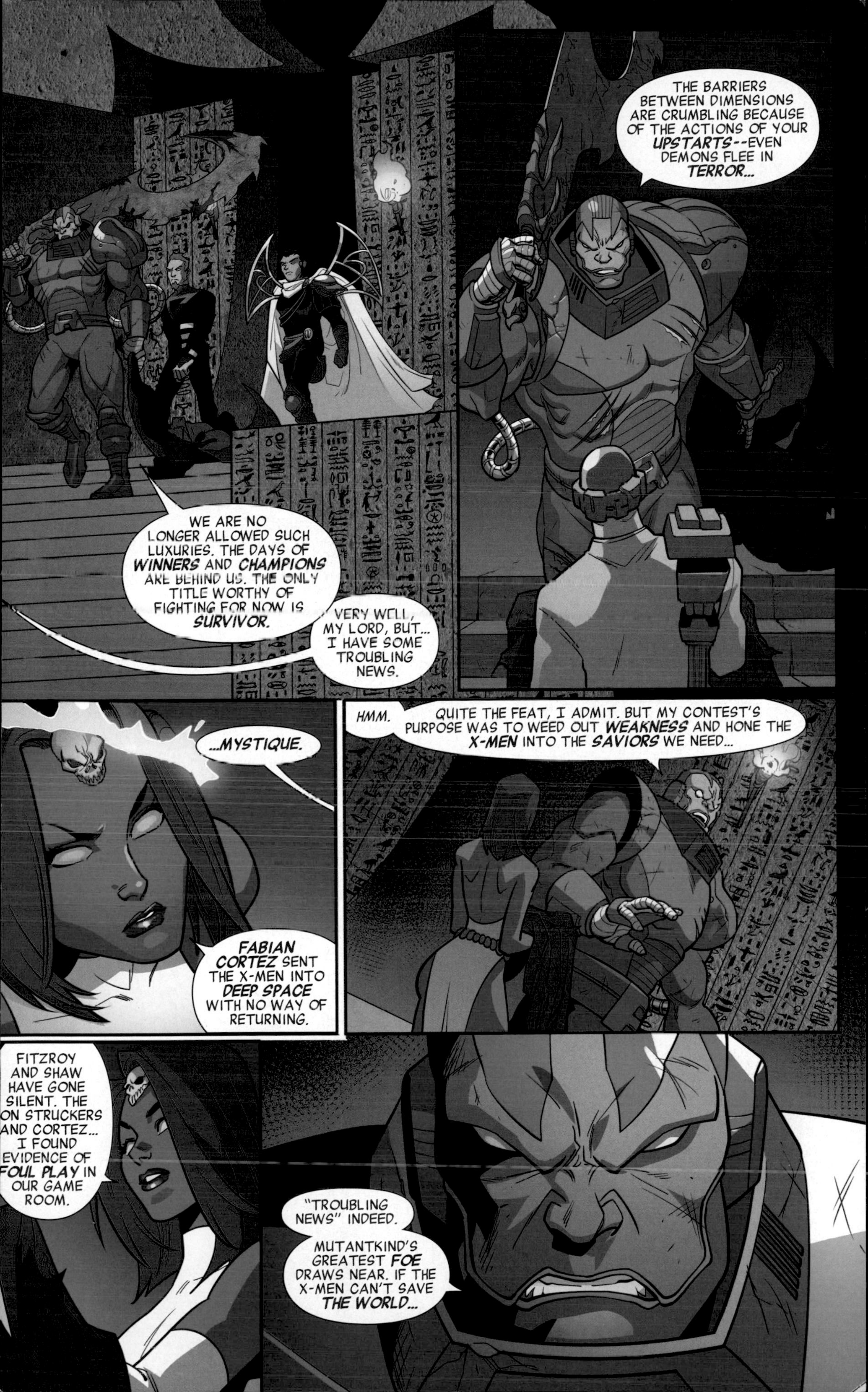

THE BARRIERS BETWEEN DIMENSIONS ARE CRUMBLING BECAUSE OF THE ACTIONS OF YOUR UPSTARTS--EVEN DEMONS FLEE IN TERROR...
WE ARE NO LONGER ALLOWED SUCH LUXURIES. THE DAYS OF WINNERS AND CHAMPIONS ARE BEHIND US. THE ONLY TITLE WORTHY OF FIGHTING FOR NOW IS SURVIVOR.
VERY WELL, MY LORD, BUT... I HAVE SOME TROUBLING NEWS.
...MYSTIQUE.
FABIAN CORTEZ SENT THE X-MEN INTO DEEP SPACE WITH NO WAY OF RETURNING.
HMM.
QUITE THE FEAT, I ADMIT. BUT MY CONTEST'S PURPOSE WAS TO WEED OUT WEAKNESS AND HONE THE X-MEN INTO THE SAVIORS WE NEED...
FITZROY AND SHAW HAVE GONE SILENT. THE VON STRUCKERS AND CORTEZ... I FOUND EVIDENCE OF FOUL PLAY IN OUR GAME ROOM.
"TROUBLING NEWS" INDEED.
MUTANTKIND'S GREATEST FOE DRAWS NEAR. IF THE X-MEN CAN'T SAVE THE WORLD...

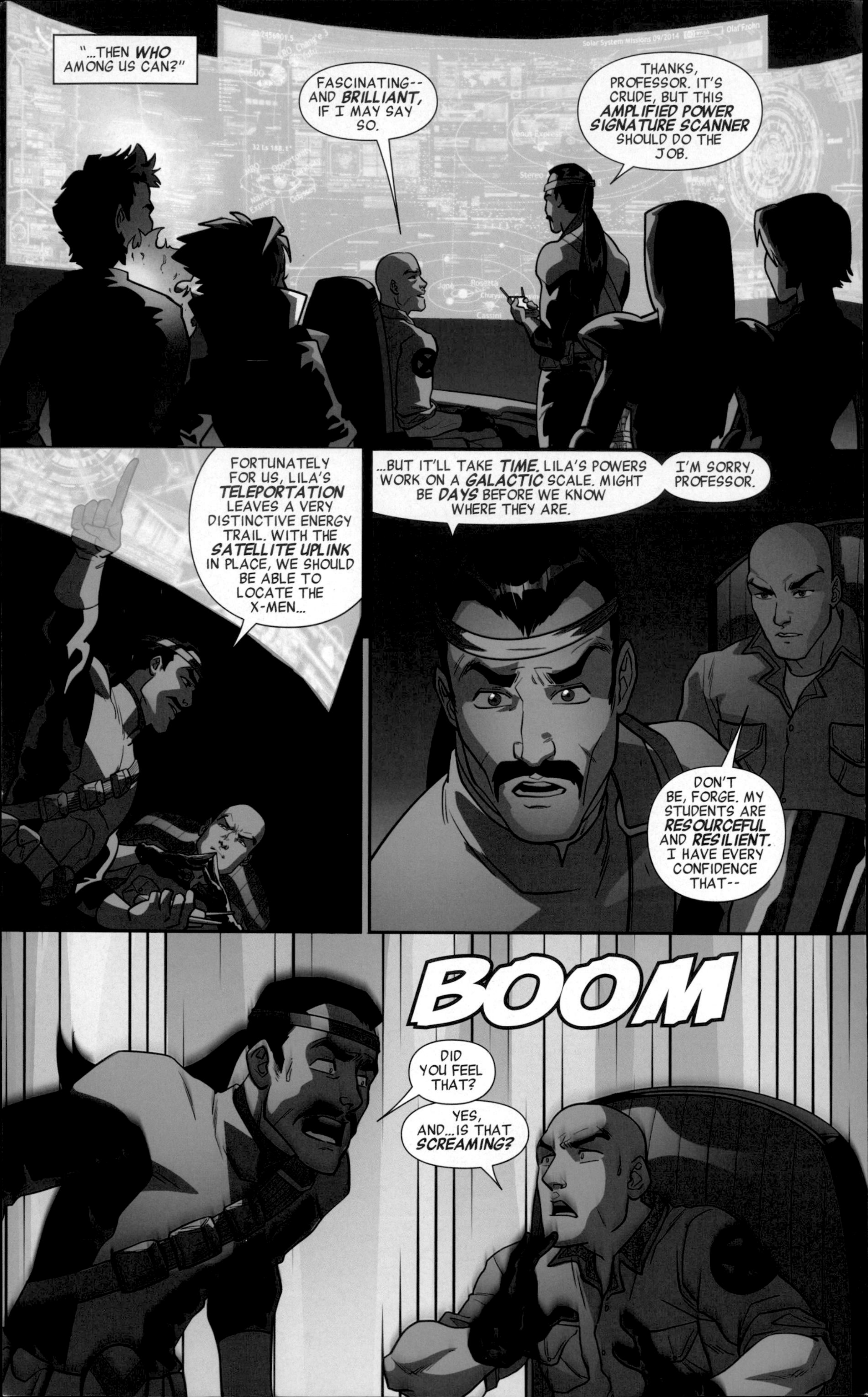
"...THEN WHO AMONG US CAN?"
FASCINATING--AND BRILLIANT, IF I MAY SAY SO.
THANKS, PROFESSOR. IT'S CRUDE, BUT THIS AMPLIFIED POWER SIGNATURE SCANNER SHOULD DO THE JOB.
FORTUNATELY FOR US, LILA'S TELEPORTATION LEAVES A VERY DISTINCTIVE ENERGY TRAIL. WITH THE SATELLITE UPLINK IN PLACE, WE SHOULD BE ABLE TO LOCATE THE X-MEN...
...BUT IT'LL TAKE TIME. LILA'S POWERS WORK ON A GALACTIC SCALE. MIGHT BE DAYS BEFORE WE KNOW WHERE THEY ARE.
I'M SORRY, PROFESSOR.
DON'T BE, FORGE. MY STUDENTS ARE RESOURCEFUL AND RESILIENT. I HAVE EVERY CONFIDENCE THAT--
BOOM
DID YOU FEEL THAT?
YES, AND...IS THAT SCREAMING?

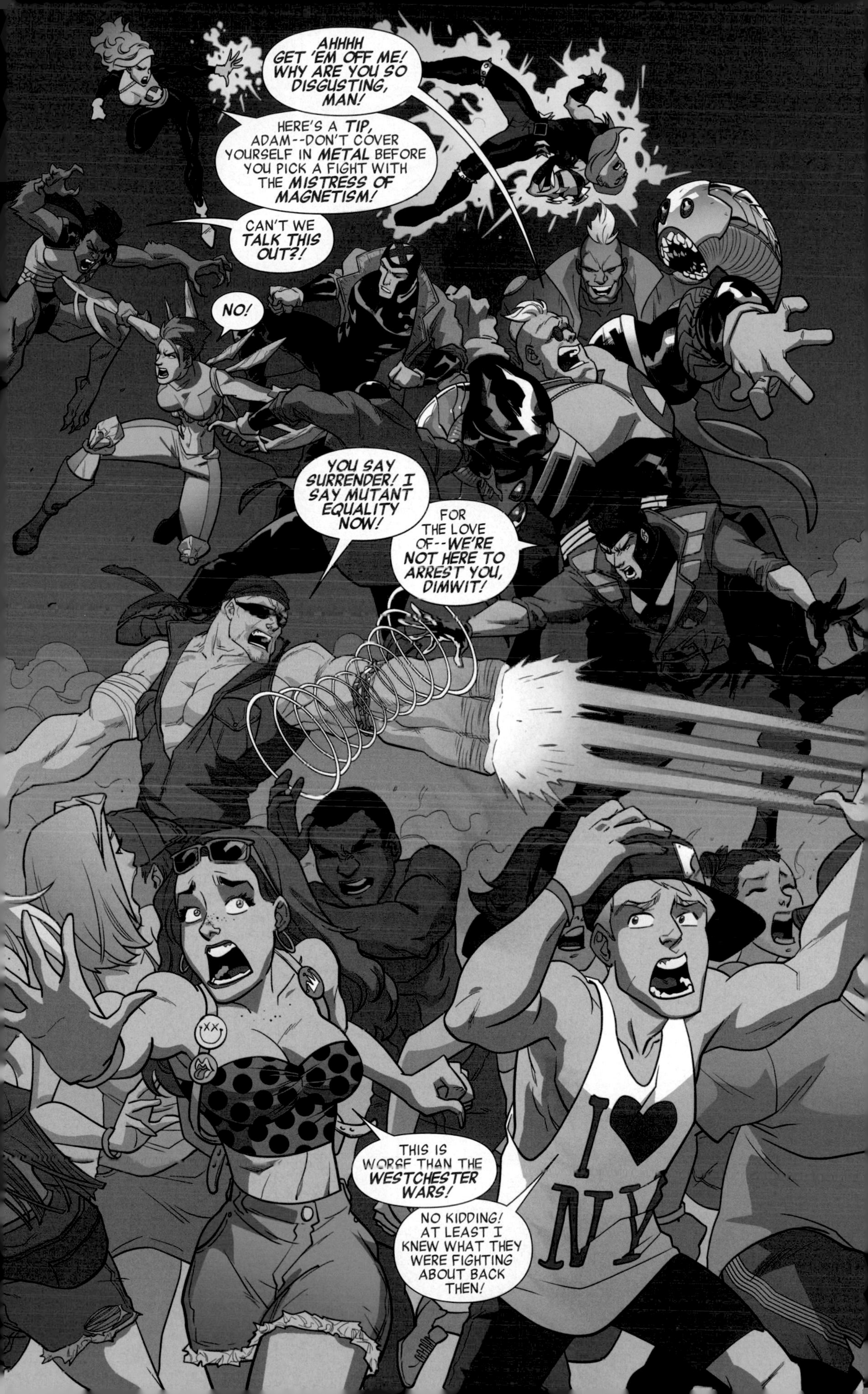
AHHHH GET 'EM OFF ME! WHY ARE YOU SO DISGUSTING, MAN!
HERE'S A TIP, ADAM--DON'T COVER YOURSELF IN METAL BEFORE YOU PICK A FIGHT WITH THE MISTRESS OF MAGNETISM!
CAN'T WE TALK THIS OUT?!
NO!
YOU SAY SURRENDER! I SAY MUTANT EQUALITY NOW!
FOR THE LOVE OF--WE'RE NOT HERE TO ARREST YOU, DIMWIT!
THIS IS WORSE THAN THE WESTCHESTER WARS!
NO KIDDING! AT LEAST I KNEW WHAT THEY WERE FIGHTING ABOUT BACK THEN!
I ♥ NY

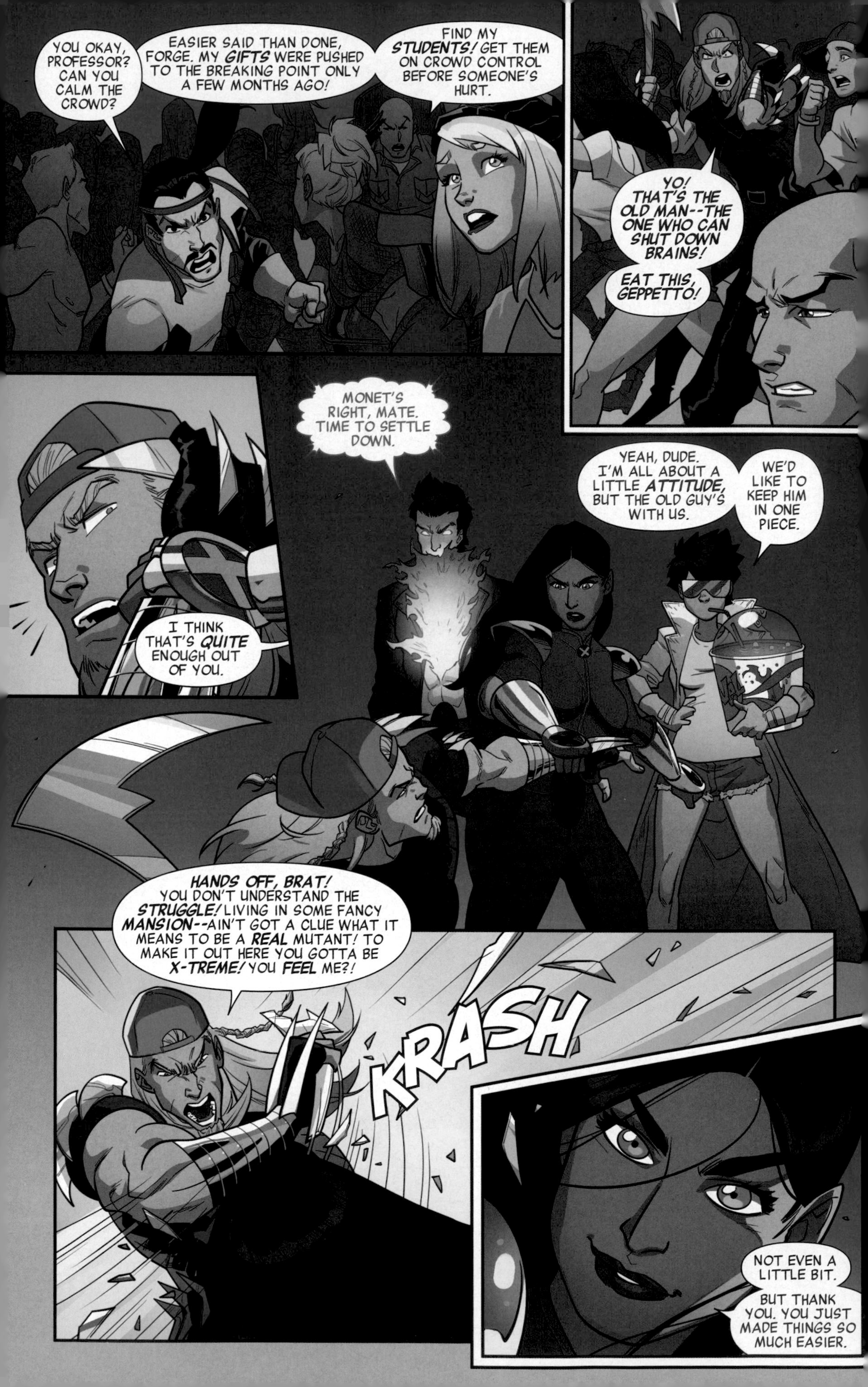

YOU OKAY, PROFESSOR? CAN YOU CALM THE CROWD?
EASIER SAID THAN DONE, FORGE. MY GIFTS WERE PUSHED TO THE BREAKING POINT ONLY A FEW MONTHS AGO!
FIND MY STUDENTS! GET THEM ON CROWD CONTROL BEFORE SOMEONE'S HURT.
YO! THAT'S THE OLD MAN--THE ONE WHO CAN SHUT DOWN BRAINS!
EAT THIS, GEPPETTO!
I THINK THAT'S QUITE ENOUGH OUT OF YOU.
MONET'S RIGHT, MATE. TIME TO SETTLE DOWN.
YEAH, DUDE. I'M ALL ABOUT A LITTLE ATTITUDE, BUT THE OLD GUY'S WITH US.
WE'D LIKE TO KEEP HIM IN ONE PIECE.
HANDS OFF, BRAT! YOU DON'T UNDERSTAND THE STRUGGLE! LIVING IN SOME FANCY MANSION--AIN'T GOT A CLUE WHAT IT MEANS TO BE A REAL MUTANT! TO MAKE IT OUT HERE YOU GOTTA BE X-TREME! YOU FEEL ME?!
KRASH
NOT EVEN A LITTLE BIT.
BUT THANK YOU. YOU JUST MADE THINGS SO MUCH EASIER.

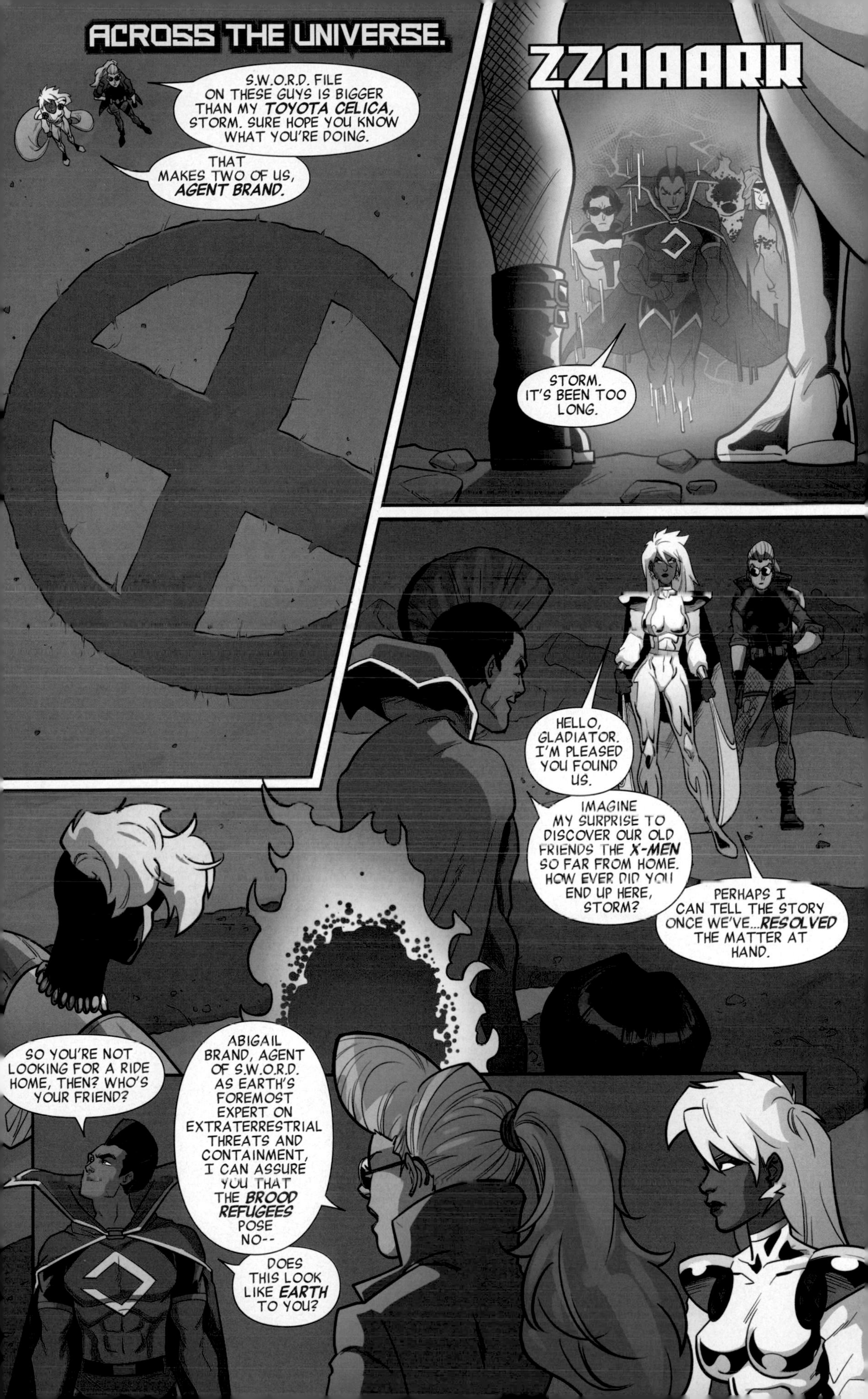
ACROSS THE UNIVERSE.
S.W.O.R.D. FILE ON THESE GUYS IS BIGGER THAN MY TOYOTA CELICA, STORM. SURE HOPE YOU KNOW WHAT YOU'RE DOING.
THAT MAKES TWO OF US, AGENT BRAND.
ZZAAAARK
STORM. IT'S BEEN TOO LONG.
HELLO, GLADIATOR. I'M PLEASED YOU FOUND US.
IMAGINE MY SURPRISE TO DISCOVER OUR OLD FRIENDS THE X-MEN SO FAR FROM HOME. HOW EVER DID YOU END UP HERE, STORM?
PERHAPS I CAN TELL THE STORY ONCE WE'VE...RESOLVED THE MATTER AT HAND.
SO YOU'RE NOT LOOKING FOR A RIDE HOME, THEN? WHO'S YOUR FRIEND?
ABIGAIL BRAND, AGENT OF S.W.O.R.D. AS EARTH'S FOREMOST EXPERT ON EXTRATERRESTRIAL THREATS AND CONTAINMENT, I CAN ASSURE YOU THAT THE BROOD REFUGEES POSE NO--
DOES THIS LOOK LIKE EARTH TO YOU?

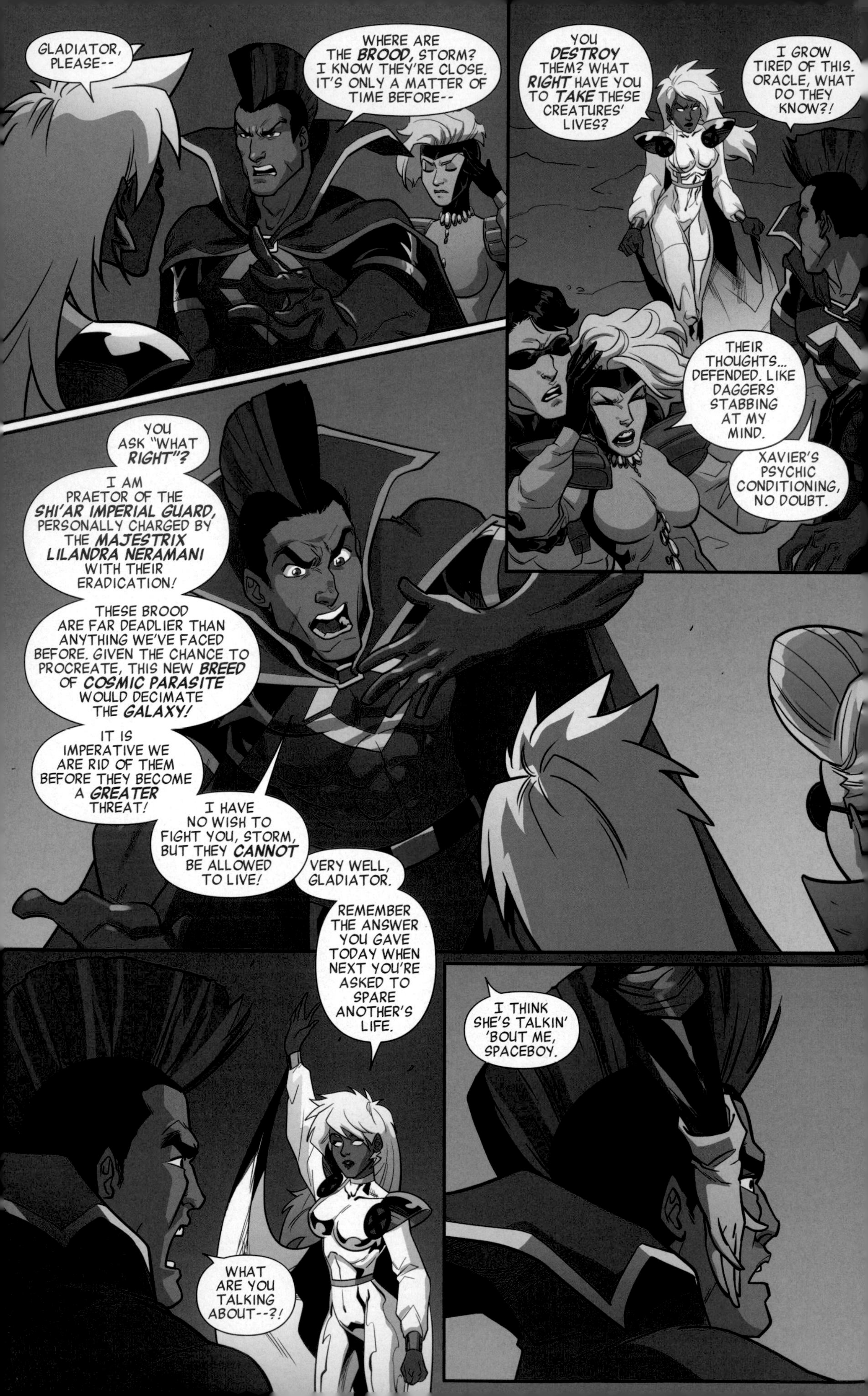
GLADIATOR, PLEASE--
WHERE ARE THE BROOD, STORM? I KNOW THEY'RE CLOSE. IT'S ONLY A MATTER OF TIME BEFORE--
YOU DESTROY THEM? WHAT RIGHT HAVE YOU TO TAKE THESE CREATURES' LIVES?
I GROW TIRED OF THIS. ORACLE, WHAT DO THEY KNOW?!
THEIR THOUGHTS... DEFENDED. LIKE DAGGERS STABBING AT MY MIND.
XAVIER'S PSYCHIC CONDITIONING, NO DOUBT.
YOU ASK "WHAT RIGHT"?
I AM PRAETOR OF THE SHI'AR IMPERIAL GUARD, PERSONALLY CHARGED BY THE MAJESTRIX LILANDRA NERAMANI WITH THEIR ERADICATION!
THESE BROOD ARE FAR DEADLIER THAN ANYTHING WE'VE FACED BEFORE. GIVEN THE CHANCE TO PROCREATE, THIS NEW BREED OF COSMIC PARASITE WOULD DECIMATE THE GALAXY!
IT IS IMPERATIVE WE ARE RID OF THEM BEFORE THEY BECOME A GREATER THREAT!
I HAVE NO WISH TO FIGHT YOU, STORM, BUT THEY CANNOT BE ALLOWED TO LIVE!
VERY WELL, GLADIATOR.
REMEMBER THE ANSWER YOU GAVE TODAY WHEN NEXT YOU'RE ASKED TO SPARE ANOTHER'S LIFE.
WHAT ARE YOU TALKING ABOUT--?!
I THINK SHE'S TALKIN' 'BOUT ME, SPACEBOY.

SUGAHTOOOOM
YOU CAN DROP THE CLOAK NOW, PHADER. I THINK THEY KNOW WE'RE HERE.
WHA--
HOW-- WHERE'D THEY COME FROM?!
X-MEN! DEFEND THE BROOD!
HEH. AIN'T NOBODY EVER SAID THAT BEFORE.
DOES YOUR SPECIES ALWAYS SPEAK THIS MUCH WHILE YOU FIGHT?
BELIEVE ME, HARDSIDE-- THIS IS THEM BEING QUIET.

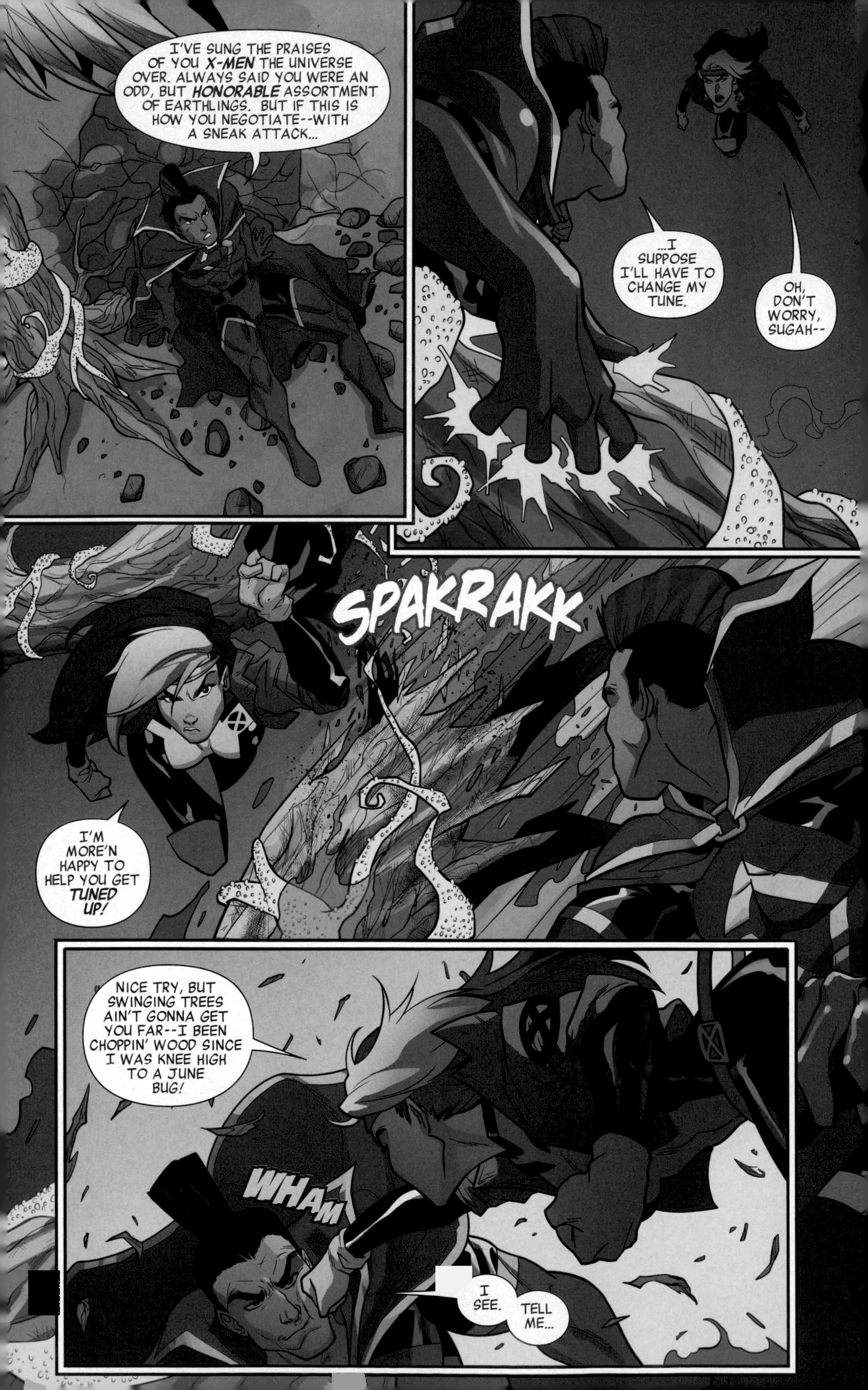
I'VE SUNG THE PRAISES OF YOU X-MEN THE UNIVERSE OVER. ALWAYS SAID YOU WERE AN ODD, BUT HONORABLE ASSORTMENT OF EARTHLINGS. BUT IF THIS IS HOW YOU NEGOTIATE--WITH A SNEAK ATTACK...
...I SUPPOSE I'LL HAVE TO CHANGE MY TUNE.
OH, DON'T WORRY, SUGAH--
SPAKRAKK
I'M MORE'N HAPPY TO HELP YOU GET TUNED UP!
NICE TRY, BUT SWINGING TREES AIN'T GONNA GET YOU FAR--I BEEN CHOPPIN' WOOD SINCE I WAS KNEE HIGH TO A JUNE BUG!
WHAM
I SEE.
TELL ME...

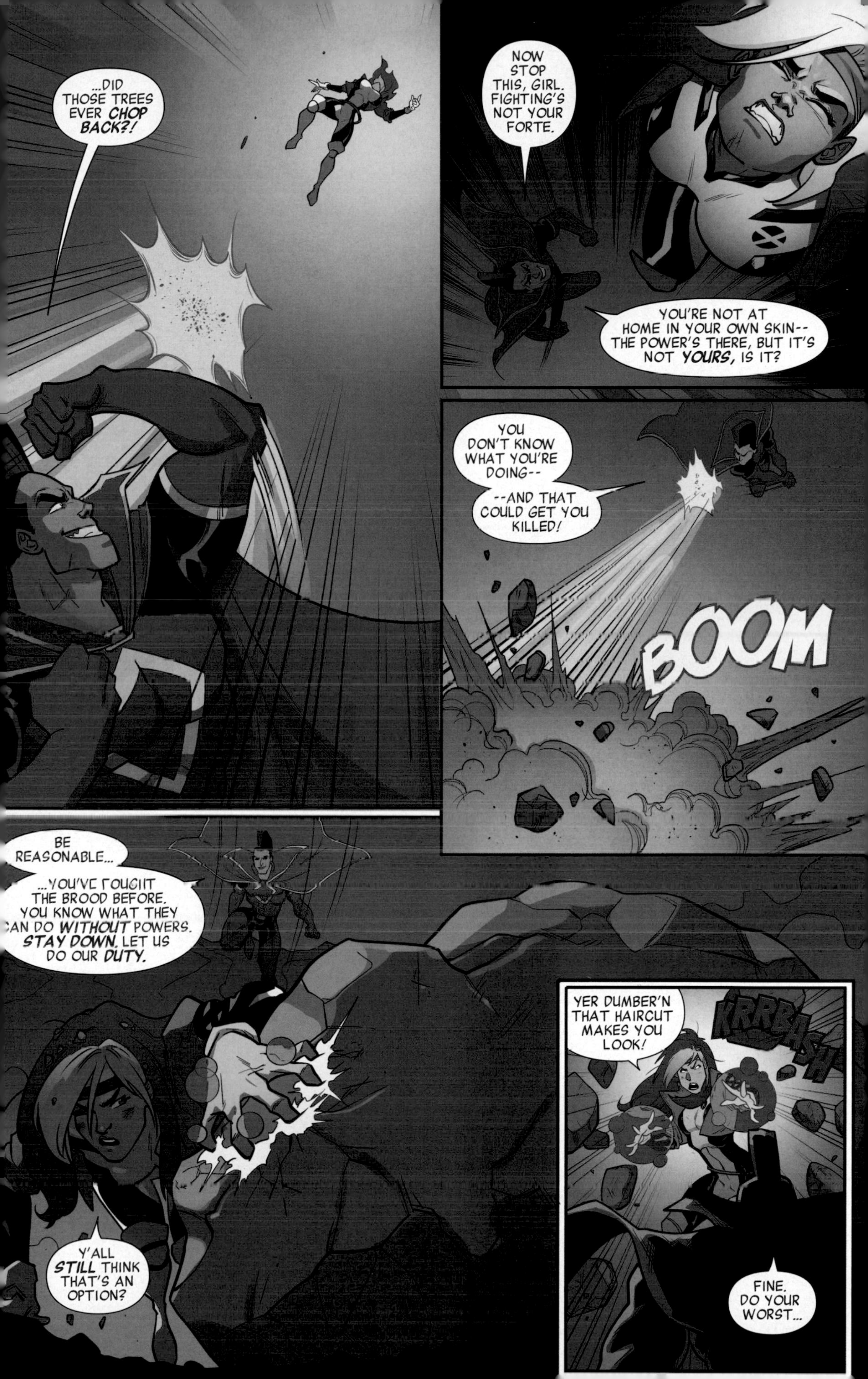

...DID THOSE TREES EVER CHOP BACK?!
NOW STOP THIS, GIRL. FIGHTING'S NOT YOUR FORTE.
YOU'RE NOT AT HOME IN YOUR OWN SKIN-- THE POWER'S THERE, BUT IT'S NOT YOURS, IS IT?
YOU DON'T KNOW WHAT YOU'RE DOING--
--AND THAT COULD GET YOU KILLED!
BOOM
BE REASONABLE...
...YOU'VE FOUGHT THE BROOD BEFORE. YOU KNOW WHAT THEY CAN DO WITHOUT POWERS. STAY DOWN, LET US DO OUR DUTY.
Y'ALL STILL THINK THAT'S AN OPTION?
YER DUMBER'N THAT HAIRCUT MAKES YOU LOOK!
KRRBASH
FINE. DO YOUR WORST...

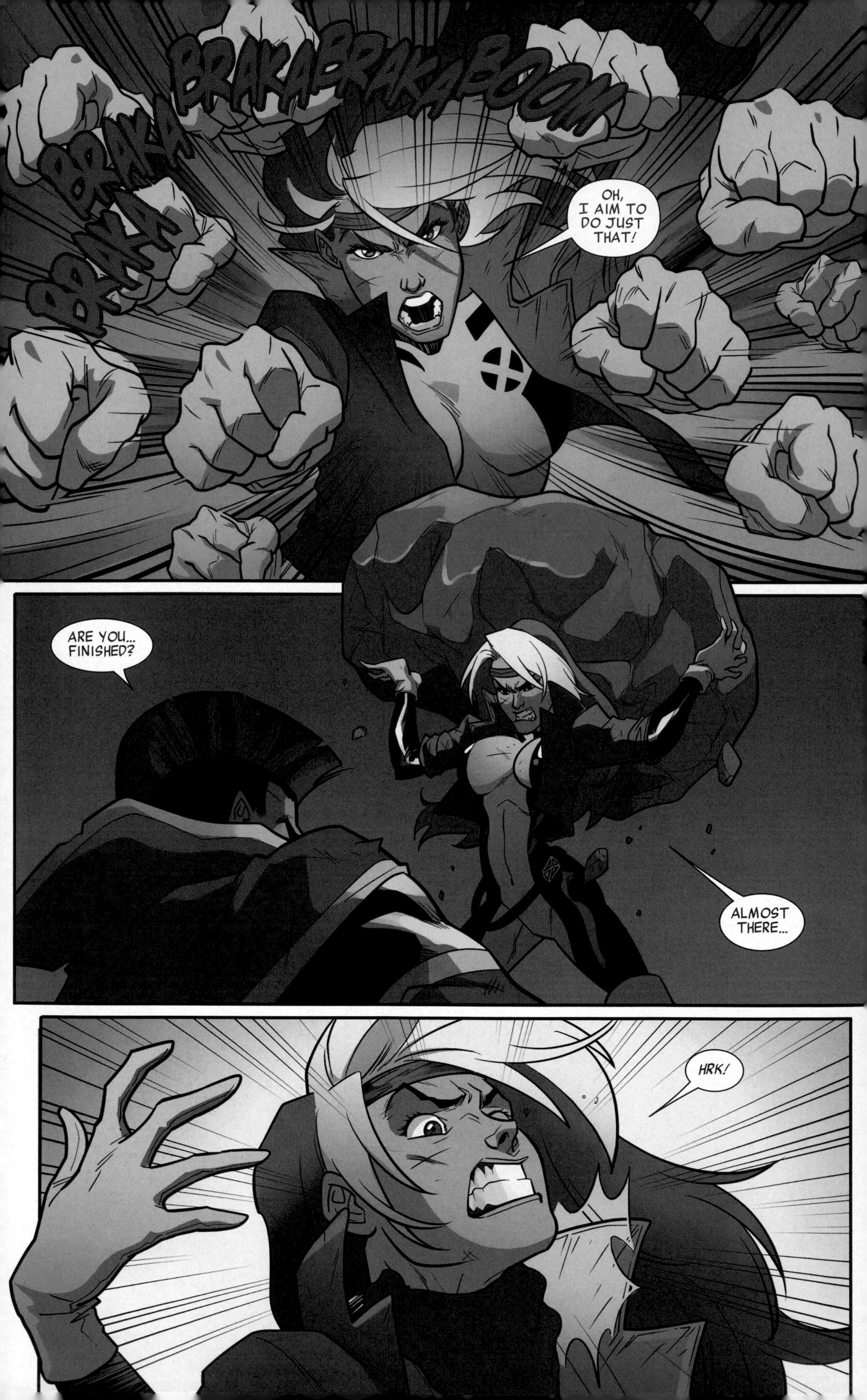
BRAKA BRAKA BRAKA BRAKA BOOM
OH, I AIM TO DO JUST THAT!
ARE YOU... FINISHED?
ALMOST THERE...
HRK!

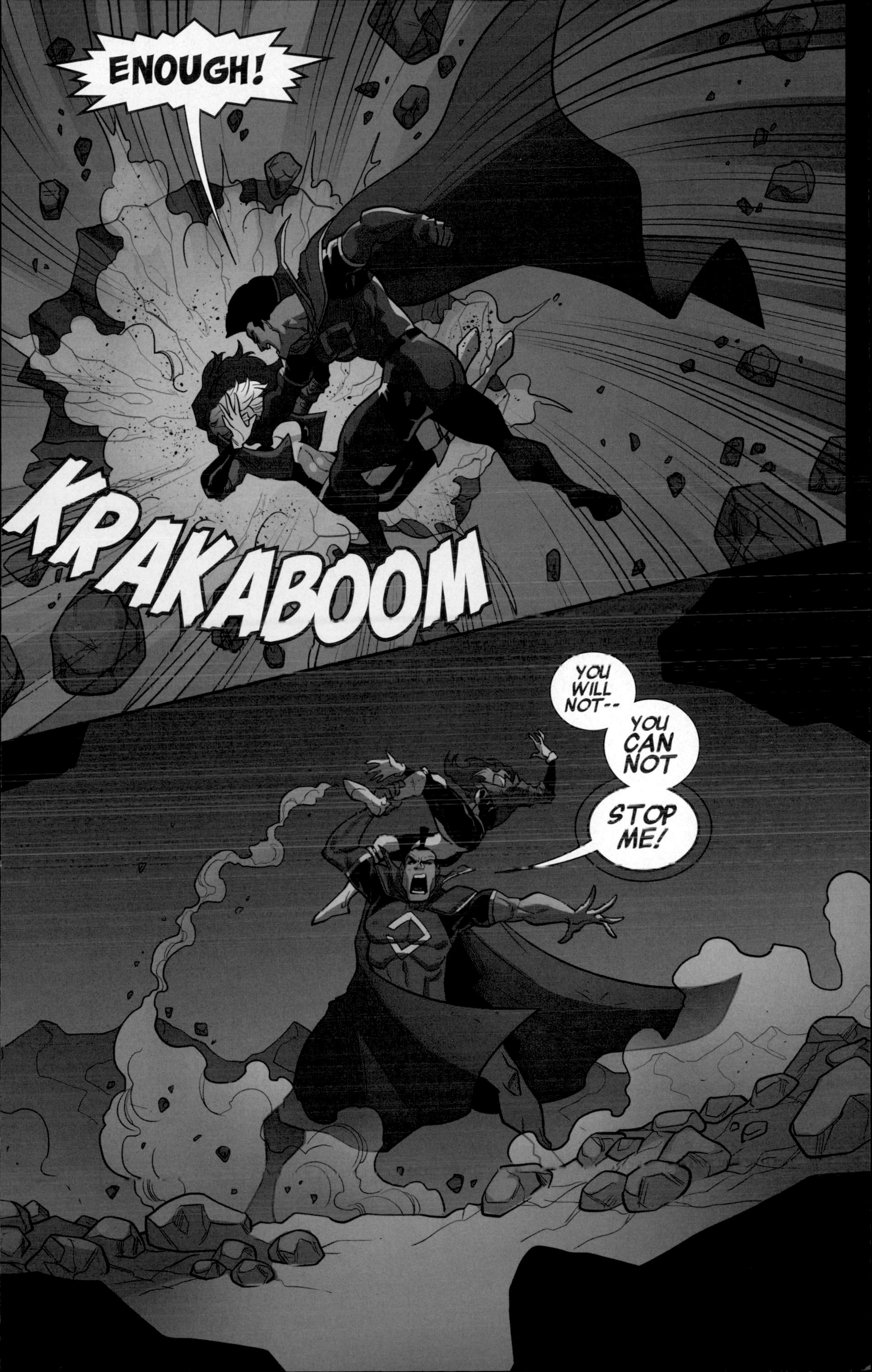
ENOUGH!
KRAKABOOM
YOU WILL NOT--
YOU CAN NOT
STOP ME!

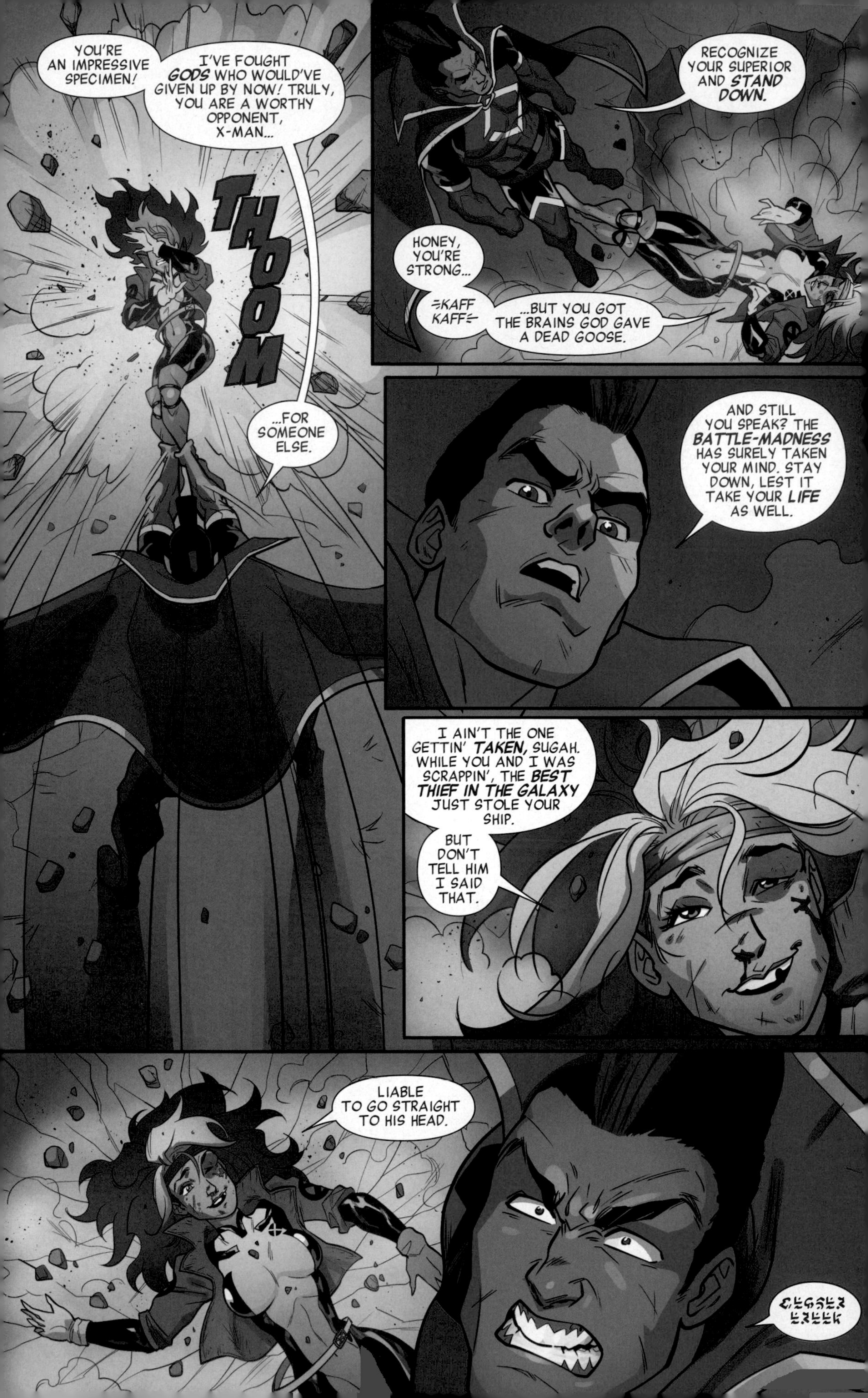

YOU'RE AN IMPRESSIVE SPECIMEN!
I'VE FOUGHT GODS WHO WOULD'VE GIVEN UP BY NOW! TRULY, YOU ARE A WORTHY OPPONENT, X-MAN...
THOOM
...FOR SOMEONE ELSE.
RECOGNIZE YOUR SUPERIOR AND STAND DOWN.
HONEY, YOU'RE STRONG...
=KAFF KAFF=
...BUT YOU GOT THE BRAINS GOD GAVE A DEAD GOOSE.
AND STILL YOU SPEAK? THE BATTLE-MADNESS HAS SURELY TAKEN YOUR MIND. STAY DOWN, LEST IT TAKE YOUR LIFE AS WELL.
I AIN'T THE ONE GETTIN' TAKEN, SUGAH. WHILE YOU AND I WAS SCRAPPIN', THE BEST THIEF IN THE GALAXY JUST STOLE YOUR SHIP.
BUT DON'T TELL HIM I SAID THAT.
LIABLE TO GO STRAIGHT TO HIS HEAD.

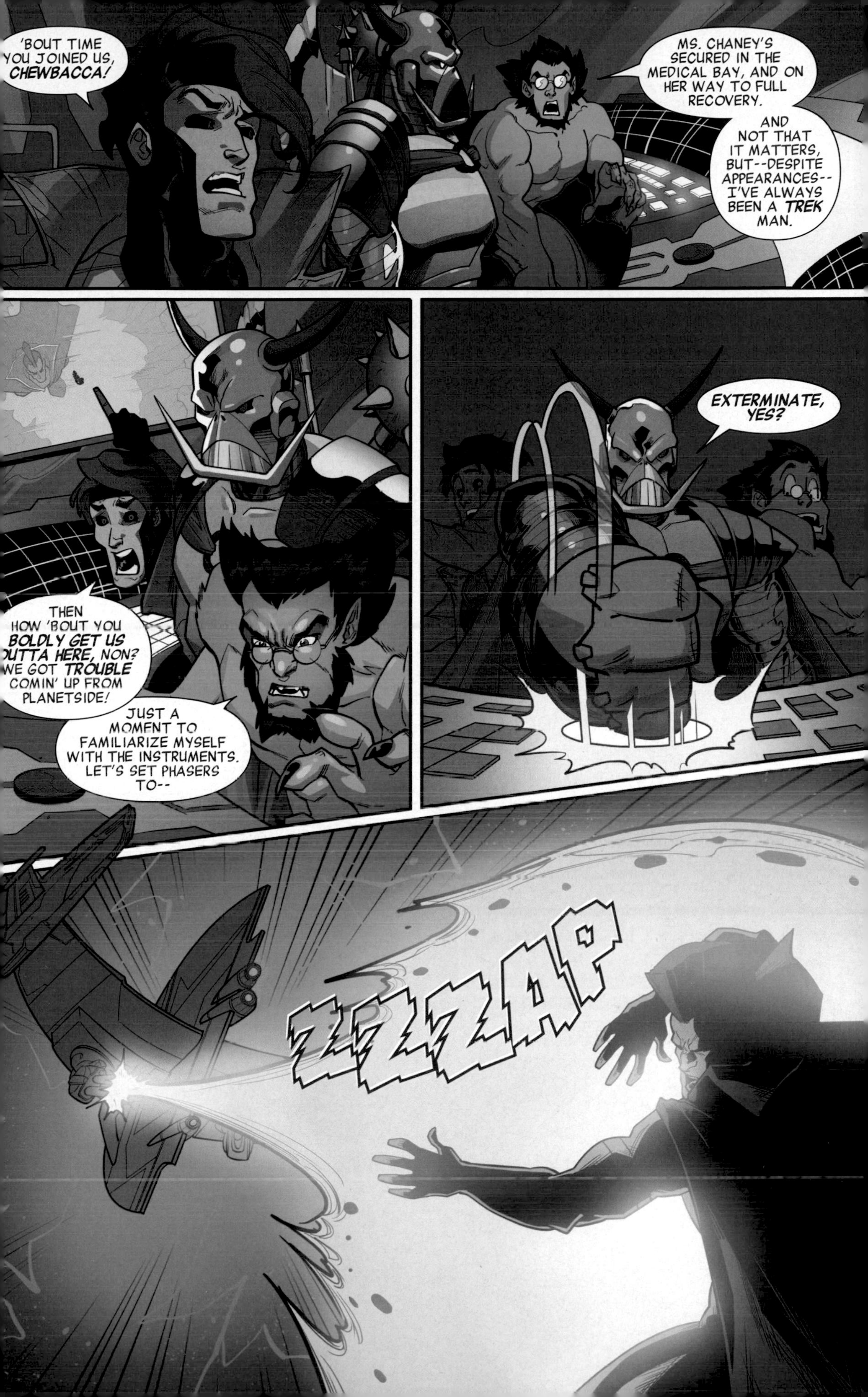
'BOUT TIME YOU JOINED US, CHEWBACCA!
MS. CHANEY'S SECURED IN THE MEDICAL BAY, AND ON HER WAY TO FULL RECOVERY.
AND NOT THAT IT MATTERS, BUT--DESPITE APPEARANCES--I'VE ALWAYS BEEN A TREK MAN.
THEN HOW 'BOUT YOU BOLDLY GET US OUTTA HERE, NON? WE GOT TROUBLE COMIN' UP FROM PLANETSIDE!
JUST A MOMENT TO FAMILIARIZE MYSELF WITH THE INSTRUMENTS. LET'S SET PHASERS TO--
EXTERMINATE, YES?
ZZZAP

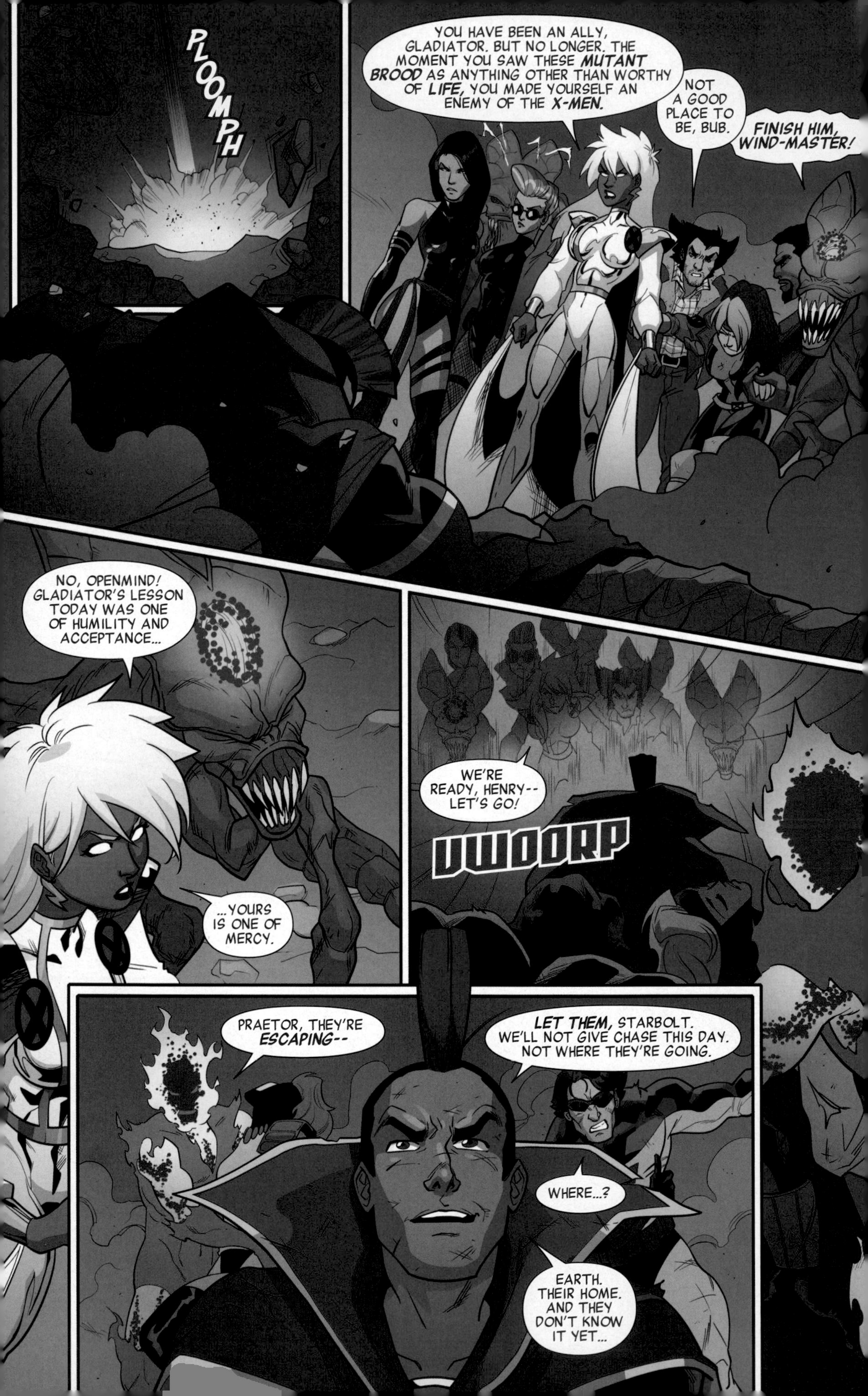
PLOOMPH
YOU HAVE BEEN AN ALLY, GLADIATOR. BUT NO LONGER. THE MOMENT YOU SAW THESE MUTANT BROOD AS ANYTHING OTHER THAN WORTHY OF LIFE, YOU MADE YOURSELF AN ENEMY OF THE X-MEN.
NOT A GOOD PLACE TO BE, BUB.
FINISH HIM, WIND-MASTER!
NO, OPENMIND! GLADIATOR'S LESSON TODAY WAS ONE OF HUMILITY AND ACCEPTANCE...
...YOURS IS ONE OF MERCY.
WE'RE READY, HENRY--LET'S GO!
VWOORP
PRAETOR, THEY'RE ESCAPING--
LET THEM, STARBOLT. WE'LL NOT GIVE CHASE THIS DAY. NOT WHERE THEY'RE GOING.
WHERE...?
EARTH. THEIR HOME. AND THEY DON'T KNOW IT YET...

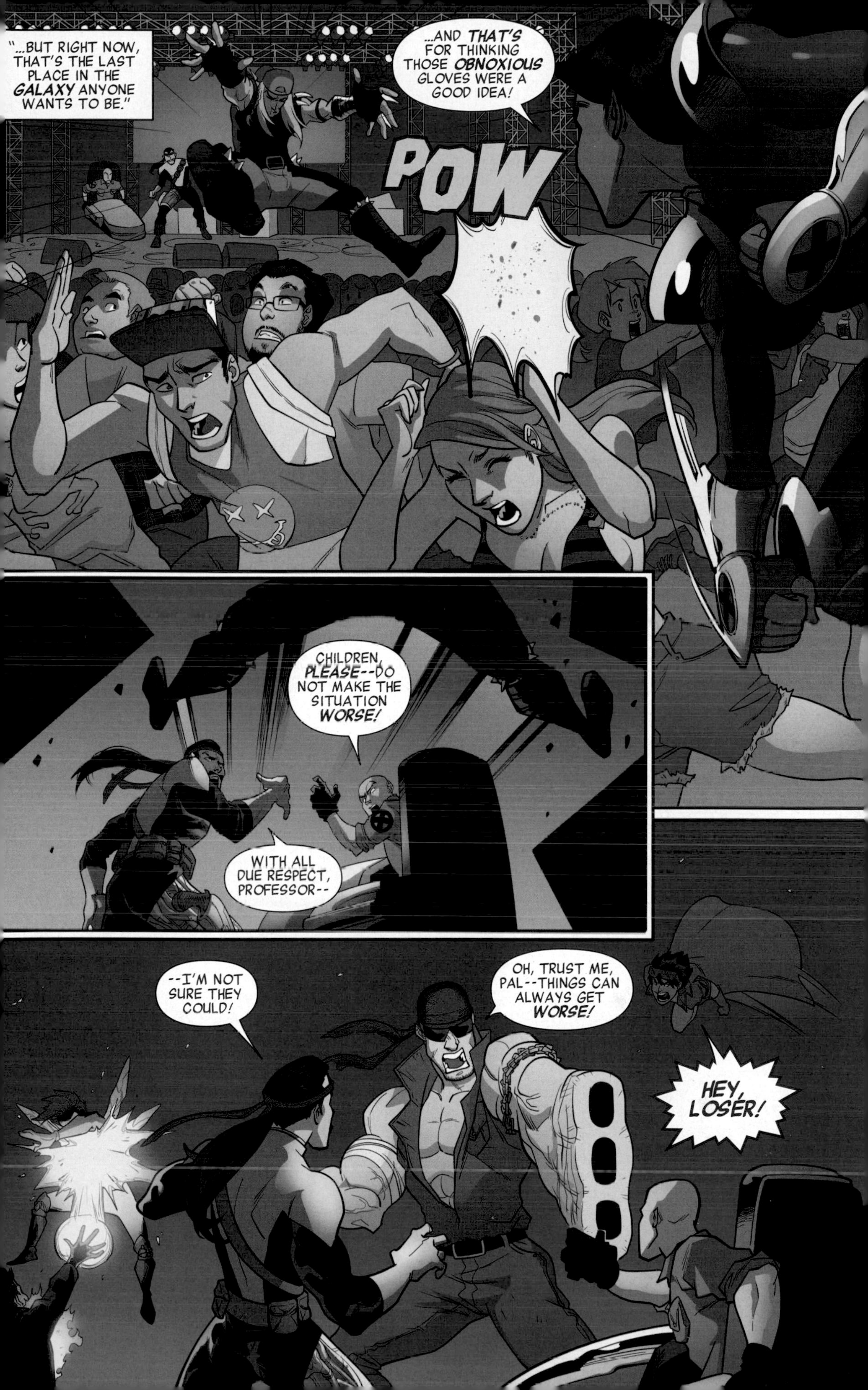
"...BUT RIGHT NOW, THAT'S THE LAST PLACE IN THE GALAXY ANYONE WANTS TO BE."
...AND THAT'S FOR THINKING THOSE OBNOXIOUS GLOVES WERE A GOOD IDEA!
POW
CHILDREN, PLEASE--DO NOT MAKE THE SITUATION WORSE!
WITH ALL DUE RESPECT, PROFESSOR--
--I'M NOT SURE THEY COULD!
OH, TRUST ME, PAL--THINGS CAN ALWAYS GET WORSE!
HEY, LOSER!

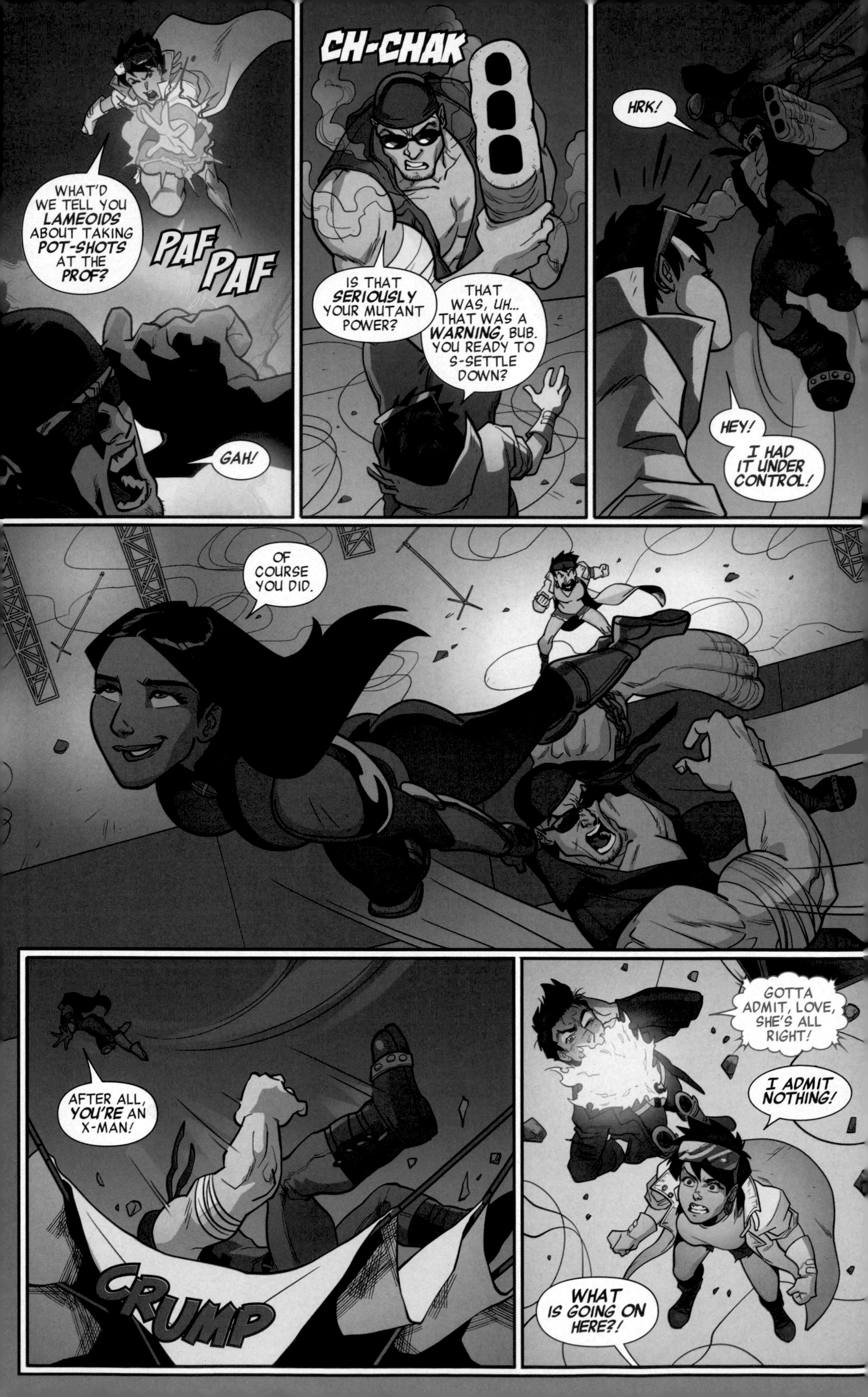
WHAT'D WE TELL YOU LAMEOIDS ABOUT TAKING POT-SHOTS AT THE PROF?
PAF PAF
GAH!
CH-CHAK
IS THAT SERIOUSLY YOUR MUTANT POWER?
THAT WAS, UH... THAT WAS A WARNING, BUB. YOU READY TO S-SETTLE DOWN?
HRK!
HEY! I HAD IT UNDER CONTROL!
OF COURSE YOU DID.
AFTER ALL, YOU'RE AN X-MAN!
CRUMP
GOTTA ADMIT, LOVE, SHE'S ALL RIGHT!
I ADMIT NOTHING!
WHAT IS GOING ON HERE?!

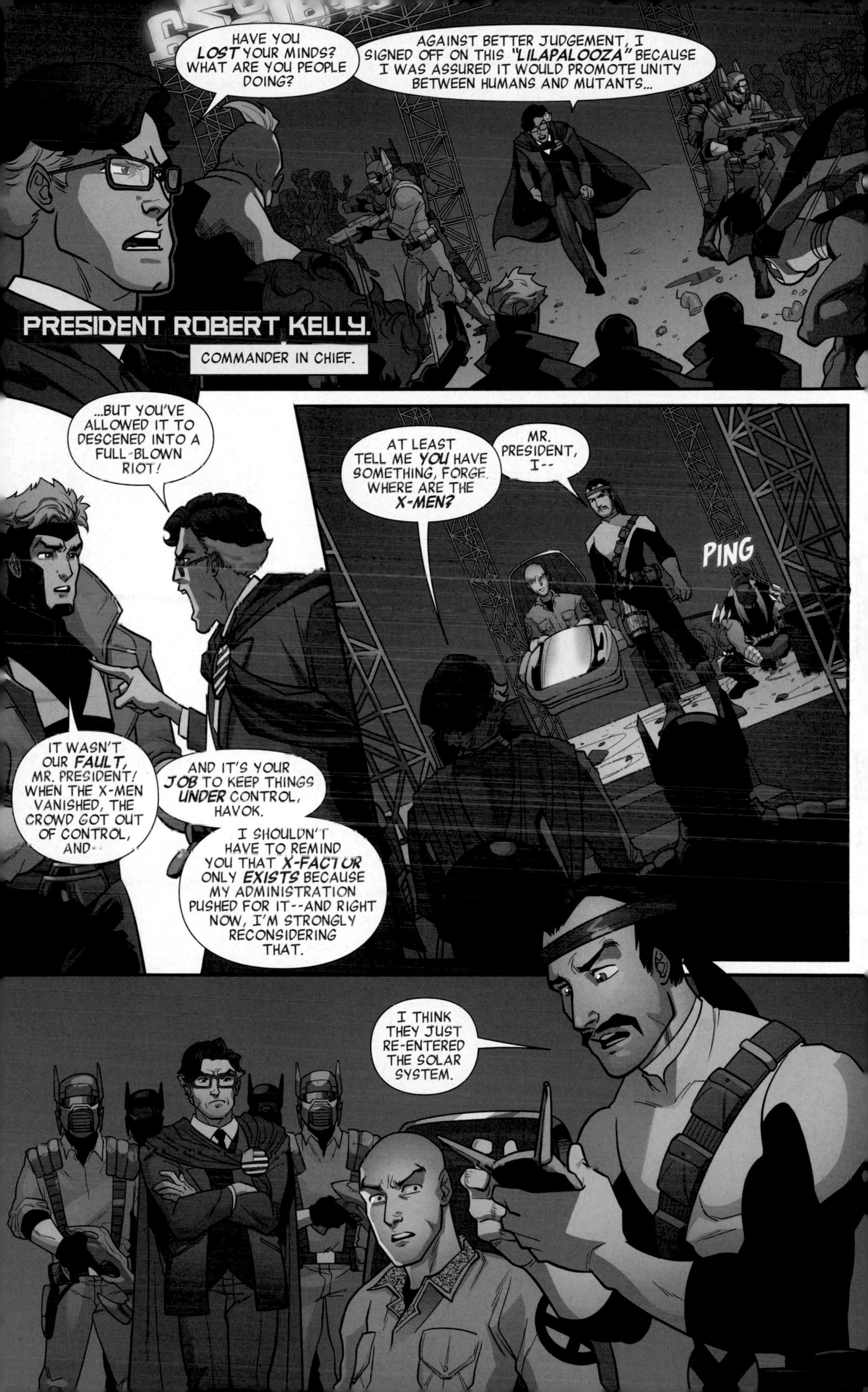
HAVE YOU LOST YOUR MINDS? WHAT ARE YOU PEOPLE DOING?
AGAINST BETTER JUDGEMENT, I SIGNED OFF ON THIS "LILAPALOOZA" BECAUSE I WAS ASSURED IT WOULD PROMOTE UNITY BETWEEN HUMANS AND MUTANTS...
PRESIDENT ROBERT KELLY.
COMMANDER IN CHIEF.
...BUT YOU'VE ALLOWED IT TO DESCENED INTO A FULL-BLOWN RIOT!
IT WASN'T OUR FAULT, MR. PRESIDENT! WHEN THE X-MEN VANISHED, THE CROWD GOT OUT OF CONTROL, AND--
AND IT'S YOUR JOB TO KEEP THINGS UNDER CONTROL, HAVOK.
I SHOULDN'T HAVE TO REMIND YOU THAT X-FACTOR ONLY EXISTS BECAUSE MY ADMINISTRATION PUSHED FOR IT--AND RIGHT NOW, I'M STRONGLY RECONSIDERING THAT.
AT LEAST TELL ME YOU HAVE SOMETHING, FORGE. WHERE ARE THE X-MEN?
MR. PRESIDENT, I--
PING
I THINK THEY JUST RE-ENTERED THE SOLAR SYSTEM.

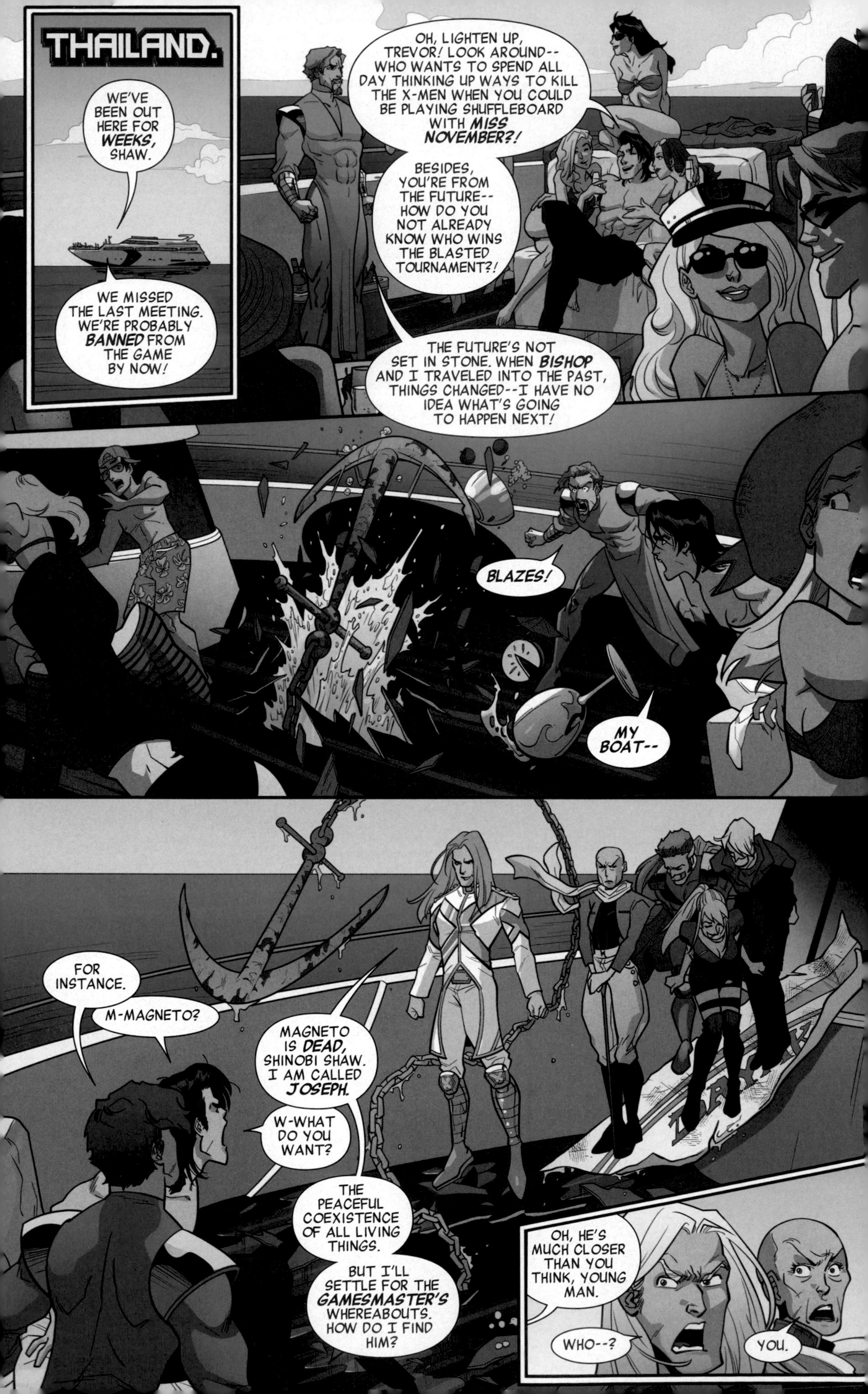
THAILAND.
WE'VE BEEN OUT HERE FOR WEEKS, SHAW.
WE MISSED THE LAST MEETING. WE'RE PROBABLY BANNED FROM THE GAME BY NOW!
OH, LIGHTEN UP, TREVOR! LOOK AROUND-- WHO WANTS TO SPEND ALL DAY THINKING UP WAYS TO KILL THE X-MEN WHEN YOU COULD BE PLAYING SHUFFLEBOARD WITH MISS NOVEMBER?!
BESIDES, YOU'RE FROM THE FUTURE-- HOW DO YOU NOT ALREADY KNOW WHO WINS THE BLASTED TOURNAMENT?!
THE FUTURE'S NOT SET IN STONE. WHEN BISHOP AND I TRAVELED INTO THE PAST, THINGS CHANGED--I HAVE NO IDEA WHAT'S GOING TO HAPPEN NEXT!
BLAZES!
MY BOAT--
FOR INSTANCE.
M-MAGNETO?
MAGNETO IS DEAD, SHINOBI SHAW. I AM CALLED JOSEPH.
W-WHAT DO YOU WANT?
THE PEACEFUL COEXISTENCE OF ALL LIVING THINGS.
BUT I'LL SETTLE FOR THE GAMESMASTER'S WHEREABOUTS. HOW DO I FIND HIM?
OH, HE'S MUCH CLOSER THAN YOU THINK, YOUNG MAN.
WHO--?
YOU.

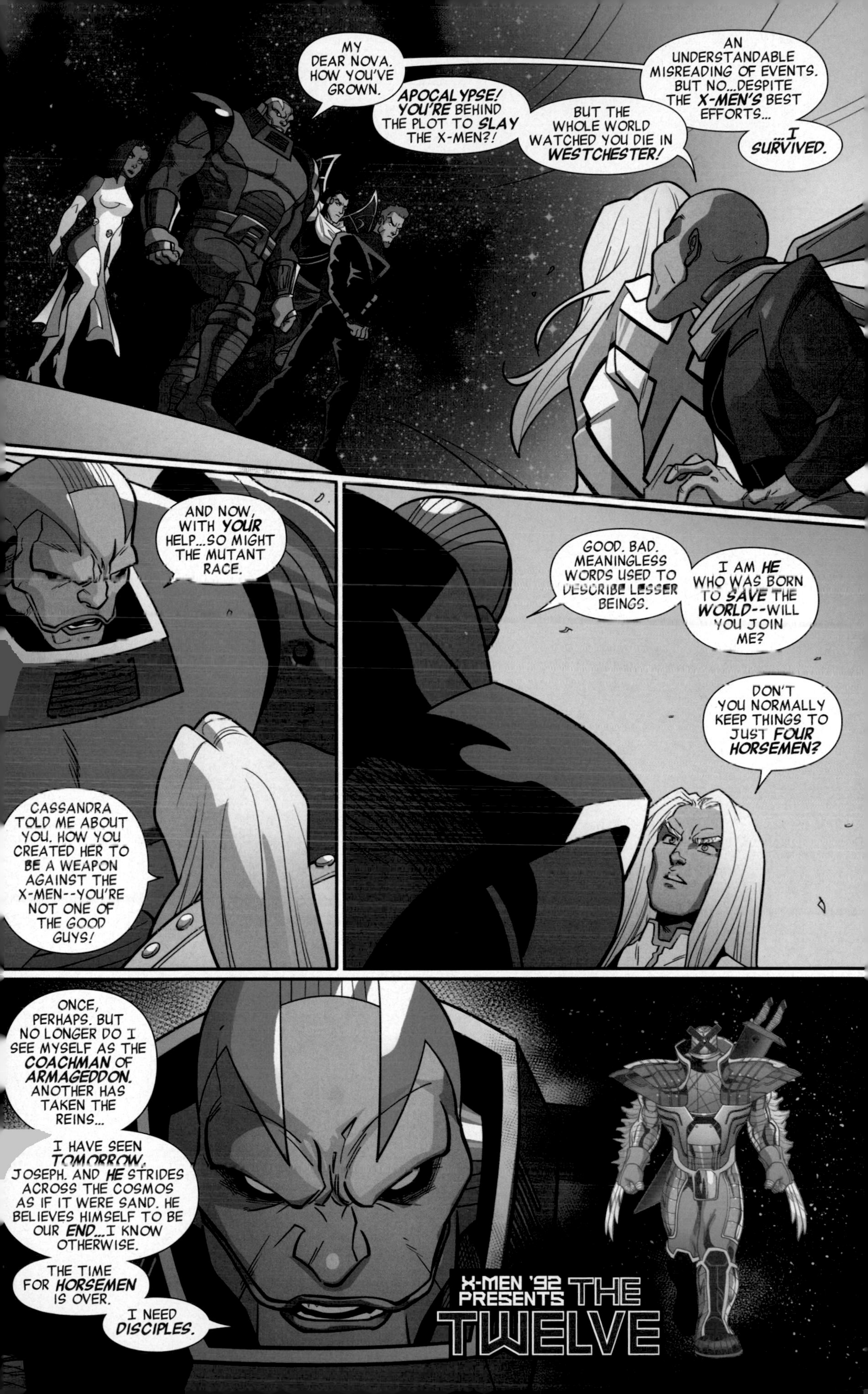
MY DEAR NOVA. HOW YOU'VE GROWN.
APOCALYPSE! YOU'RE BEHIND THE PLOT TO SLAY THE X-MEN?!
BUT THE WHOLE WORLD WATCHED YOU DIE IN WESTCHESTER!
AN UNDERSTANDABLE MISREADING OF EVENTS. BUT NO...DESPITE THE X-MEN'S BEST EFFORTS...
...I SURVIVED.
AND NOW, WITH YOUR HELP...SO MIGHT THE MUTANT RACE.
CASSANDRA TOLD ME ABOUT YOU. HOW YOU CREATED HER TO BE A WEAPON AGAINST THE X-MEN--YOU'RE NOT ONE OF THE GOOD GUYS!
GOOD. BAD. MEANINGLESS WORDS USED TO DESCRIBE LESSER BEINGS.
I AM HE WHO WAS BORN TO SAVE THE WORLD--WILL YOU JOIN ME?
DON'T YOU NORMALLY KEEP THINGS TO JUST FOUR HORSEMEN?
ONCE, PERHAPS. BUT NO LONGER DO I SEE MYSELF AS THE COACHMAN OF ARMAGEDDON. ANOTHER HAS TAKEN THE REINS...
I HAVE SEEN TOMORROW, JOSEPH. AND HE STRIDES ACROSS THE COSMOS AS IF IT WERE SAND. HE BELIEVES HIMSELF TO BE OUR END...I KNOW OTHERWISE.
THE TIME FOR HORSEMEN IS OVER.
I NEED DISCIPLES.
X-MEN '92 PRESENTS THE TWELVE

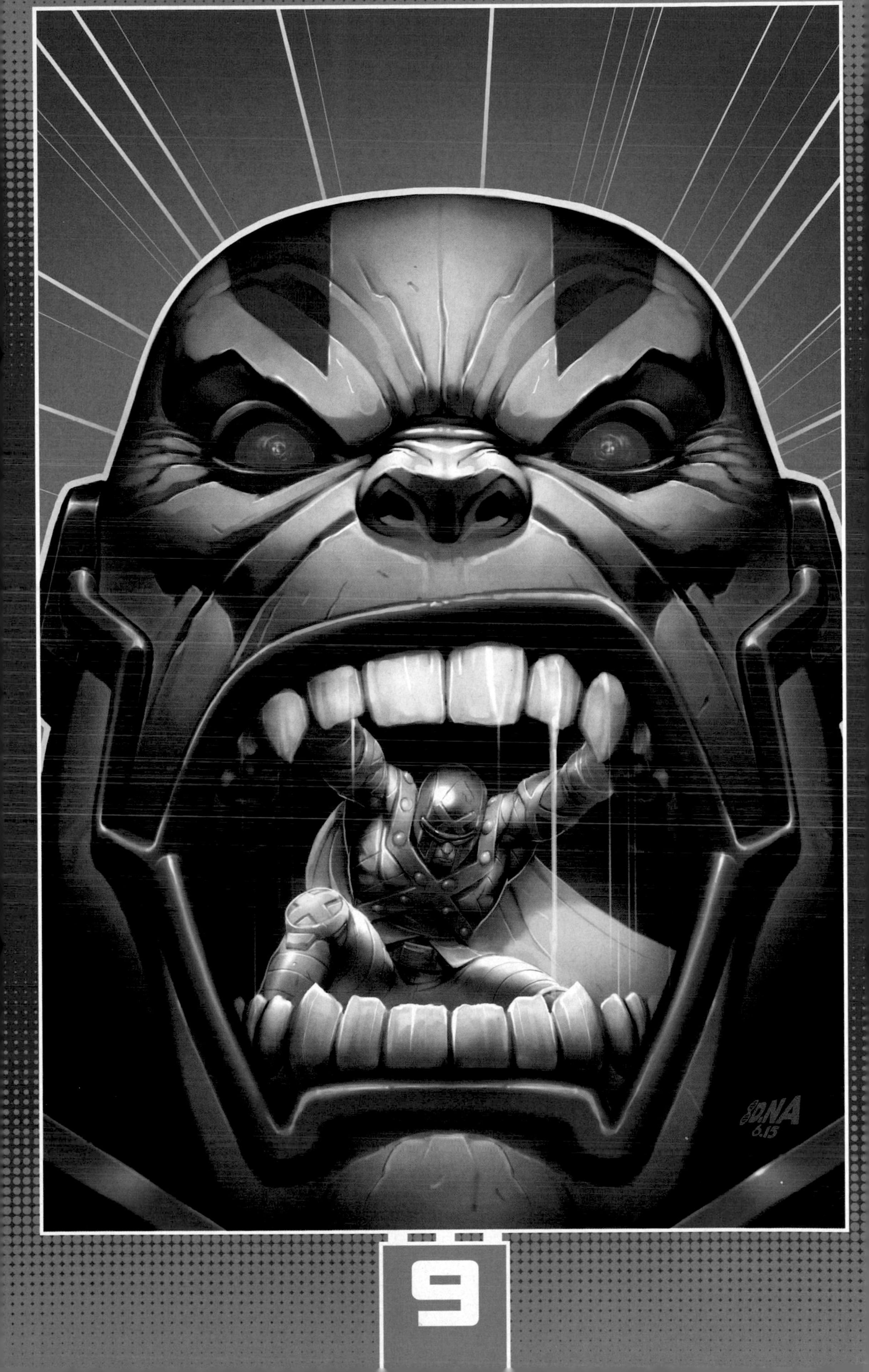

9

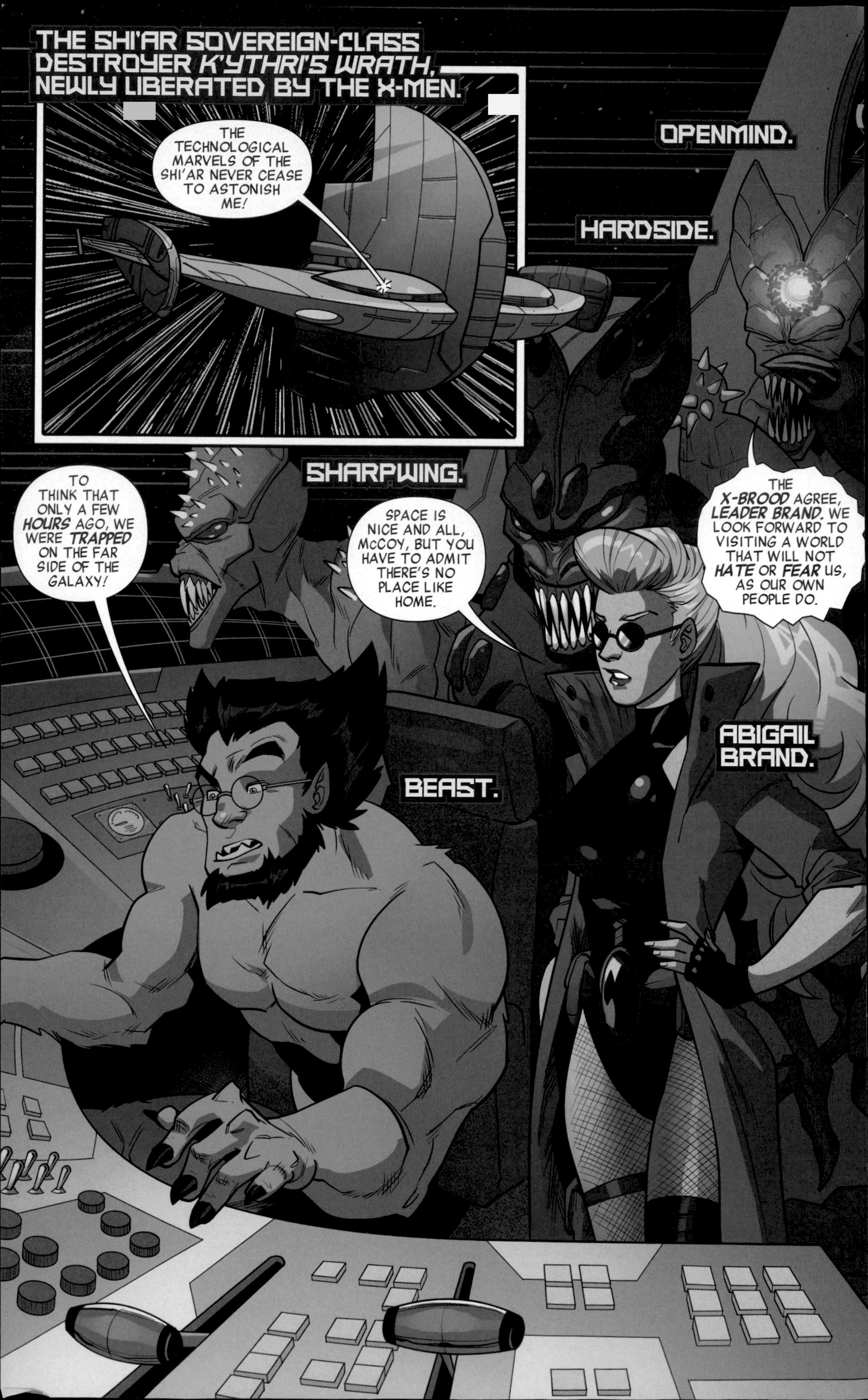
THE SHI'AR SOVEREIGN-CLASS DESTROYER K'YTHRI'S WRATH, NEWLY LIBERATED BY THE X-MEN.
THE TECHNOLOGICAL MARVELS OF THE SHI'AR NEVER CEASE TO ASTONISH ME!
OPENMIND.
HARDSIDE.
SHARPWING.
TO THINK THAT ONLY A FEW HOURS AGO, WE WERE TRAPPED ON THE FAR SIDE OF THE GALAXY!
SPACE IS NICE AND ALL, McCOY, BUT YOU HAVE TO ADMIT THERE'S NO PLACE LIKE HOME.
THE X-BROOD AGREE, LEADER BRAND. WE LOOK FORWARD TO VISITING A WORLD THAT WILL NOT HATE OR FEAR US, AS OUR OWN PEOPLE DO.
ABIGAIL BRAND.
BEAST.

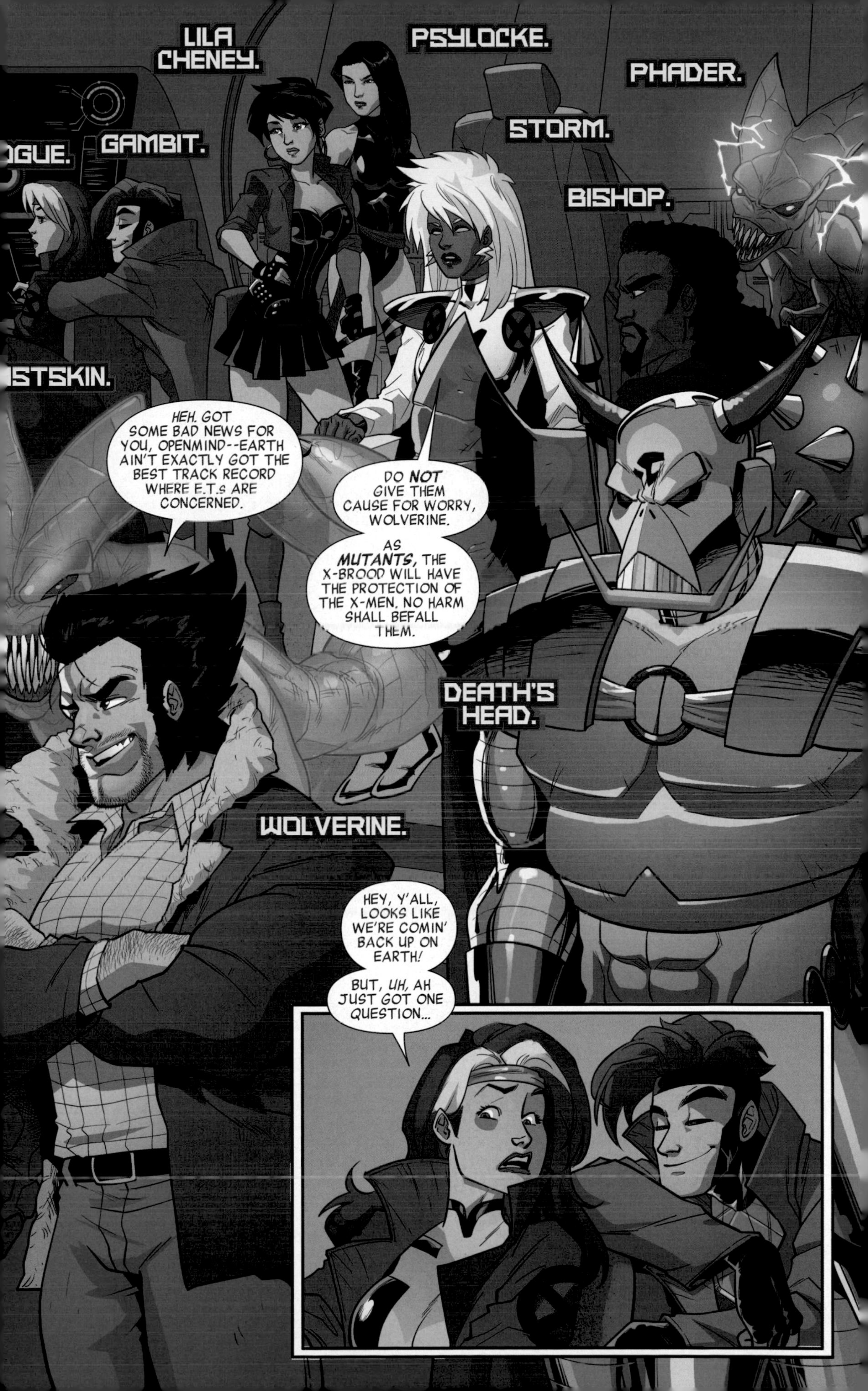

OGUE.
GAMBIT.
LILA CHENEY.
PSYLOCKE.
STORM.
BISHOP.
PHADER.
ISTSKIN.
HEH. GOT SOME BAD NEWS FOR YOU, OPENMIND--EARTH AIN'T EXACTLY GOT THE BEST TRACK RECORD WHERE E.T.s ARE CONCERNED.
DO NOT GIVE THEM CAUSE FOR WORRY, WOLVERINE.
AS MUTANTS, THE X-BROOD WILL HAVE THE PROTECTION OF THE X-MEN. NO HARM SHALL BEFALL THEM.
DEATH'S HEAD.
WOLVERINE.
HEY, Y'ALL, LOOKS LIKE WE'RE COMIN' BACK UP ON EARTH!
BUT, UH, AH JUST GOT ONE QUESTION...

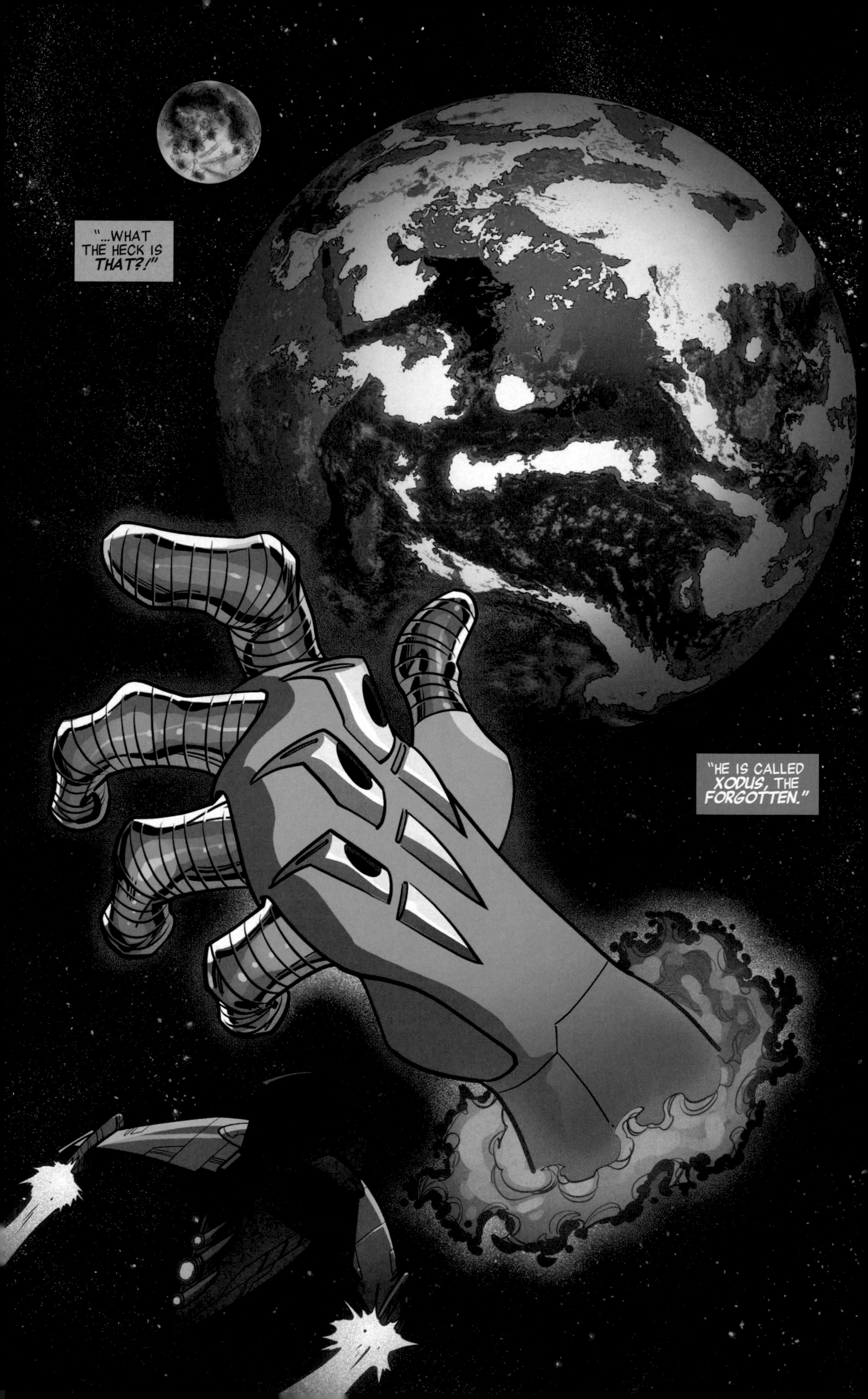
"...WHAT THE HECK IS THAT?!"
"HE IS CALLED XODUS, THE FORGOTTEN."

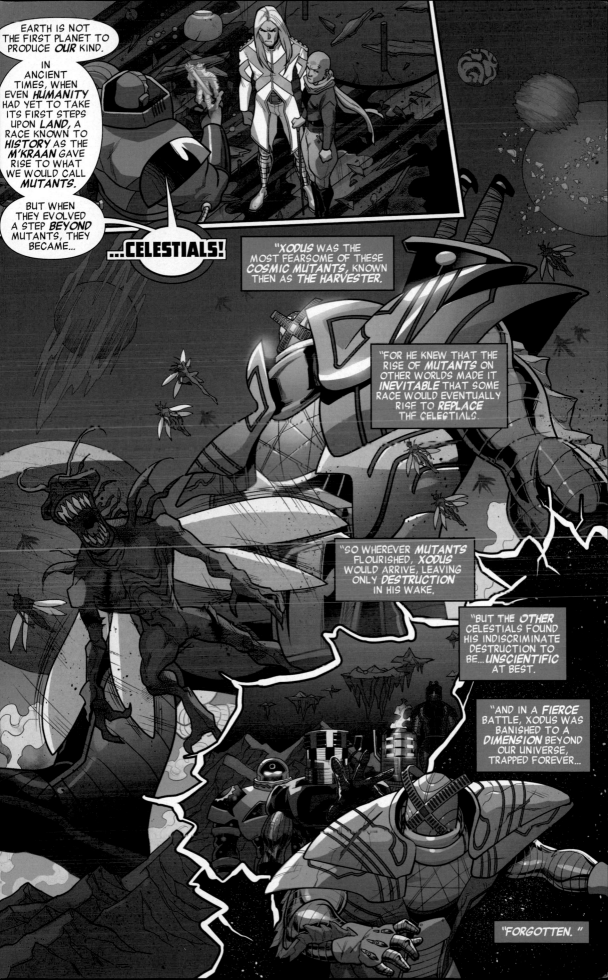

EARTH IS NOT THE FIRST PLANET TO PRODUCE *OUR* KIND.

IN ANCIENT TIMES, WHEN EVEN *HUMANITY* HAD YET TO TAKE ITS FIRST STEPS UPON *LAND,* A RACE KNOWN TO *HISTORY* AS THE *M'KRAAN* GAVE RISE TO WHAT WE WOULD CALL *MUTANTS.*

BUT WHEN THEY EVOLVED A STEP *BEYOND* MUTANTS, THEY BECAME...

...CELESTIALS!

"*XODUS* WAS THE MOST FEARSOME OF THESE *COSMIC MUTANTS,* KNOWN THEN AS *THE HARVESTER.*

"FOR HE KNEW THAT THE RISE OF *MUTANTS* ON OTHER WORLDS MADE IT *INEVITABLE* THAT SOME RACE WOULD EVENTUALLY RISE TO *REPLACE* THE CELESTIALS.

"SO WHEREVER *MUTANTS* FLOURISHED, *XODUS* WOULD ARRIVE, LEAVING ONLY *DESTRUCTION* IN HIS WAKE.

"BUT THE *OTHER* CELESTIALS FOUND HIS INDISCRIMINATE DESTRUCTION TO BE...*UNSCIENTIFIC* AT BEST.

"AND IN A *FIERCE* BATTLE, XODUS WAS BANISHED TO A *DIMENSION* BEYOND OUR UNIVERSE, TRAPPED FOREVER...

"FORGOTTEN."

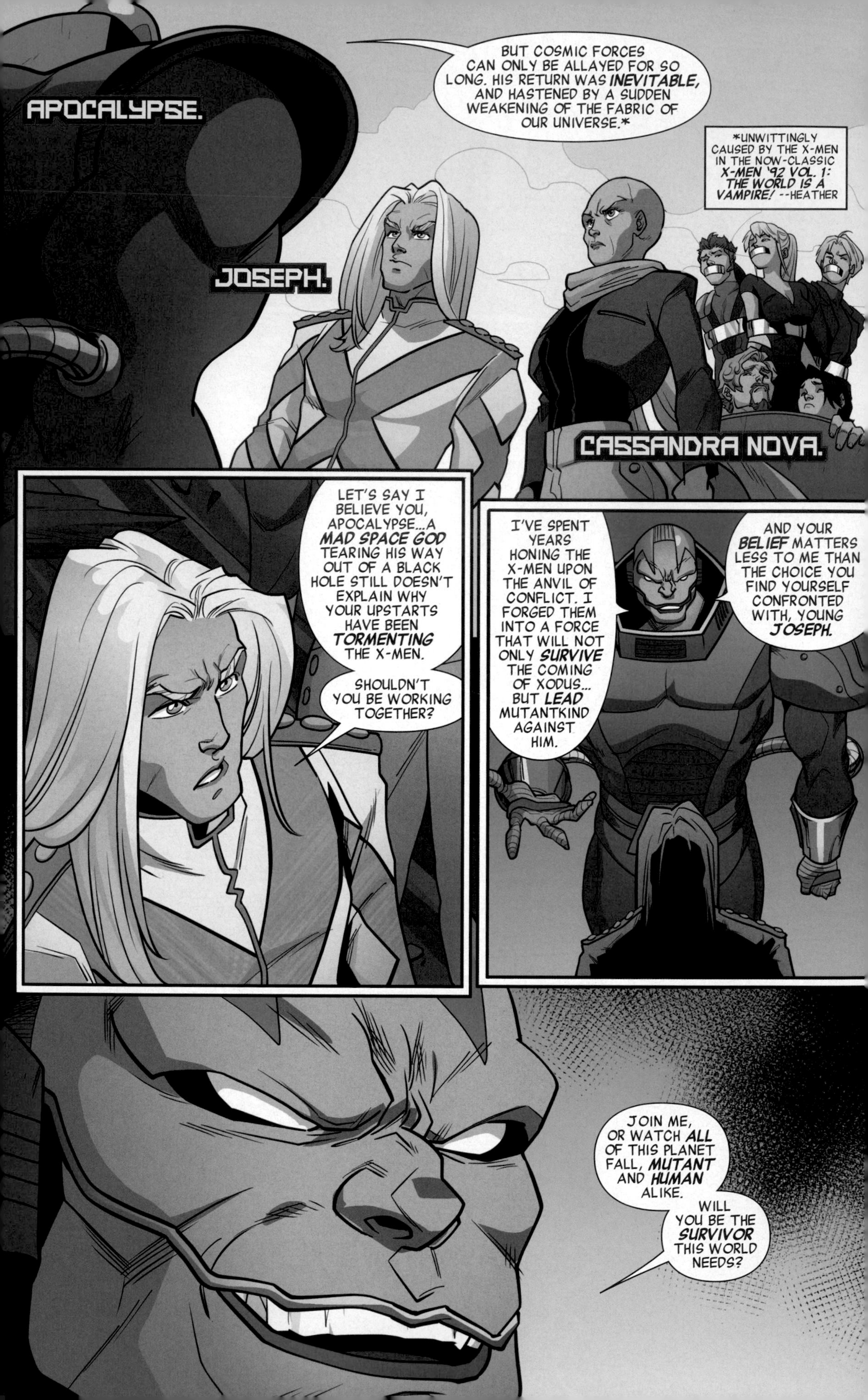
APOCALYPSE.
BUT COSMIC FORCES CAN ONLY BE ALLAYED FOR SO LONG. HIS RETURN WAS INEVITABLE, AND HASTENED BY A SUDDEN WEAKENING OF THE FABRIC OF OUR UNIVERSE.*
*UNWITTINGLY CAUSED BY THE X-MEN IN THE NOW-CLASSIC X-MEN '92 VOL. 1: THE WORLD IS A VAMPIRE! --HEATHER
JOSEPH.
CASSANDRA NOVA.
LET'S SAY I BELIEVE YOU, APOCALYPSE...A MAD SPACE GOD TEARING HIS WAY OUT OF A BLACK HOLE STILL DOESN'T EXPLAIN WHY YOUR UPSTARTS HAVE BEEN TORMENTING THE X-MEN.
SHOULDN'T YOU BE WORKING TOGETHER?
I'VE SPENT YEARS HONING THE X-MEN UPON THE ANVIL OF CONFLICT. I FORGED THEM INTO A FORCE THAT WILL NOT ONLY SURVIVE THE COMING OF XODUS... BUT LEAD MUTANTKIND AGAINST HIM.
AND YOUR BELIEF MATTERS LESS TO ME THAN THE CHOICE YOU FIND YOURSELF CONFRONTED WITH, YOUNG JOSEPH.
JOIN ME, OR WATCH ALL OF THIS PLANET FALL, MUTANT AND HUMAN ALIKE.
WILL YOU BE THE SURVIVOR THIS WORLD NEEDS?

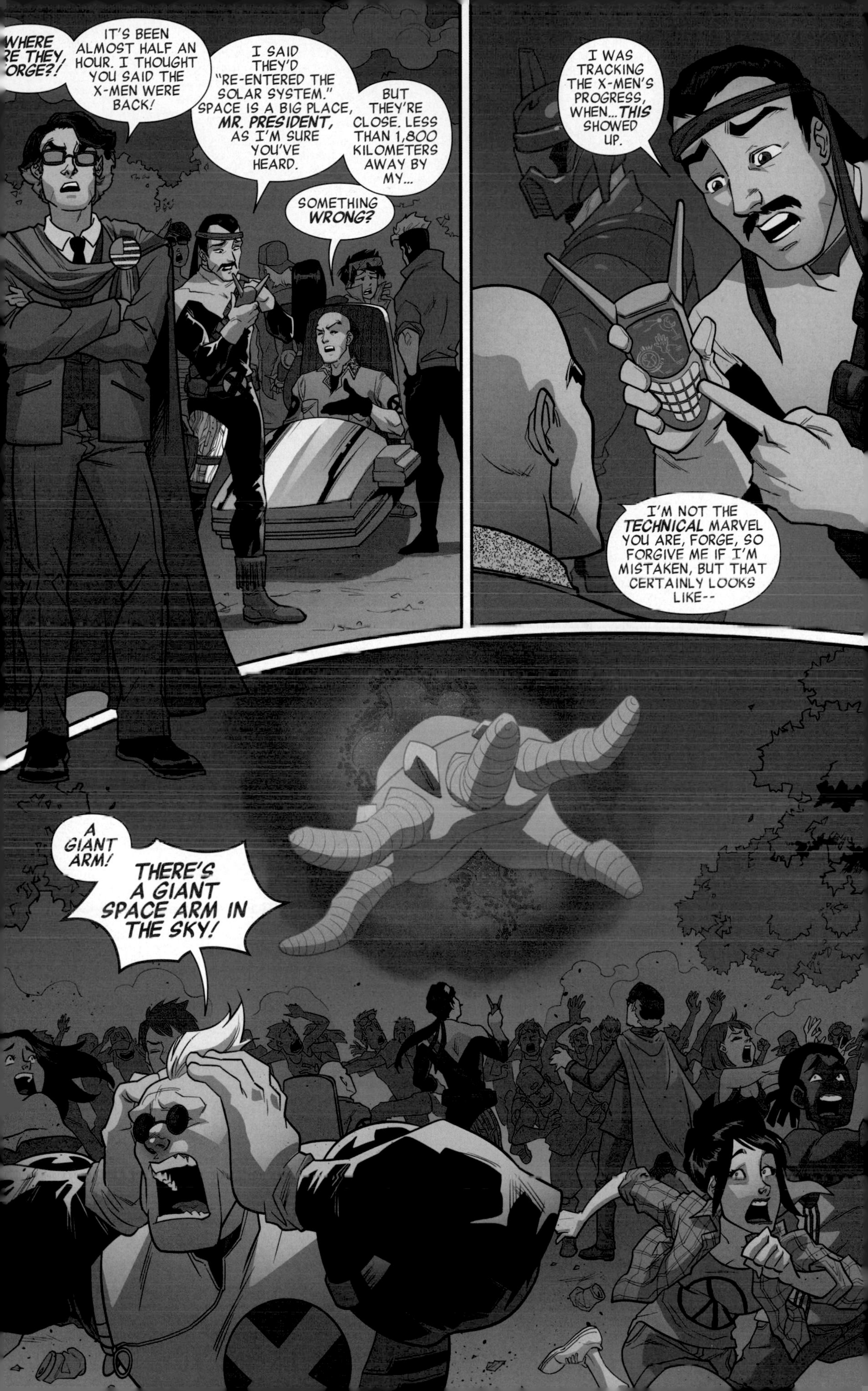
WHERE ARE THEY, FORGE?!
IT'S BEEN ALMOST HALF AN HOUR. I THOUGHT YOU SAID THE X-MEN WERE BACK!
I SAID THEY'D "RE-ENTERED THE SOLAR SYSTEM." SPACE IS A BIG PLACE, MR. PRESIDENT, AS I'M SURE YOU'VE HEARD.
BUT THEY'RE CLOSE. LESS THAN 1,800 KILOMETERS AWAY BY MY...
SOMETHING WRONG?
I WAS TRACKING THE X-MEN'S PROGRESS, WHEN...THIS SHOWED UP.
I'M NOT THE TECHNICAL MARVEL YOU ARE, FORGE, SO FORGIVE ME IF I'M MISTAKEN, BUT THAT CERTAINLY LOOKS LIKE--
A GIANT ARM!
THERE'S A GIANT SPACE ARM IN THE SKY!

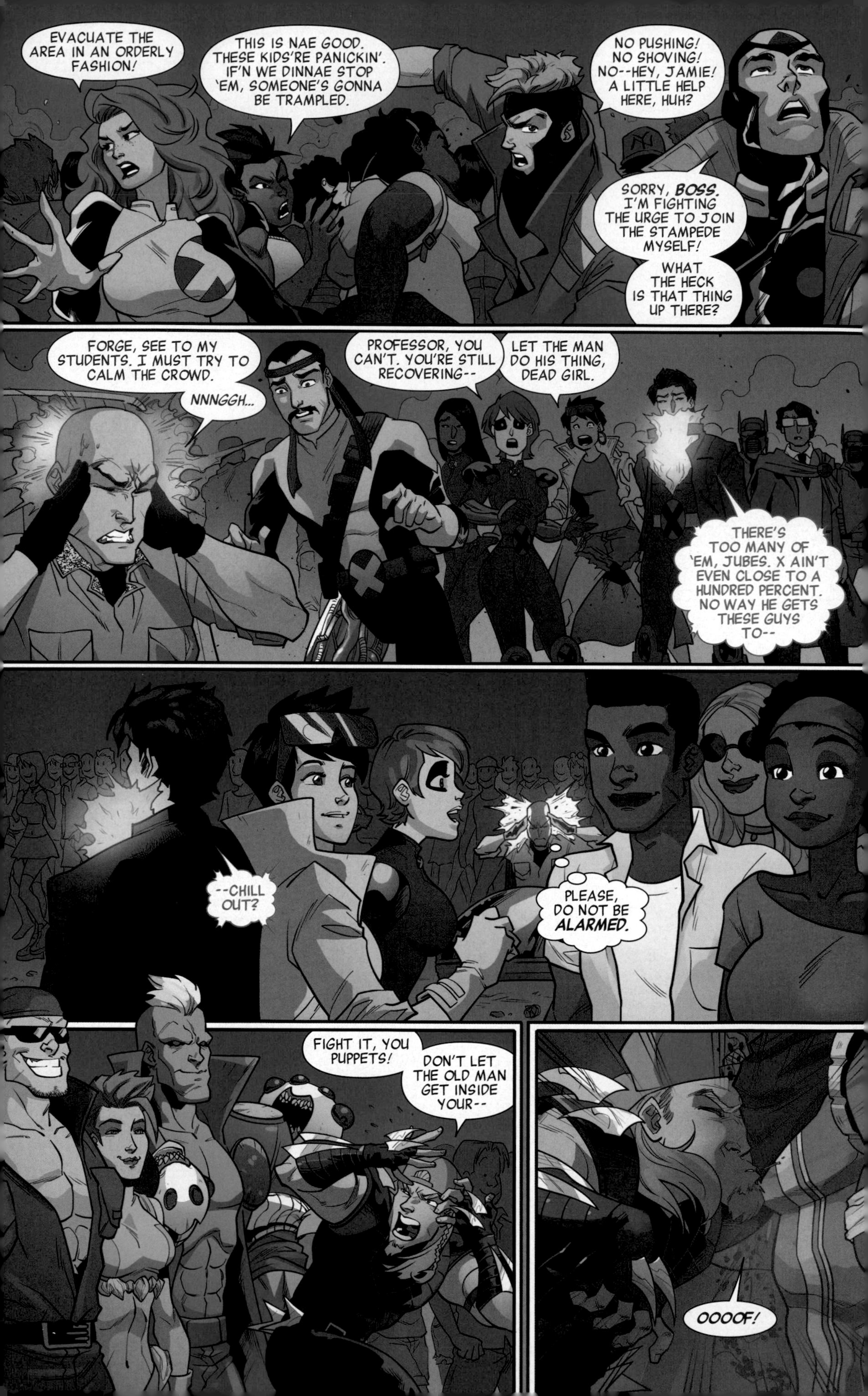
EVACUATE THE AREA IN AN ORDERLY FASHION!
THIS IS NAE GOOD. THESE KIDS'RE PANICKIN'. IF'N WE DINNAE STOP 'EM, SOMEONE'S GONNA BE TRAMPLED.
NO PUSHING! NO SHOVING! NO--HEY, JAMIE! A LITTLE HELP HERE, HUH?
SORRY, BOSS. I'M FIGHTING THE URGE TO JOIN THE STAMPEDE MYSELF!
WHAT THE HECK IS THAT THING UP THERE?
FORGE, SEE TO MY STUDENTS. I MUST TRY TO CALM THE CROWD.
NNNGGH...
PROFESSOR, YOU CAN'T. YOU'RE STILL RECOVERING--
LET THE MAN DO HIS THING, DEAD GIRL.
THERE'S TOO MANY OF 'EM, JUBES. X AIN'T EVEN CLOSE TO A HUNDRED PERCENT. NO WAY HE GETS THESE GUYS TO--
--CHILL OUT?
PLEASE, DO NOT BE ALARMED.
FIGHT IT, YOU PUPPETS!
DON'T LET THE OLD MAN GET INSIDE YOUR--
OOOOF!

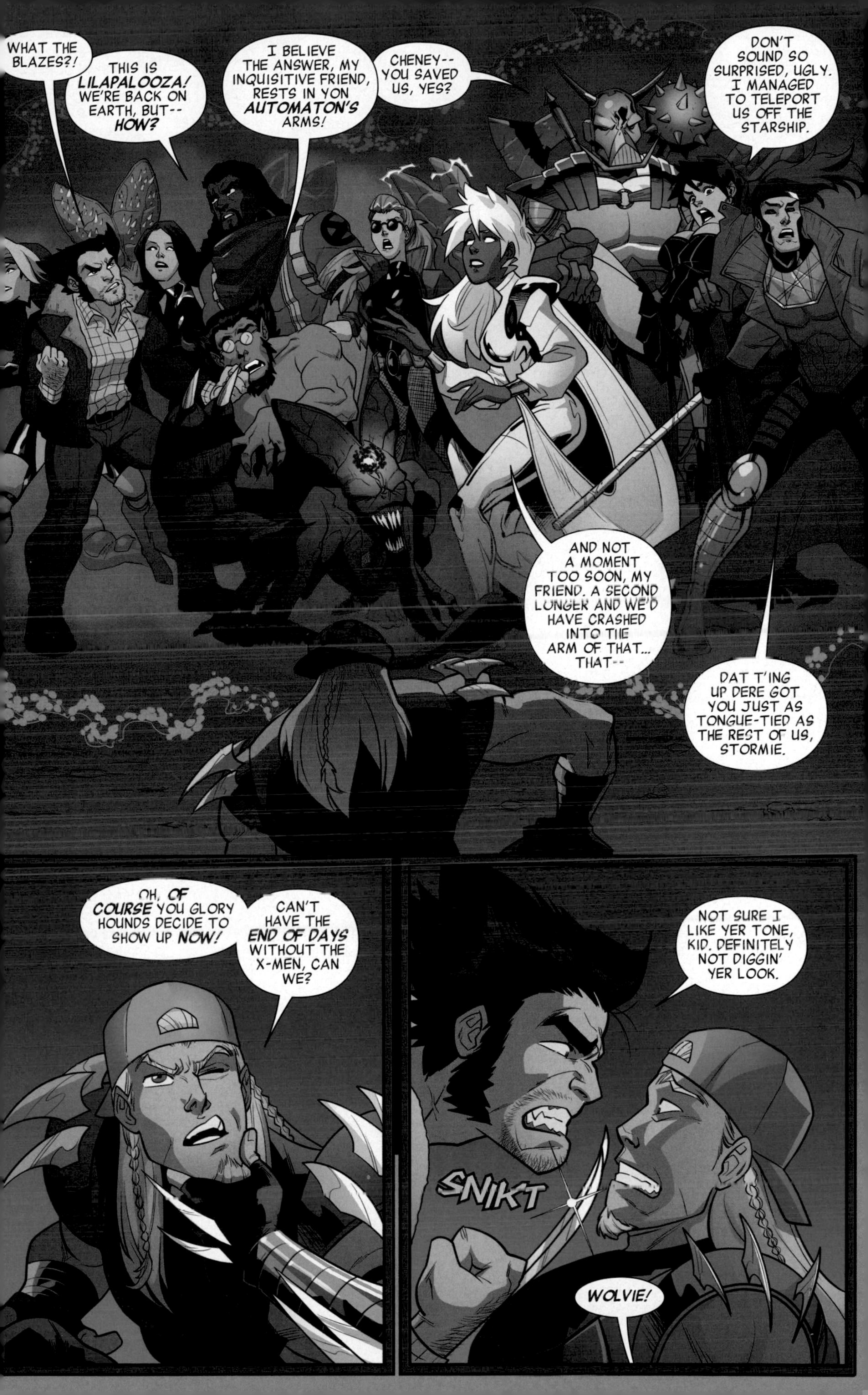

WHAT THE BLAZES?!
THIS IS LILAPALOOZA! WE'RE BACK ON EARTH, BUT-- HOW?
I BELIEVE THE ANSWER, MY INQUISITIVE FRIEND, RESTS IN YON AUTOMATON'S ARMS!
CHENEY-- YOU SAVED US, YES?
DON'T SOUND SO SURPRISED, UGLY. I MANAGED TO TELEPORT US OFF THE STARSHIP.
AND NOT A MOMENT TOO SOON, MY FRIEND. A SECOND LONGER AND WE'D HAVE CRASHED INTO THE ARM OF THAT... THAT--
DAT T'ING UP DERE GOT YOU JUST AS TONGUE-TIED AS THE REST OF US, STORMIE.
OH, OF COURSE YOU GLORY HOUNDS DECIDE TO SHOW UP NOW!
CAN'T HAVE THE END OF DAYS WITHOUT THE X-MEN, CAN WE?
NOT SURE I LIKE YER TONE, KID. DEFINITELY NOT DIGGIN' YER LOOK.
SNIKT
WOLVIE!

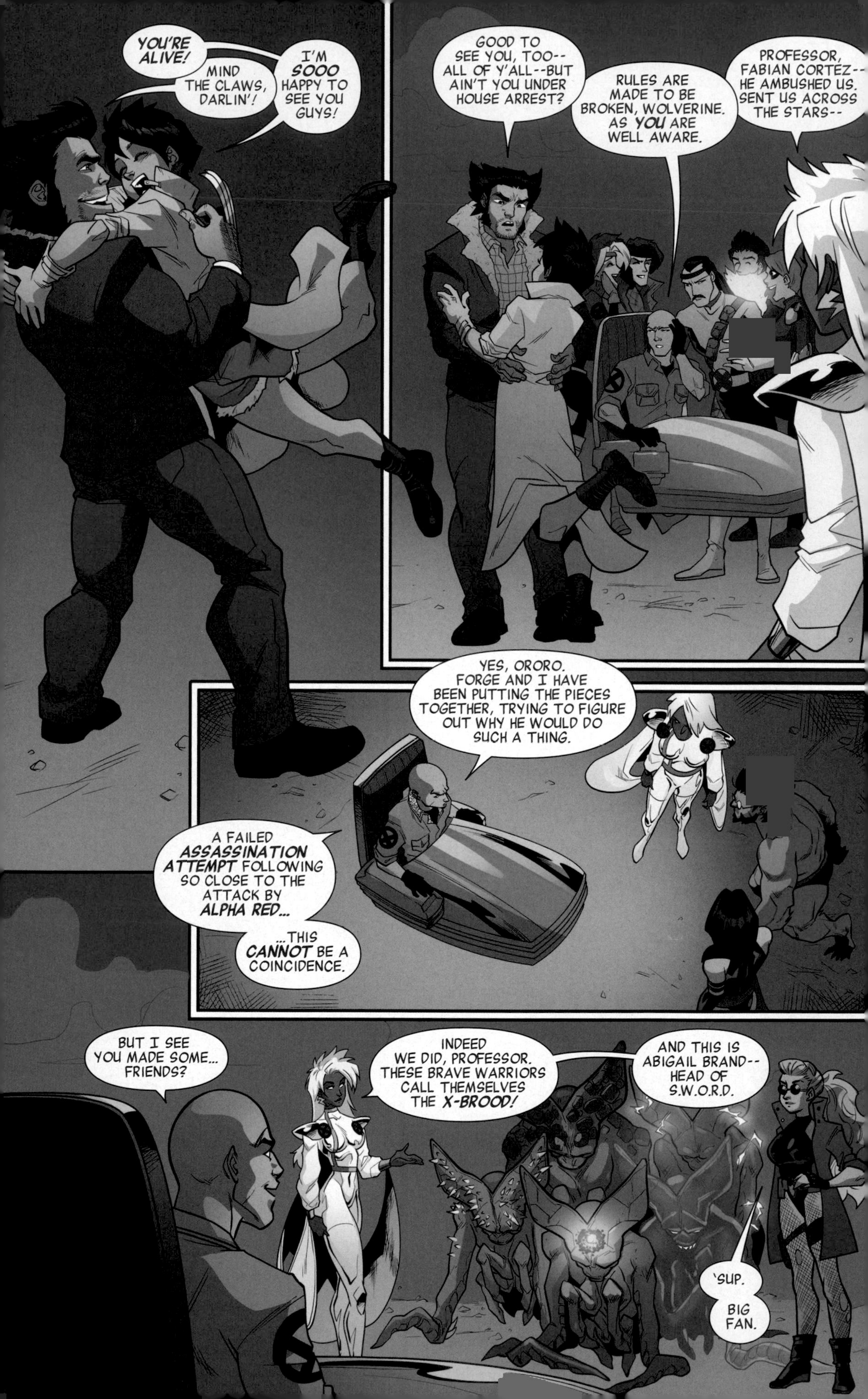
YOU'RE ALIVE!
I'M SOOO HAPPY TO SEE YOU GUYS!
MIND THE CLAWS, DARLIN'!
GOOD TO SEE YOU, TOO-- ALL OF Y'ALL--BUT AIN'T YOU UNDER HOUSE ARREST?
RULES ARE MADE TO BE BROKEN, WOLVERINE. AS YOU ARE WELL AWARE.
PROFESSOR, FABIAN CORTEZ-- HE AMBUSHED US. SENT US ACROSS THE STARS--
YES, ORORO. FORGE AND I HAVE BEEN PUTTING THE PIECES TOGETHER, TRYING TO FIGURE OUT WHY HE WOULD DO SUCH A THING.
A FAILED ASSASSINATION ATTEMPT FOLLOWING SO CLOSE TO THE ATTACK BY ALPHA RED...
...THIS CANNOT BE A COINCIDENCE.
BUT I SEE YOU MADE SOME... FRIENDS?
INDEED WE DID, PROFESSOR. THESE BRAVE WARRIORS CALL THEMSELVES THE X-BROOD!
AND THIS IS ABIGAIL BRAND-- HEAD OF S.W.O.R.D.
'SUP.
BIG FAN.

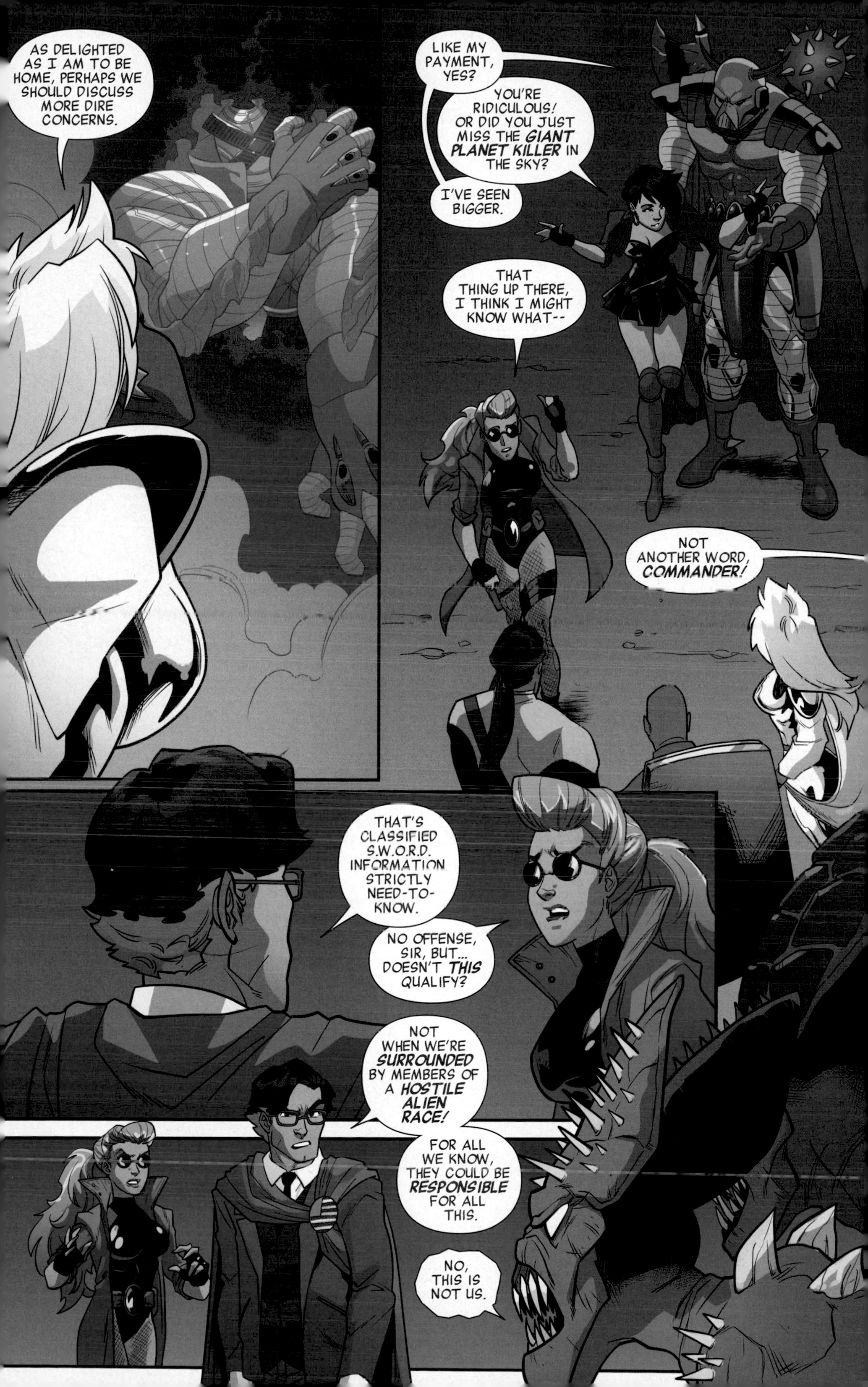
AS DELIGHTED AS I AM TO BE HOME, PERHAPS WE SHOULD DISCUSS MORE DIRE CONCERNS.
LIKE MY PAYMENT, YES?
YOU'RE RIDICULOUS! OR DID YOU JUST MISS THE GIANT PLANET KILLER IN THE SKY?
I'VE SEEN BIGGER.
THAT THING UP THERE, I THINK I MIGHT KNOW WHAT--
NOT ANOTHER WORD, COMMANDER!
THAT'S CLASSIFIED S.W.O.R.D. INFORMATION STRICTLY NEED-TO-KNOW.
NO OFFENSE, SIR, BUT... DOESN'T THIS QUALIFY?
NOT WHEN WE'RE SURROUNDED BY MEMBERS OF A HOSTILE ALIEN RACE!
FOR ALL WE KNOW, THEY COULD BE RESPONSIBLE FOR ALL THIS.
NO, THIS IS NOT US.

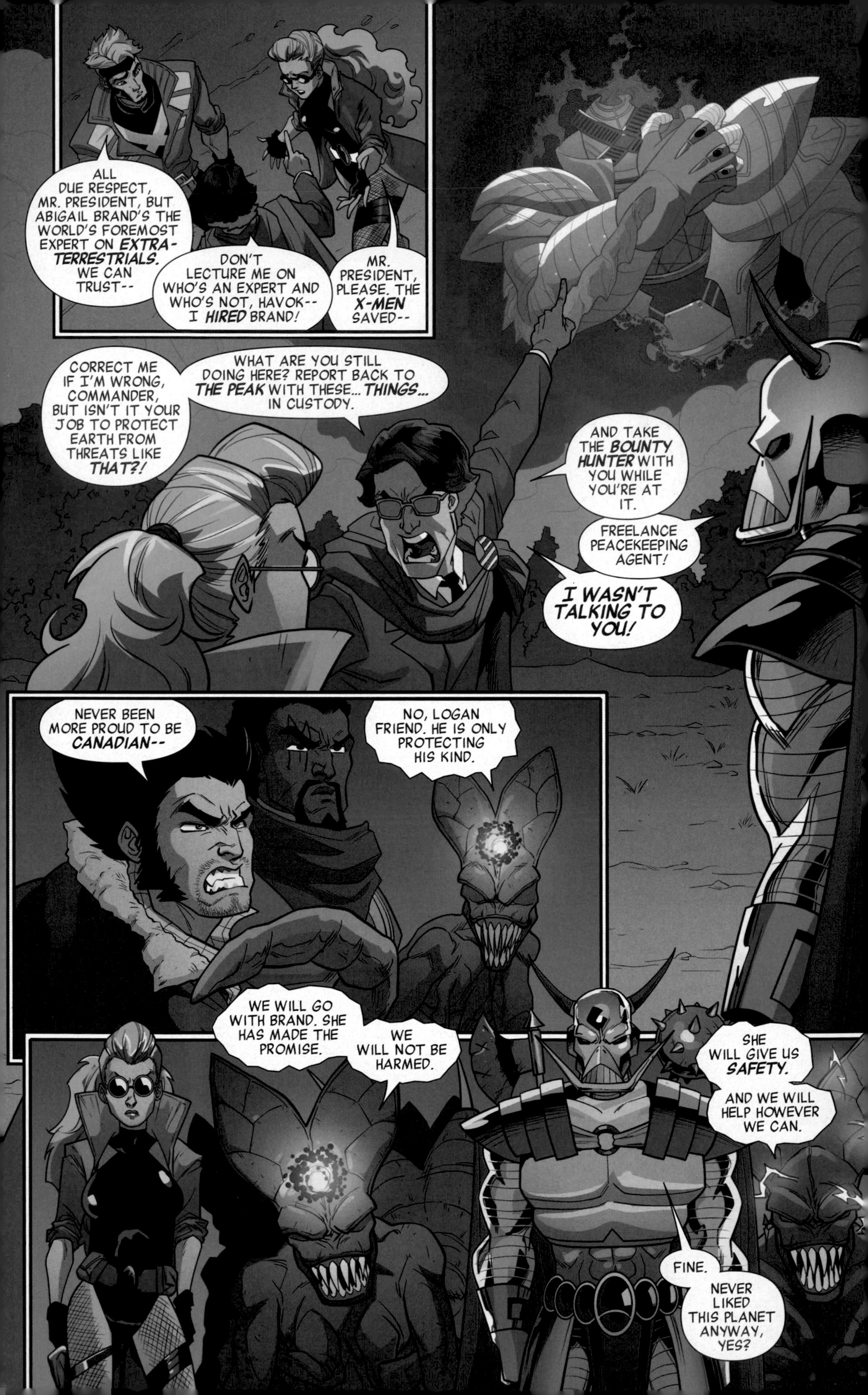

ALL DUE RESPECT, MR. PRESIDENT, BUT ABIGAIL BRAND'S THE WORLD'S FOREMOST EXPERT ON EXTRA-TERRESTRIALS. WE CAN TRUST--
DON'T LECTURE ME ON WHO'S AN EXPERT AND WHO'S NOT, HAVOK-- I HIRED BRAND!
MR. PRESIDENT, PLEASE. THE X-MEN SAVED--
CORRECT ME IF I'M WRONG, COMMANDER, BUT ISN'T IT YOUR JOB TO PROTECT EARTH FROM THREATS LIKE THAT?!
WHAT ARE YOU STILL DOING HERE? REPORT BACK TO THE PEAK WITH THESE... THINGS... IN CUSTODY.
AND TAKE THE BOUNTY HUNTER WITH YOU WHILE YOU'RE AT IT.
FREELANCE PEACEKEEPING AGENT!
I WASN'T TALKING TO YOU!
NEVER BEEN MORE PROUD TO BE CANADIAN--
NO, LOGAN FRIEND. HE IS ONLY PROTECTING HIS KIND.
WE WILL GO WITH BRAND. SHE HAS MADE THE PROMISE.
WE WILL NOT BE HARMED.
SHE WILL GIVE US SAFETY.
AND WE WILL HELP HOWEVER WE CAN.
FINE.
NEVER LIKED THIS PLANET ANYWAY, YES?

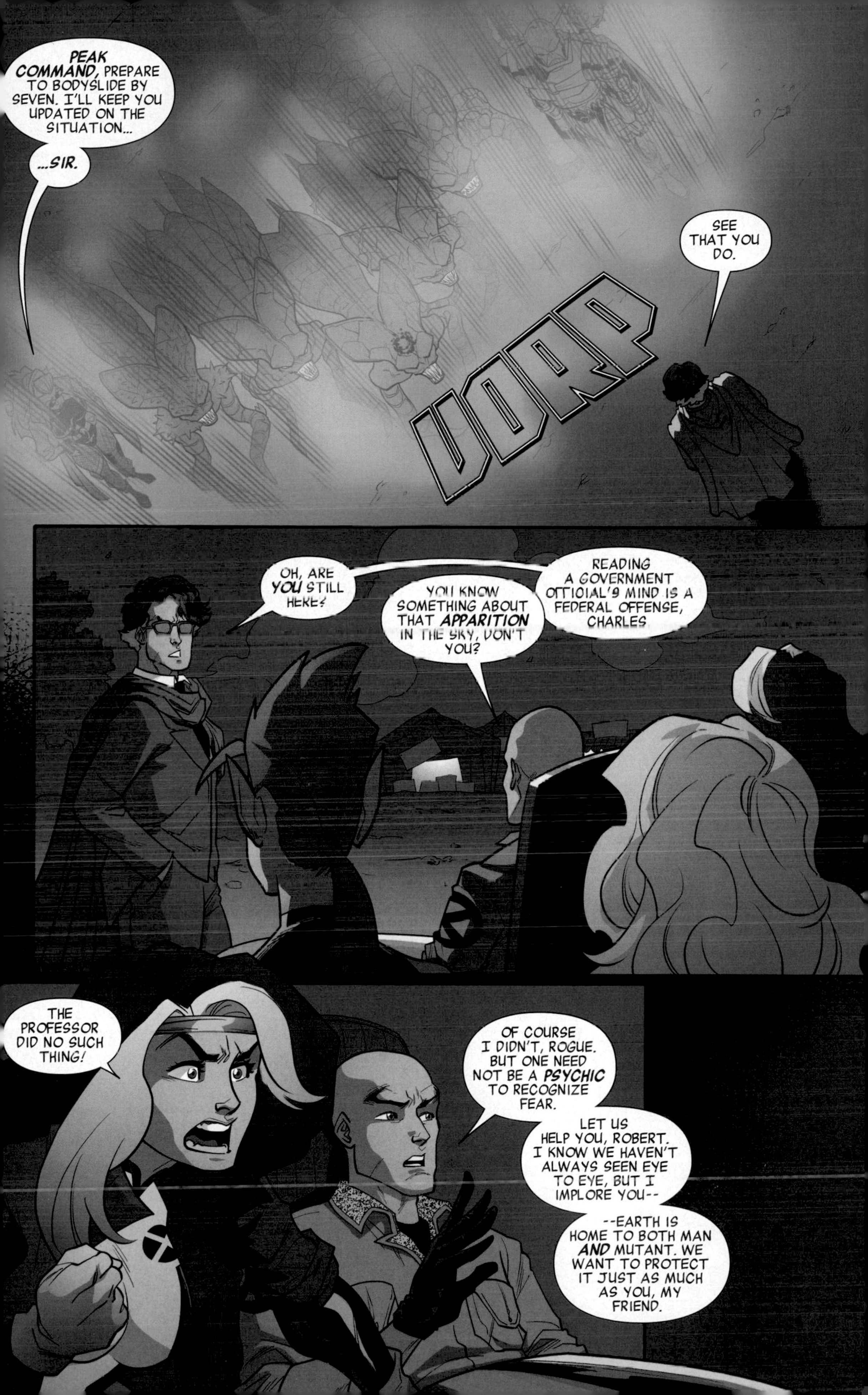
PEAK COMMAND, PREPARE TO BODYSLIDE BY SEVEN. I'LL KEEP YOU UPDATED ON THE SITUATION...
...SIR.
SEE THAT YOU DO.
VORP
OH, ARE YOU STILL HERE?
READING A GOVERNMENT OFFICIAL'S MIND IS A FEDERAL OFFENSE, CHARLES
YOU KNOW SOMETHING ABOUT THAT APPARITION IN THE SKY, DON'T YOU?
THE PROFESSOR DID NO SUCH THING!
OF COURSE I DIDN'T, ROGUE. BUT ONE NEED NOT BE A PSYCHIC TO RECOGNIZE FEAR.
LET US HELP YOU, ROBERT. I KNOW WE HAVEN'T ALWAYS SEEN EYE TO EYE, BUT I IMPLORE YOU--
--EARTH IS HOME TO BOTH MAN AND MUTANT. WE WANT TO PROTECT IT JUST AS MUCH AS YOU, MY FRIEND.

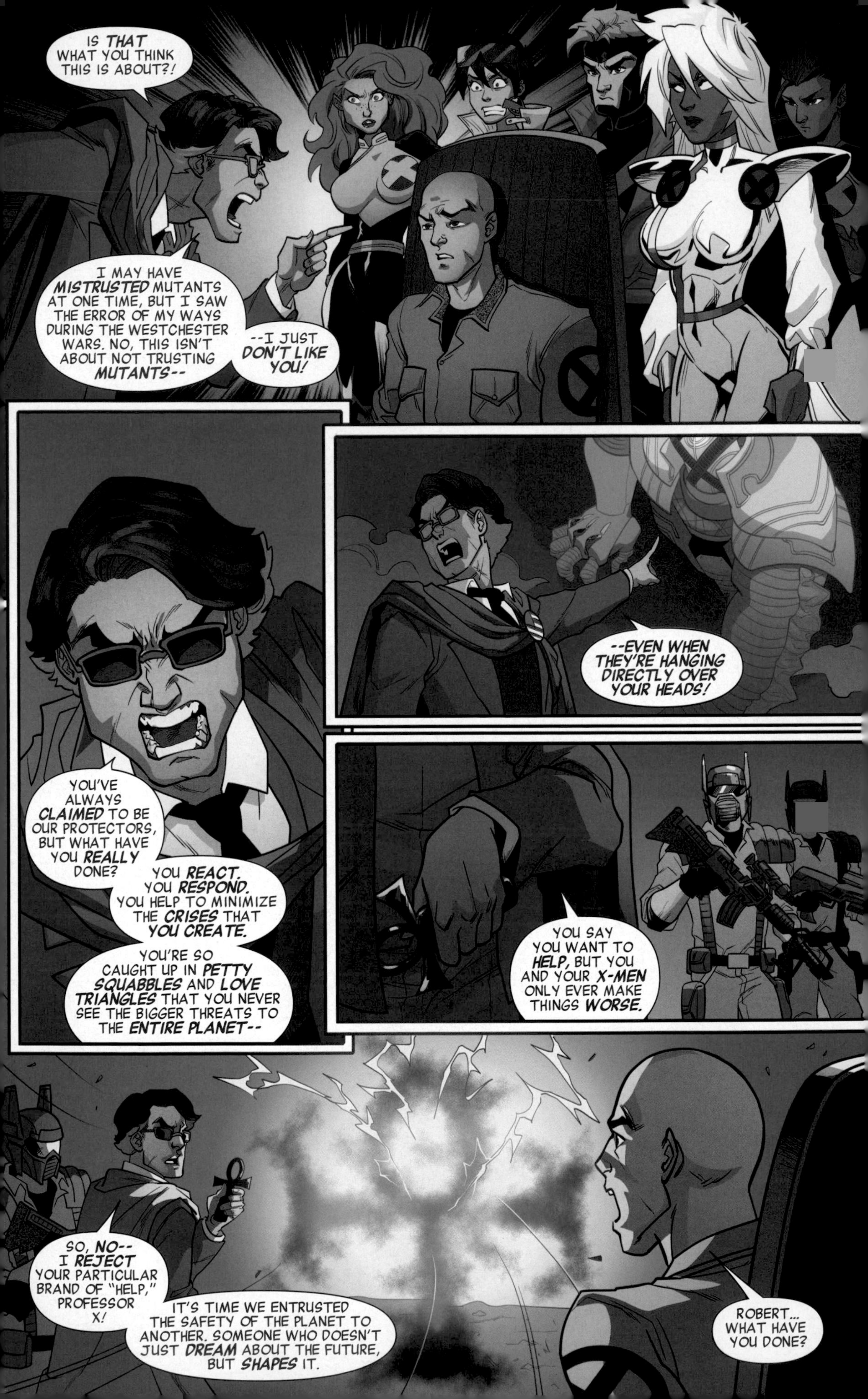

IS THAT WHAT YOU THINK THIS IS ABOUT?!
I MAY HAVE MISTRUSTED MUTANTS AT ONE TIME, BUT I SAW THE ERROR OF MY WAYS DURING THE WESTCHESTER WARS. NO, THIS ISN'T ABOUT NOT TRUSTING MUTANTS--
--I JUST DON'T LIKE YOU!
YOU'VE ALWAYS CLAIMED TO BE OUR PROTECTORS, BUT WHAT HAVE YOU REALLY DONE?
YOU REACT. YOU RESPOND. YOU HELP TO MINIMIZE THE CRISES THAT YOU CREATE.
YOU'RE SO CAUGHT UP IN PETTY SQUABBLES AND LOVE TRIANGLES THAT YOU NEVER SEE THE BIGGER THREATS TO THE ENTIRE PLANET--
--EVEN WHEN THEY'RE HANGING DIRECTLY OVER YOUR HEADS!
YOU SAY YOU WANT TO HELP, BUT YOU AND YOUR X-MEN ONLY EVER MAKE THINGS WORSE.
SO, NO-- I REJECT YOUR PARTICULAR BRAND OF "HELP," PROFESSOR X!
IT'S TIME WE ENTRUSTED THE SAFETY OF THE PLANET TO ANOTHER. SOMEONE WHO DOESN'T JUST DREAM ABOUT THE FUTURE, BUT SHAPES IT.
ROBERT... WHAT HAVE YOU DONE?

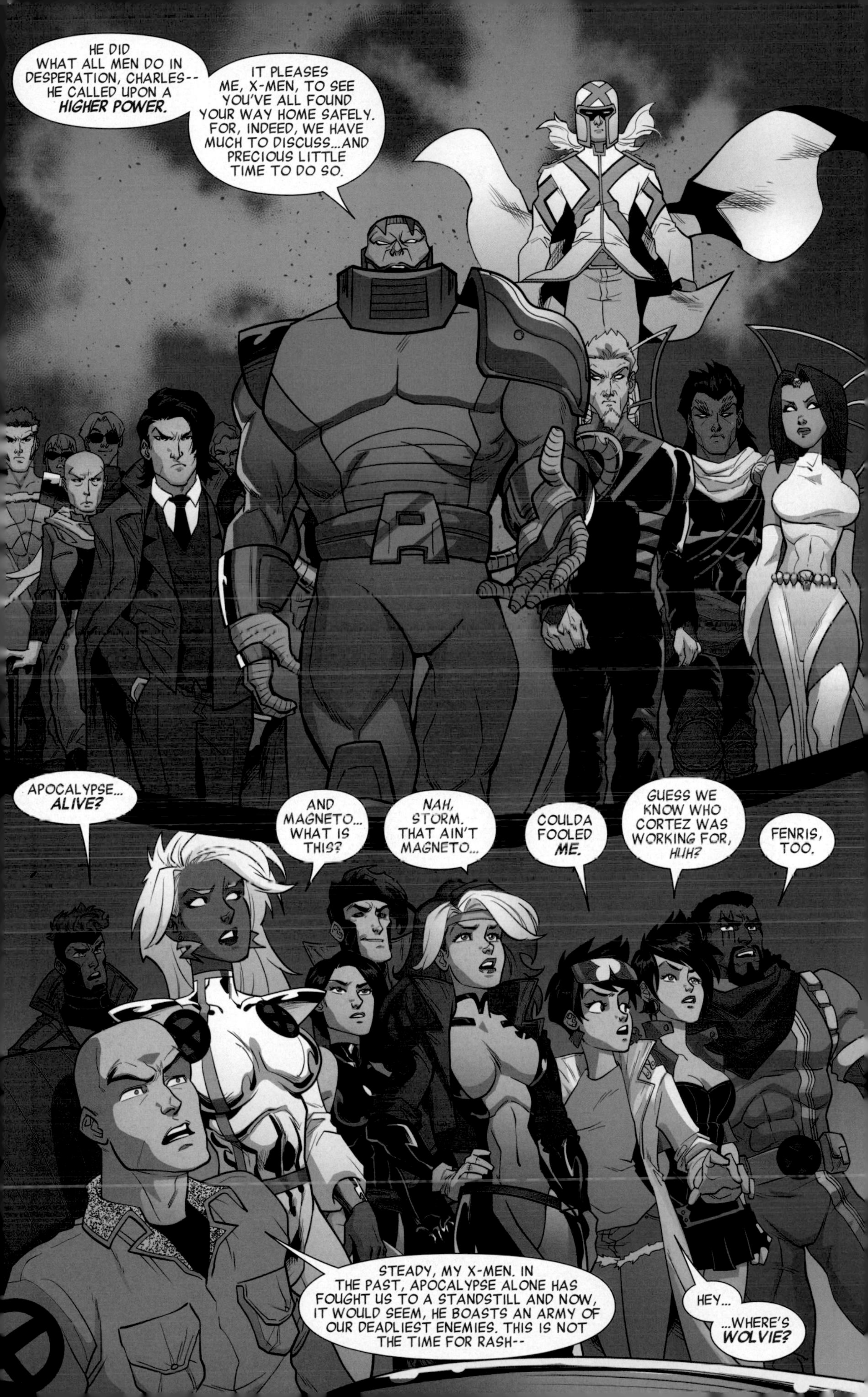
HE DID WHAT ALL MEN DO IN DESPERATION, CHARLES-- HE CALLED UPON A **HIGHER POWER.**
IT PLEASES ME, X-MEN, TO SEE YOU'VE ALL FOUND YOUR WAY HOME SAFELY. FOR, INDEED, WE HAVE MUCH TO DISCUSS...AND PRECIOUS LITTLE TIME TO DO SO.
APOCALYPSE... **ALIVE?**
AND MAGNETO... WHAT IS THIS?
NAH, STORM. THAT AIN'T MAGNETO...
COULDA FOOLED **ME.**
GUESS WE KNOW WHO CORTEZ WAS WORKING FOR, *HUH?*
FENRIS, TOO.
STEADY, MY X-MEN. IN THE PAST, APOCALYPSE ALONE HAS FOUGHT US TO A STANDSTILL AND NOW, IT WOULD SEEM, HE BOASTS AN ARMY OF OUR DEADLIEST ENEMIES. THIS IS NOT THE TIME FOR RASH--
HEY...
...WHERE'S **WOLVIE?**

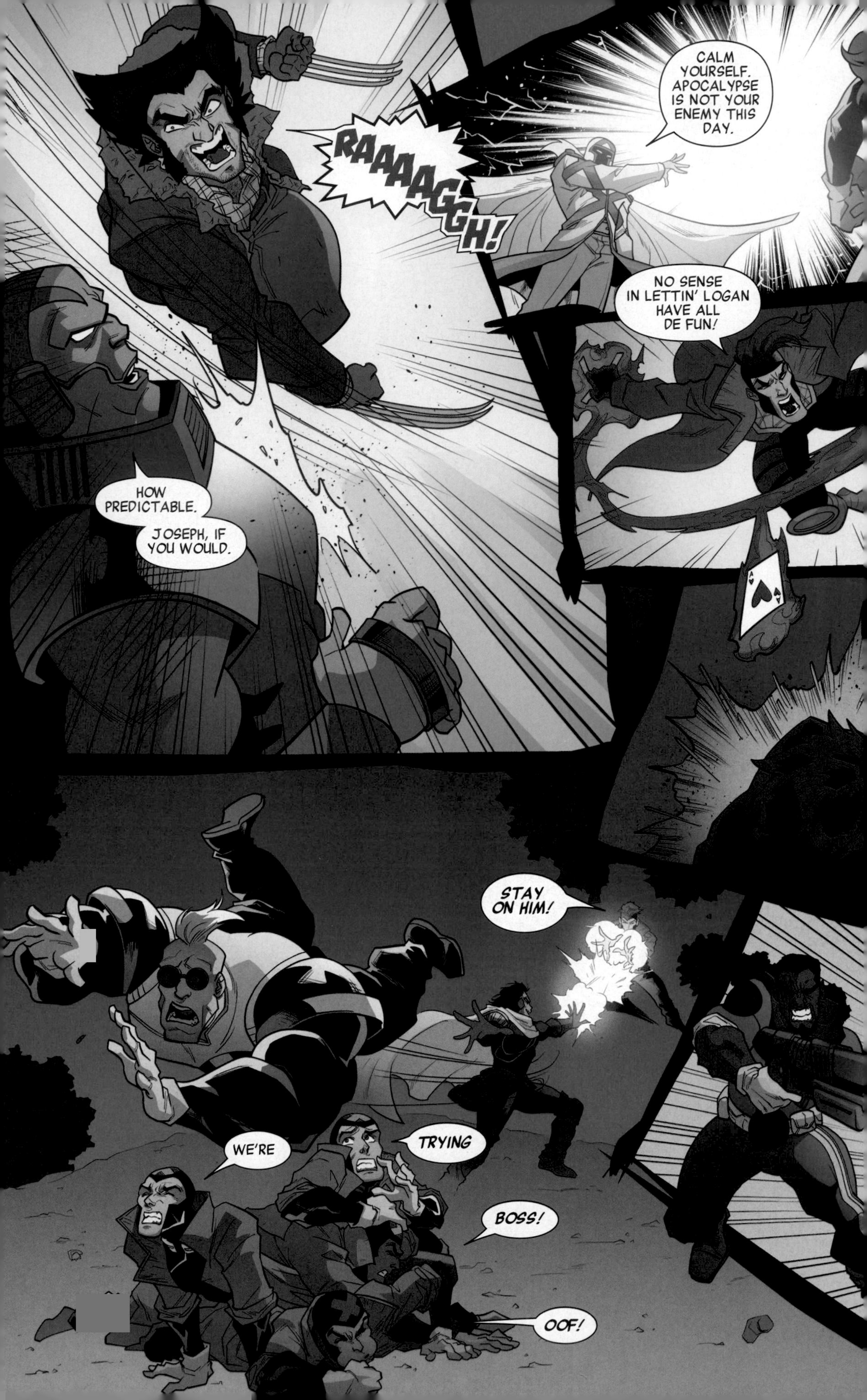
RAAAAAGGH!
CALM YOURSELF. APOCALYPSE IS NOT YOUR ENEMY THIS DAY.
NO SENSE IN LETTIN' LOGAN HAVE ALL DE FUN!
HOW PREDICTABLE.
JOSEPH, IF YOU WOULD.
STAY ON HIM!
WE'RE
TRYING
BOSS!
OOF!

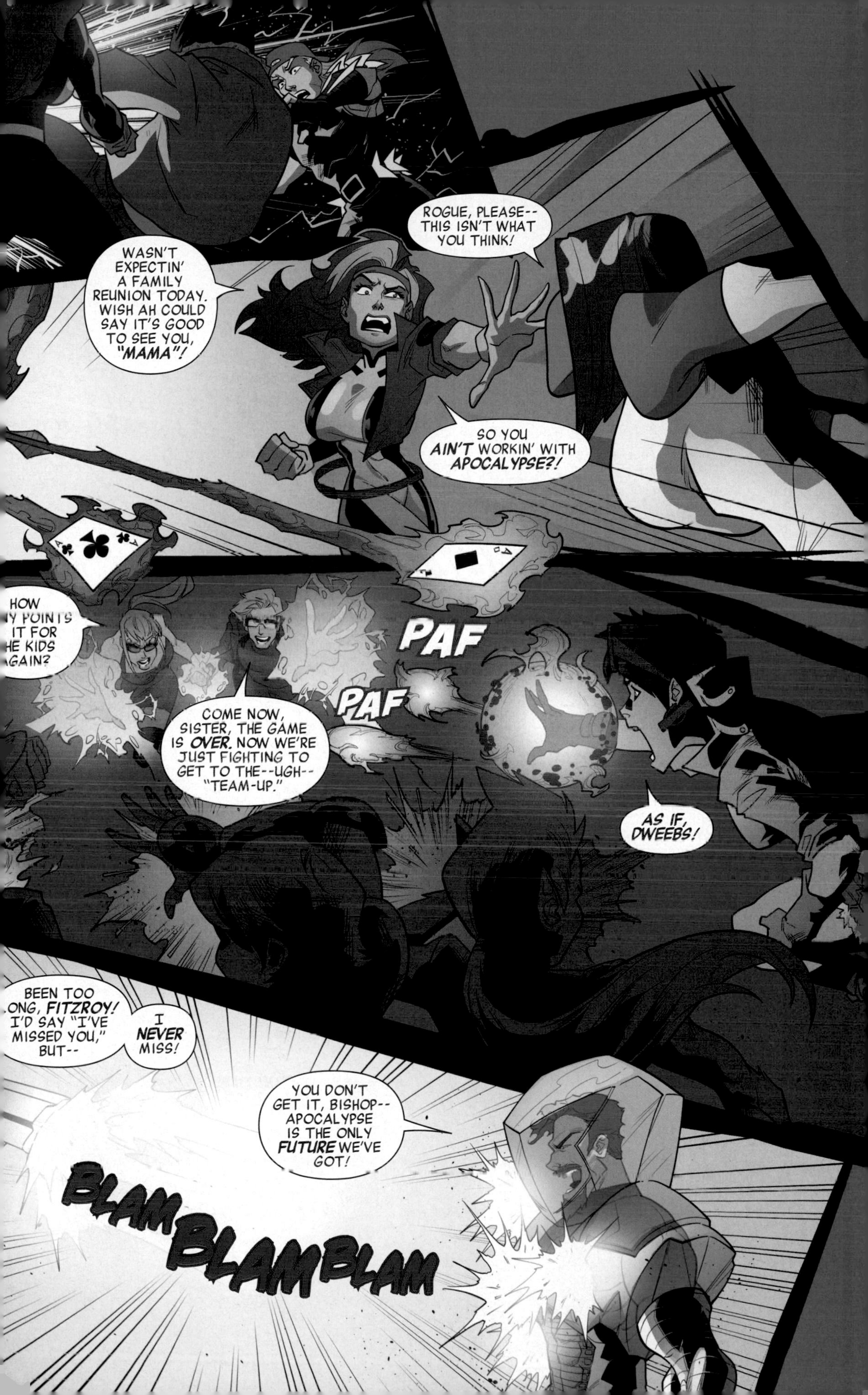

WASN'T EXPECTIN' A FAMILY REUNION TODAY. WISH AH COULD SAY IT'S GOOD TO SEE YOU, "MAMA"!
ROGUE, PLEASE-- THIS ISN'T WHAT YOU THINK!
SO YOU AIN'T WORKIN' WITH APOCALYPSE?!
HOW
IT FOR
AGAIN?
PAF
PAF
COME NOW, SISTER, THE GAME IS OVER. NOW WE'RE JUST FIGHTING TO GET TO THE--UGH-- "TEAM-UP."
AS IF, DWEEBS!
BEEN TOO LONG, FITZROY! I'D SAY "I'VE MISSED YOU," BUT--
I NEVER MISS!
YOU DON'T GET IT, BISHOP-- APOCALYPSE IS THE ONLY FUTURE WE'VE GOT!
BLAM BLAM BLAM BLAM

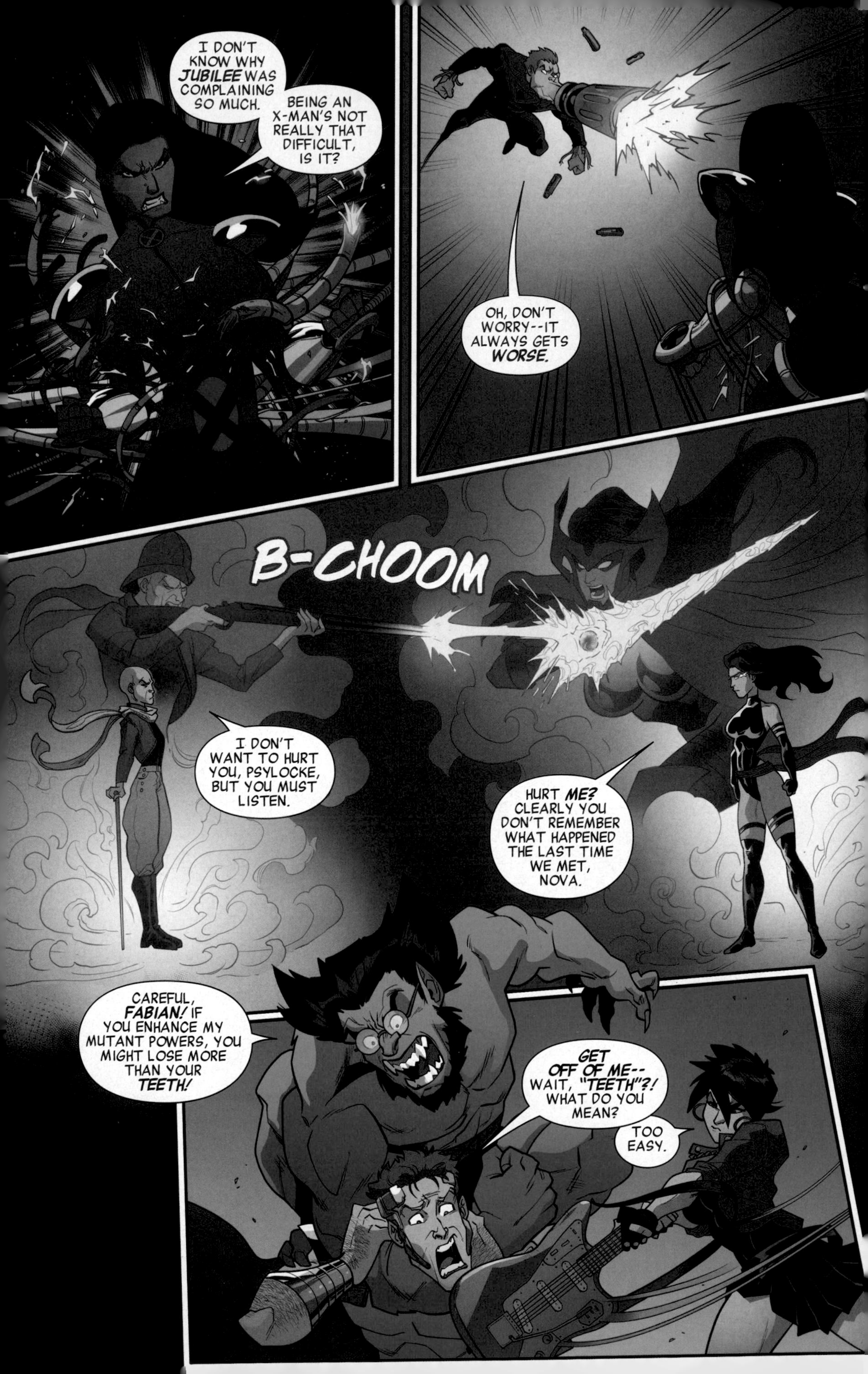

I DON'T KNOW WHY JUBILEE WAS COMPLAINING SO MUCH.
BEING AN X-MAN'S NOT REALLY THAT DIFFICULT, IS IT?
OH, DON'T WORRY--IT ALWAYS GETS WORSE.
B-CHOOM
I DON'T WANT TO HURT YOU, PSYLOCKE, BUT YOU MUST LISTEN.
HURT ME? CLEARLY YOU DON'T REMEMBER WHAT HAPPENED THE LAST TIME WE MET, NOVA.
CAREFUL, FABIAN! IF YOU ENHANCE MY MUTANT POWERS, YOU MIGHT LOSE MORE THAN YOUR TEETH!
GET OFF OF ME-- WAIT, "TEETH"?! WHAT DO YOU MEAN?
TOO EASY.

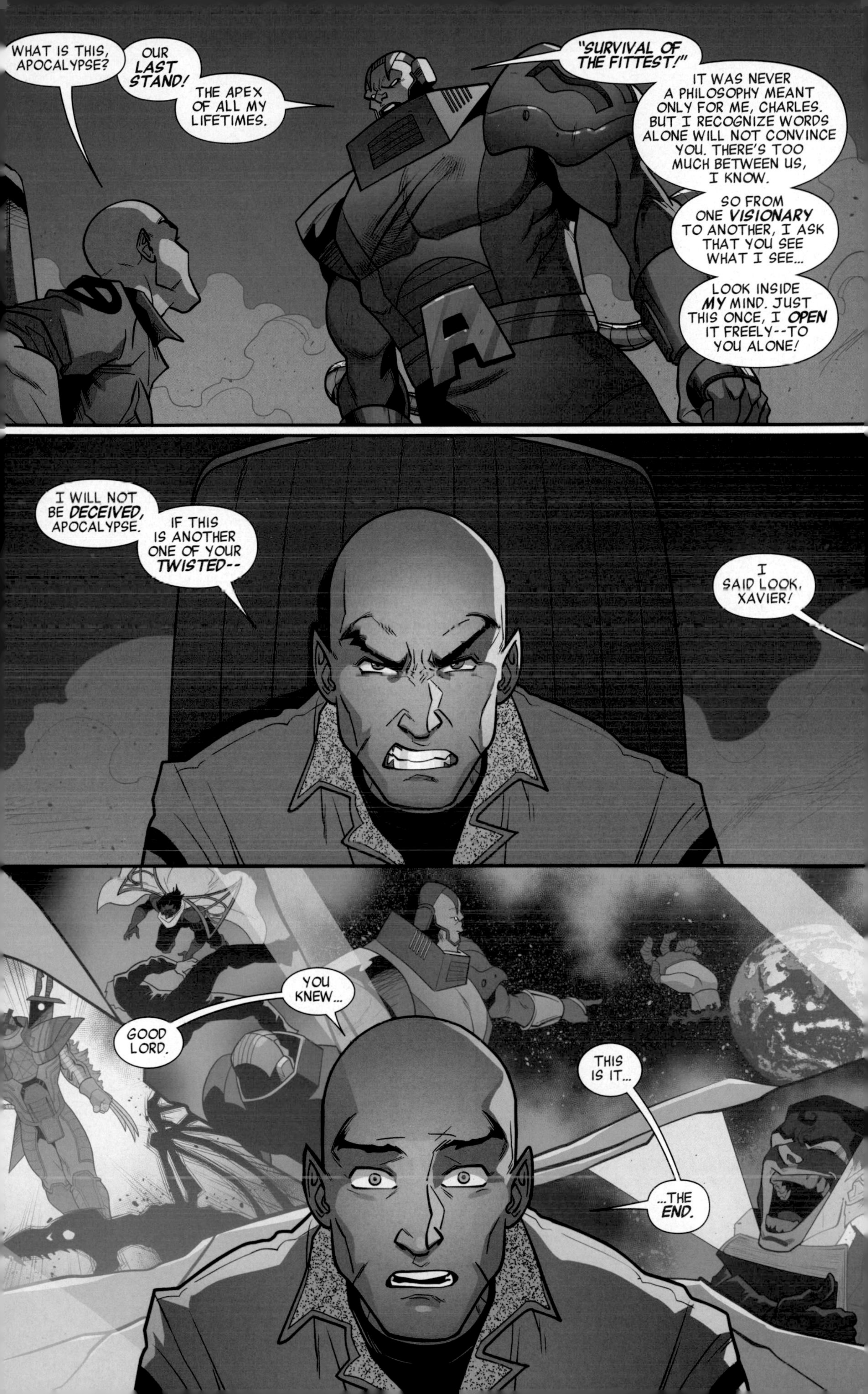
WHAT IS THIS, APOCALYPSE?
OUR LAST STAND!
THE APEX OF ALL MY LIFETIMES.
"SURVIVAL OF THE FITTEST!"
IT WAS NEVER A PHILOSOPHY MEANT ONLY FOR ME, CHARLES. BUT I RECOGNIZE WORDS ALONE WILL NOT CONVINCE YOU. THERE'S TOO MUCH BETWEEN US, I KNOW.
SO FROM ONE VISIONARY TO ANOTHER, I ASK THAT YOU SEE WHAT I SEE...
LOOK INSIDE MY MIND. JUST THIS ONCE, I OPEN IT FREELY--TO YOU ALONE!
I WILL NOT BE DECEIVED, APOCALYPSE.
IF THIS IS ANOTHER ONE OF YOUR TWISTED--
I SAID LOOK, XAVIER!
GOOD LORD.
YOU KNEW...
THIS IS IT...
...THE END.

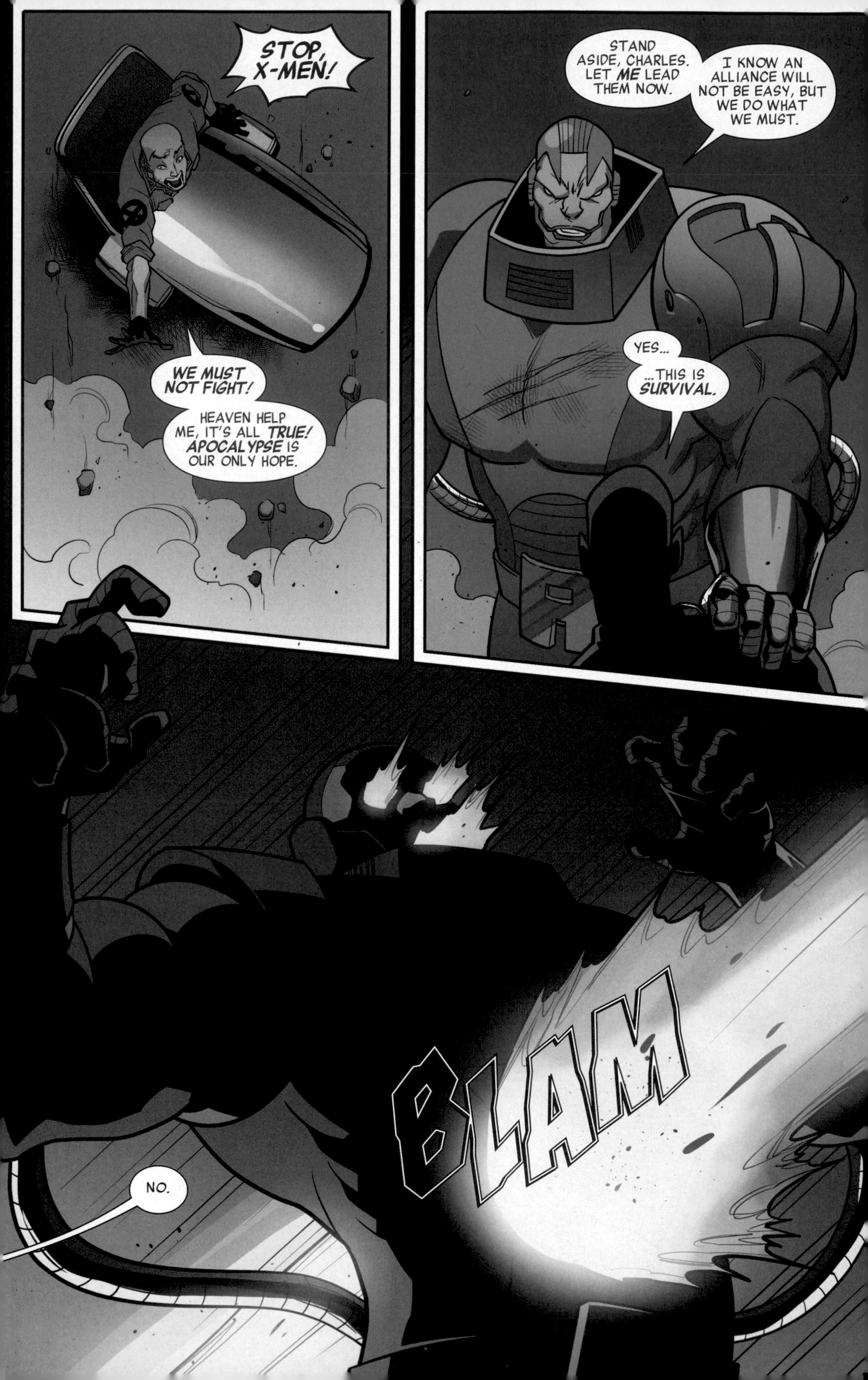
STOP, X-MEN!
WE MUST NOT FIGHT!
HEAVEN HELP ME, IT'S ALL TRUE! APOCALYPSE IS OUR ONLY HOPE.
STAND ASIDE, CHARLES. LET ME LEAD THEM NOW.
I KNOW AN ALLIANCE WILL NOT BE EASY, BUT WE DO WHAT WE MUST.
YES...
...THIS IS SURVIVAL.
BLAM
NO.

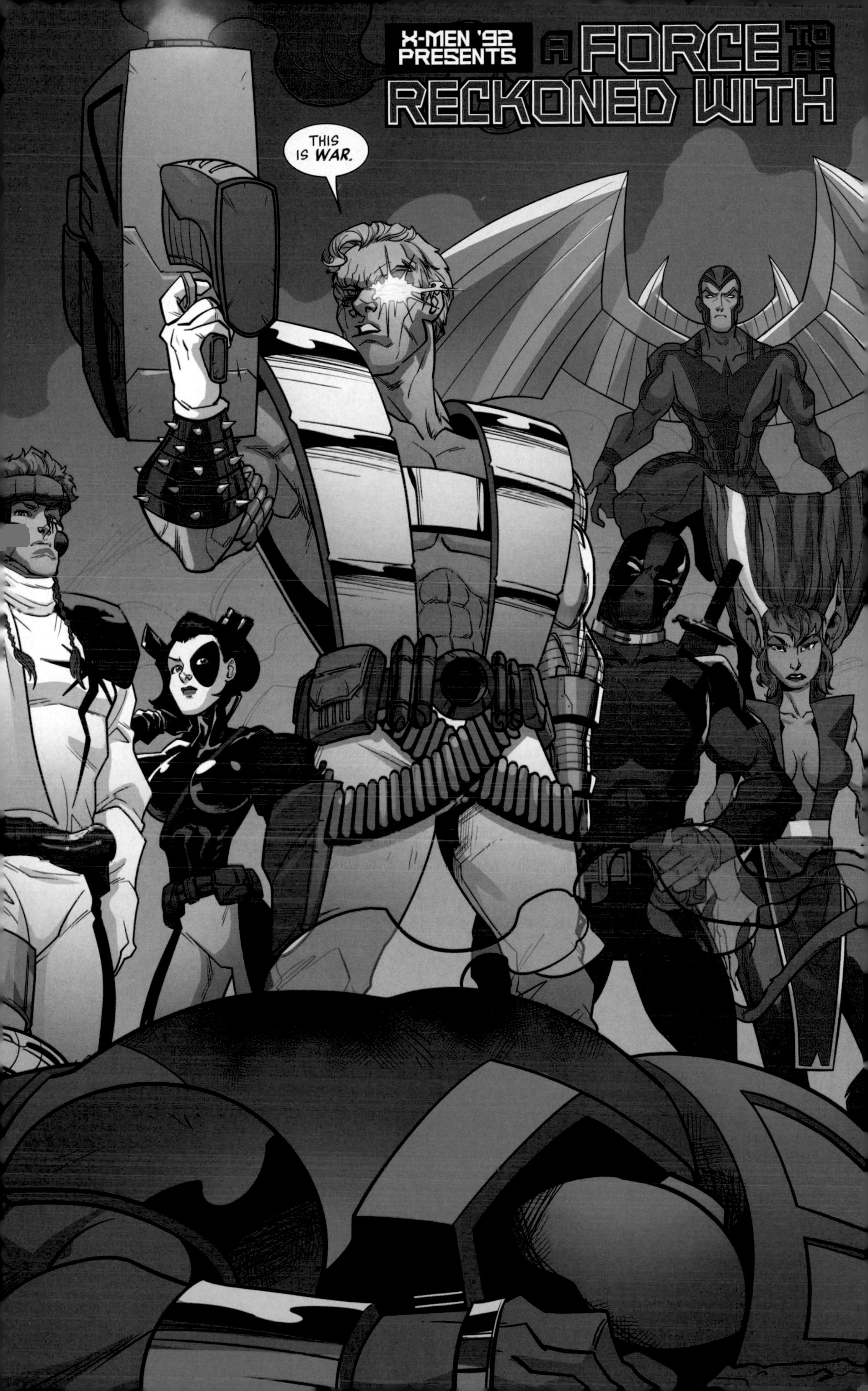
X-MEN '92 PRESENTS
A FORCE TO BE RECKONED WITH
THIS IS WAR.

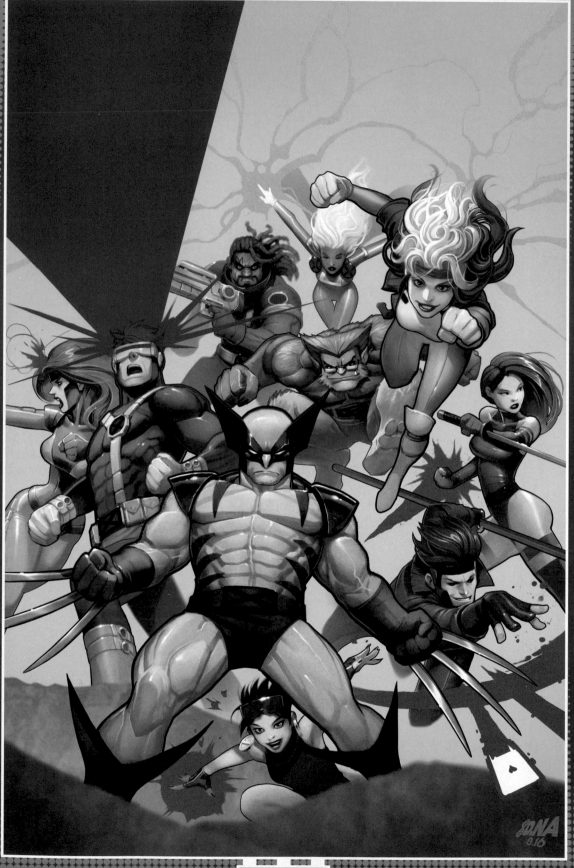

10

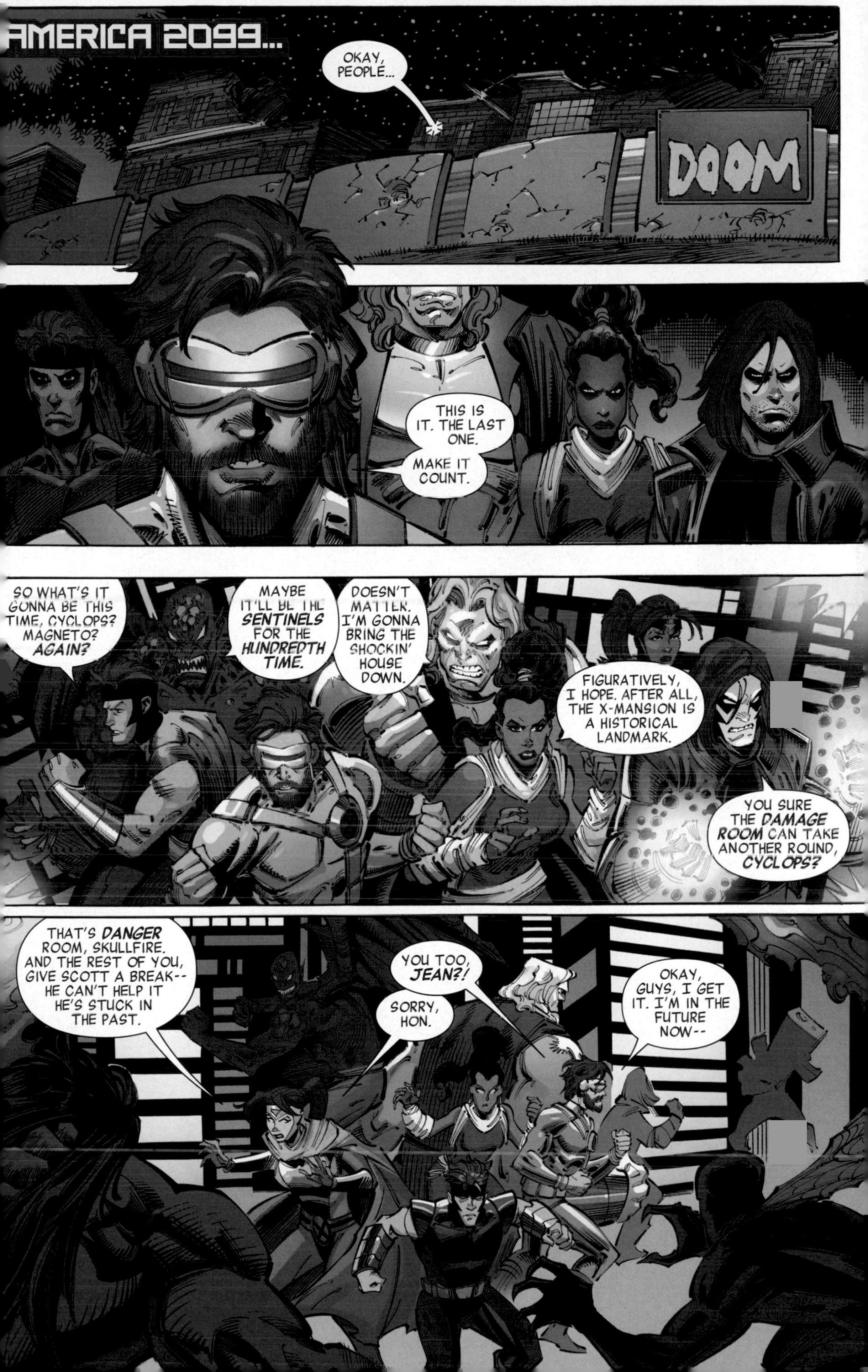
AMERICA 2099...
OKAY, PEOPLE...
DOOM
THIS IS IT. THE LAST ONE.
MAKE IT COUNT.
SO WHAT'S IT GONNA BE THIS TIME, CYCLOPS? MAGNETO? AGAIN?
MAYBE IT'LL BE THE SENTINELS FOR THE HUNDREDTH TIME.
DOESN'T MATTER. I'M GONNA BRING THE SHOCKIN' HOUSE DOWN.
FIGURATIVELY, I HOPE. AFTER ALL, THE X-MANSION IS A HISTORICAL LANDMARK.
YOU SURE THE DAMAGE ROOM CAN TAKE ANOTHER ROUND, CYCLOPS?
THAT'S DANGER ROOM, SKULLFIRE. AND THE REST OF YOU, GIVE SCOTT A BREAK-- HE CAN'T HELP IT HE'S STUCK IN THE PAST.
YOU TOO, JEAN?!
SORRY, HON.
OKAY, GUYS, I GET IT. I'M IN THE FUTURE NOW--

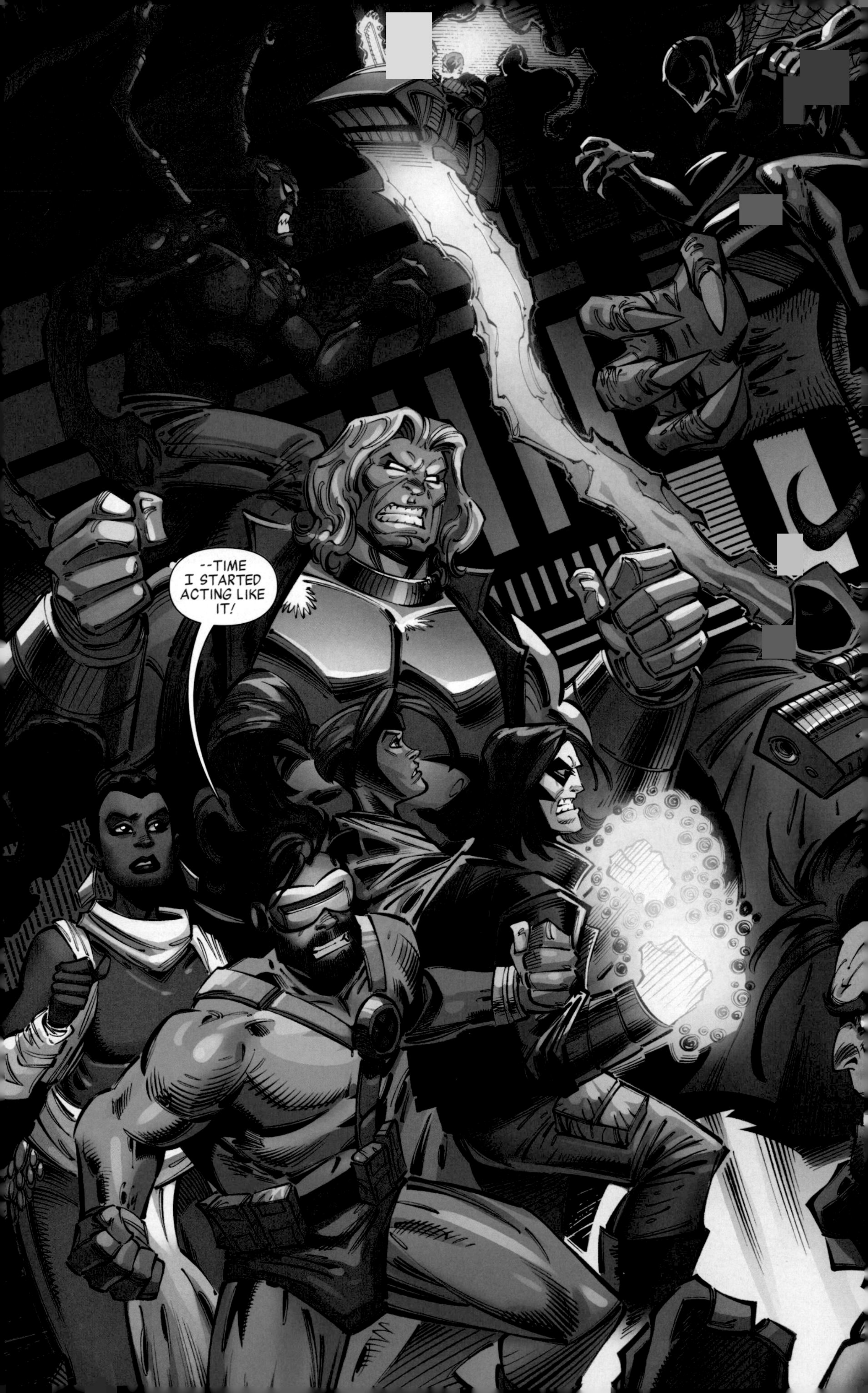
--TIME I STARTED ACTING LIKE IT!

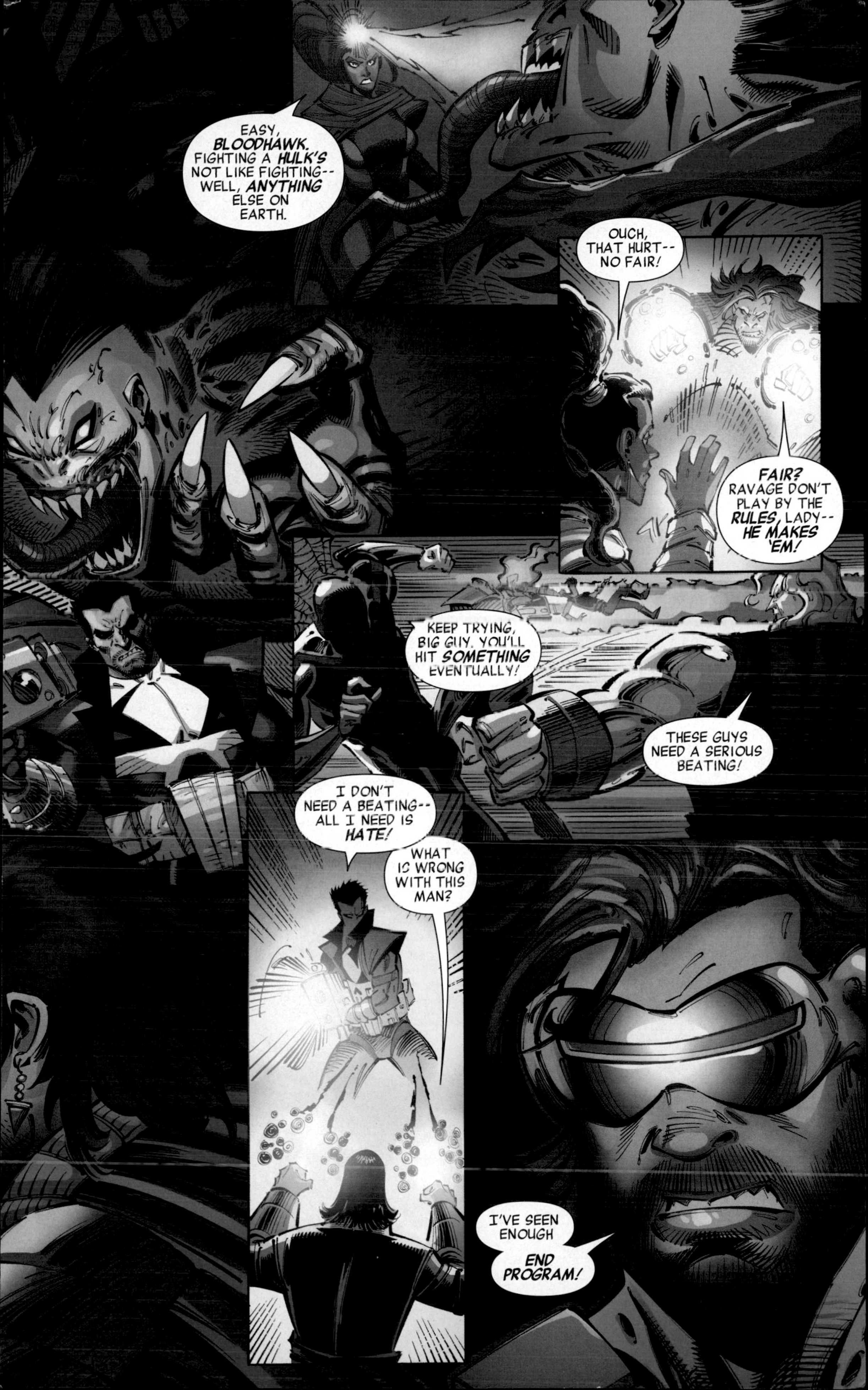
EASY, BLOODHAWK. FIGHTING A HULK'S NOT LIKE FIGHTING-- WELL, ANYTHING ELSE ON EARTH.
OUCH, THAT HURT-- NO FAIR!
FAIR? RAVAGE DON'T PLAY BY THE RULES, LADY-- HE MAKES 'EM!
KEEP TRYING, BIG GUY. YOU'LL HIT SOMETHING EVENTUALLY!
THESE GUYS NEED A SERIOUS BEATING!
I DON'T NEED A BEATING-- ALL I NEED IS HATE!
WHAT IS WRONG WITH THIS MAN?
I'VE SEEN ENOUGH
END PROGRAM!

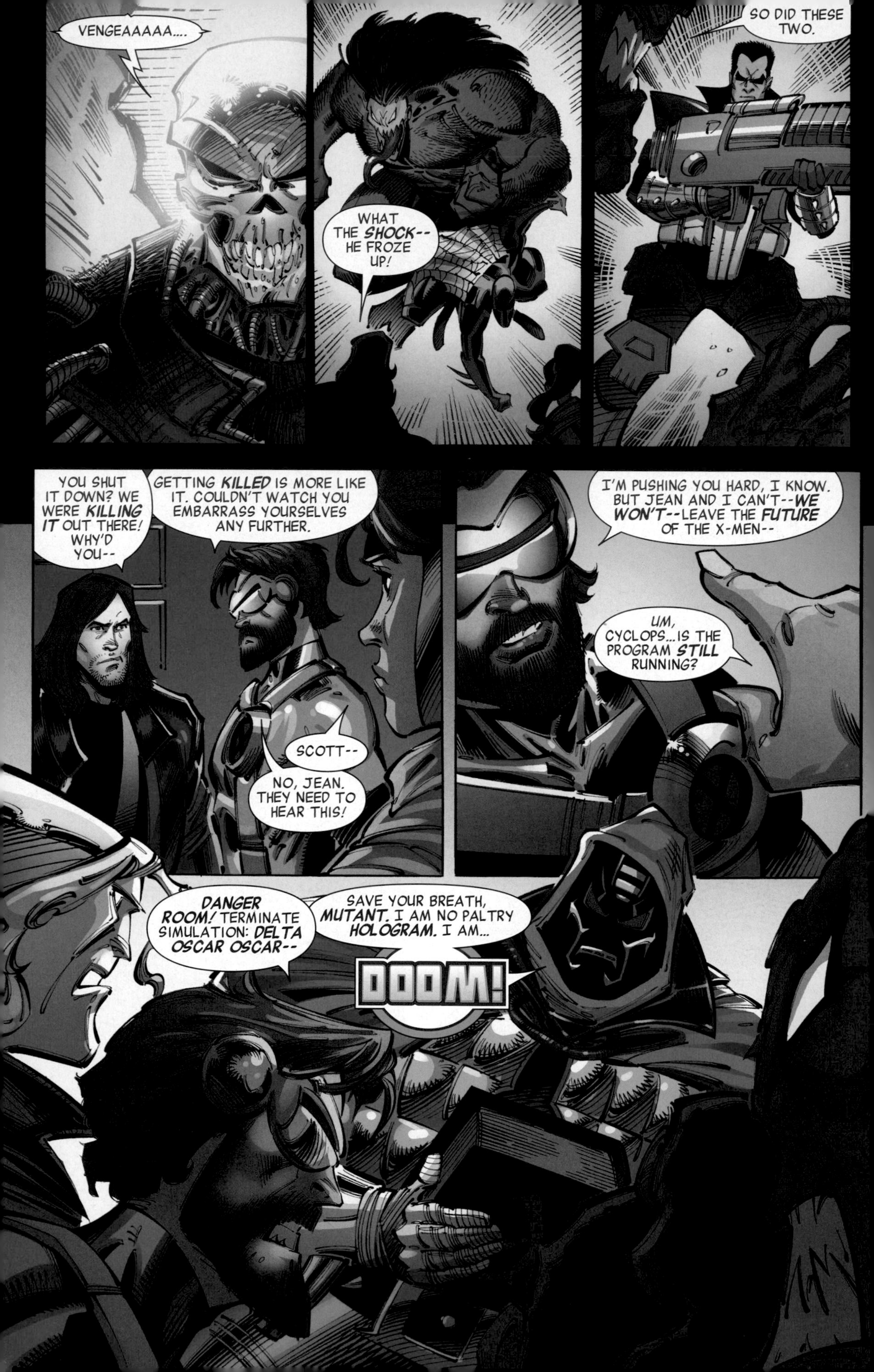
VENGEAAAAA....
WHAT THE SHOCK-- HE FROZE UP!
SO DID THESE TWO.
YOU SHUT IT DOWN? WE WERE KILLING IT OUT THERE! WHY'D YOU--
GETTING KILLED IS MORE LIKE IT. COULDN'T WATCH YOU EMBARRASS YOURSELVES ANY FURTHER.
SCOTT--
NO, JEAN. THEY NEED TO HEAR THIS!
I'M PUSHING YOU HARD, I KNOW. BUT JEAN AND I CAN'T--WE WON'T--LEAVE THE FUTURE OF THE X-MEN--
UM, CYCLOPS...IS THE PROGRAM STILL RUNNING?
DANGER ROOM! TERMINATE SIMULATION: DELTA OSCAR OSCAR--
SAVE YOUR BREATH, MUTANT. I AM NO PALTRY HOLOGRAM. I AM...
DOOM!

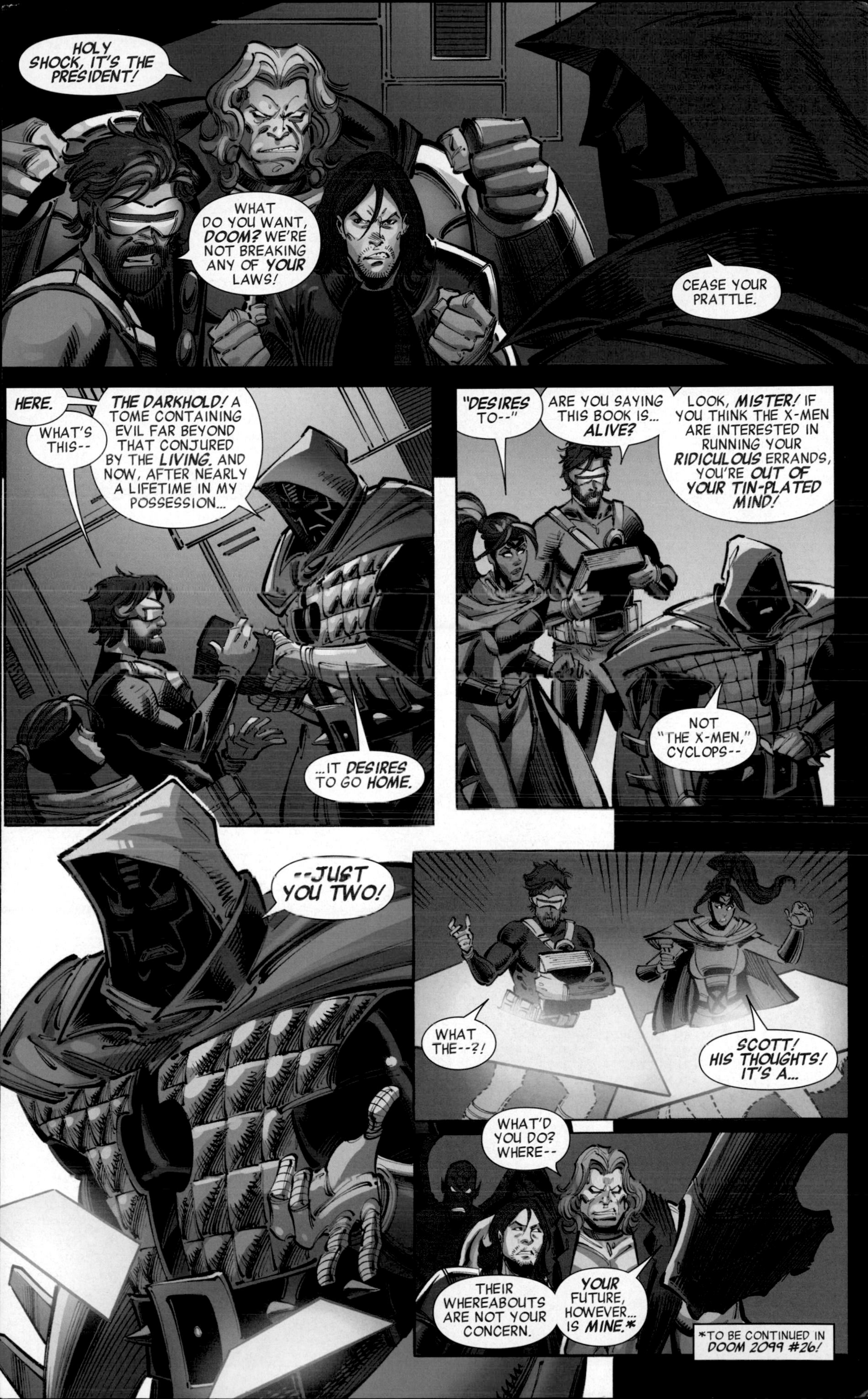
HOLY SHOCK, IT'S THE PRESIDENT!
WHAT DO YOU WANT, DOOM? WE'RE NOT BREAKING ANY OF YOUR LAWS!
CEASE YOUR PRATTLE.
HERE.
WHAT'S THIS--
THE DARKHOLD! A TOME CONTAINING EVIL FAR BEYOND THAT CONJURED BY THE LIVING. AND NOW, AFTER NEARLY A LIFETIME IN MY POSSESSION...
...IT DESIRES TO GO HOME.
"DESIRES TO--"
ARE YOU SAYING THIS BOOK IS... ALIVE?
LOOK, MISTER! IF YOU THINK THE X-MEN ARE INTERESTED IN RUNNING YOUR RIDICULOUS ERRANDS, YOU'RE OUT OF YOUR TIN-PLATED MIND!
NOT "THE X-MEN," CYCLOPS--
--JUST YOU TWO!
WHAT THE--?!
SCOTT! HIS THOUGHTS! IT'S A...
WHAT'D YOU DO? WHERE--
THEIR WHEREABOUTS ARE NOT YOUR CONCERN.
YOUR FUTURE, HOWEVER... IS MINE.*
*TO BE CONTINUED IN DOOM 2099 #26!

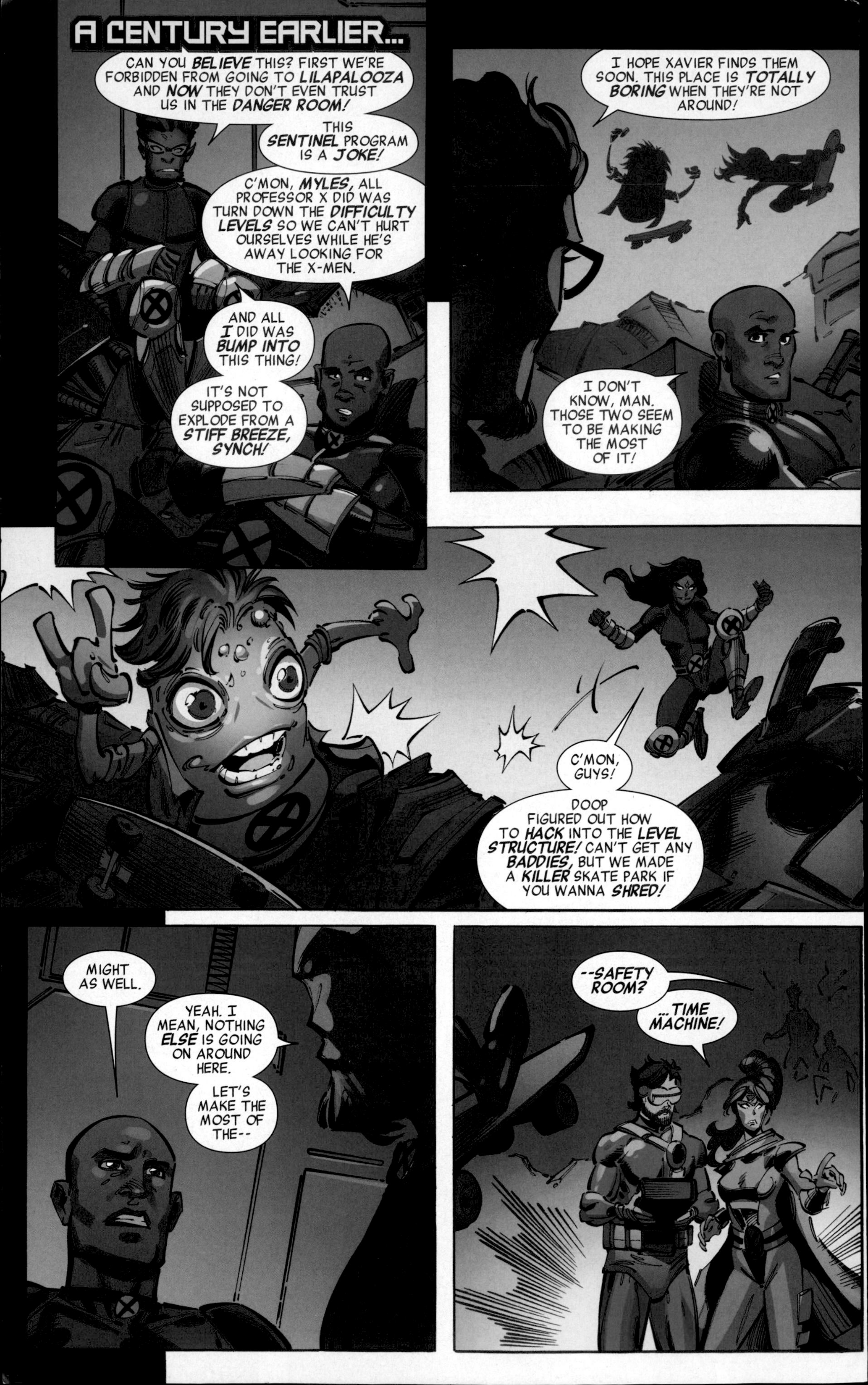
A CENTURY EARLIER...
CAN YOU BELIEVE THIS? FIRST WE'RE FORBIDDEN FROM GOING TO LILAPALOOZA AND NOW THEY DON'T EVEN TRUST US IN THE DANGER ROOM!
THIS SENTINEL PROGRAM IS A JOKE!
C'MON, MYLES, ALL PROFESSOR X DID WAS TURN DOWN THE DIFFICULTY LEVELS SO WE CAN'T HURT OURSELVES WHILE HE'S AWAY LOOKING FOR THE X-MEN.
AND ALL I DID WAS BUMP INTO THIS THING!
IT'S NOT SUPPOSED TO EXPLODE FROM A STIFF BREEZE, SYNCH!
I HOPE XAVIER FINDS THEM SOON. THIS PLACE IS TOTALLY BORING WHEN THEY'RE NOT AROUND!
I DON'T KNOW, MAN. THOSE TWO SEEM TO BE MAKING THE MOST OF IT!
C'MON, GUYS!
DOOP FIGURED OUT HOW TO HACK INTO THE LEVEL STRUCTURE! CAN'T GET ANY BADDIES, BUT WE MADE A KILLER SKATE PARK IF YOU WANNA SHRED!
MIGHT AS WELL.
YEAH. I MEAN, NOTHING ELSE IS GOING ON AROUND HERE.
LET'S MAKE THE MOST OF THE--
--SAFETY ROOM?
...TIME MACHINE!

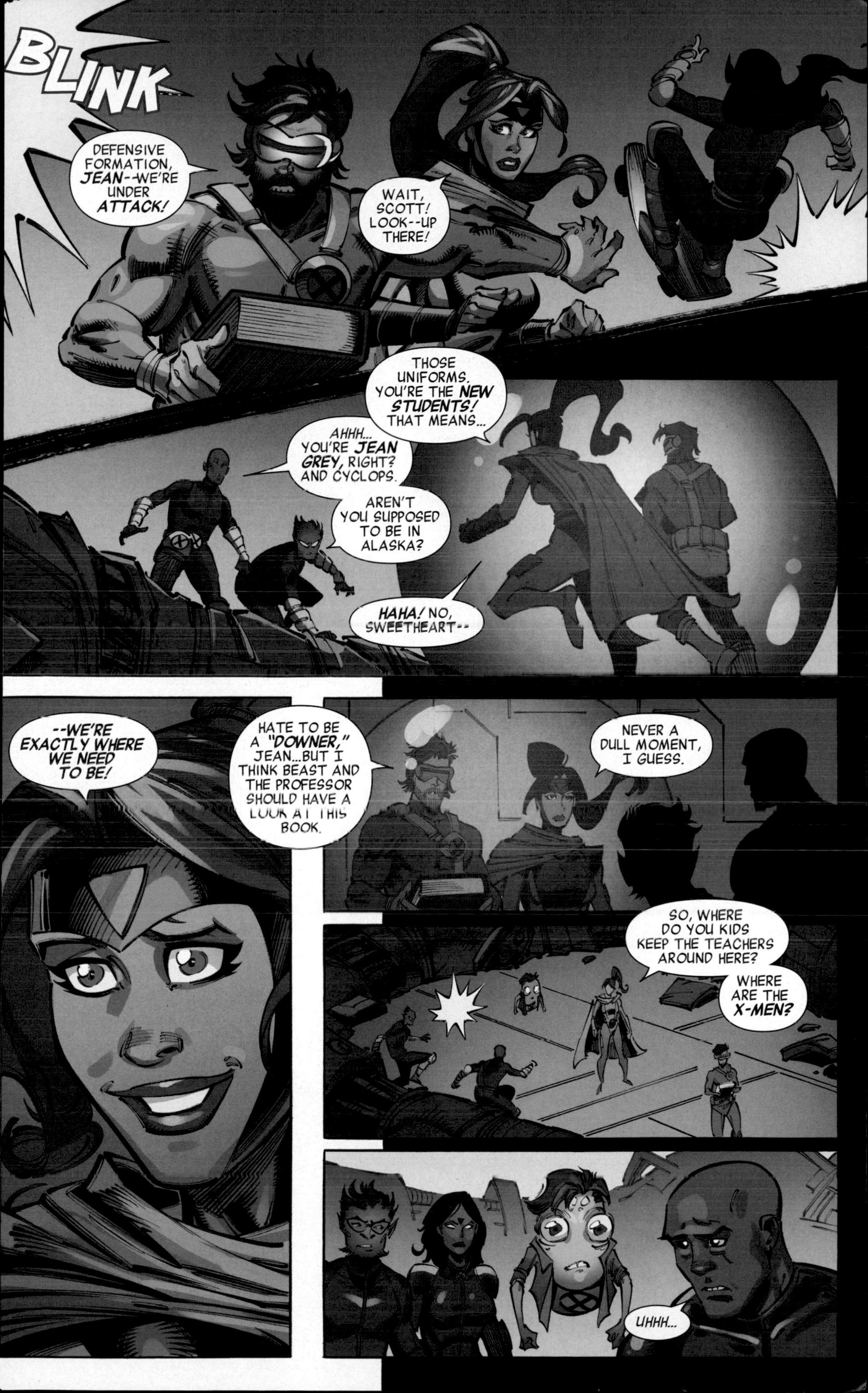
BLINK
DEFENSIVE FORMATION, JEAN--WE'RE UNDER ATTACK!
WAIT, SCOTT! LOOK--UP THERE!
THOSE UNIFORMS. YOU'RE THE NEW STUDENTS! THAT MEANS...
AHHH... YOU'RE JEAN GREY, RIGHT? AND CYCLOPS.
AREN'T YOU SUPPOSED TO BE IN ALASKA?
HAHA! NO, SWEETHEART--
--WE'RE EXACTLY WHERE WE NEED TO BE!
HATE TO BE A "DOWNER," JEAN...BUT I THINK BEAST AND THE PROFESSOR SHOULD HAVE A LOOK AT THIS BOOK.
NEVER A DULL MOMENT, I GUESS.
SO, WHERE DO YOU KIDS KEEP THE TEACHERS AROUND HERE?
WHERE ARE THE X-MEN?
UHHH...

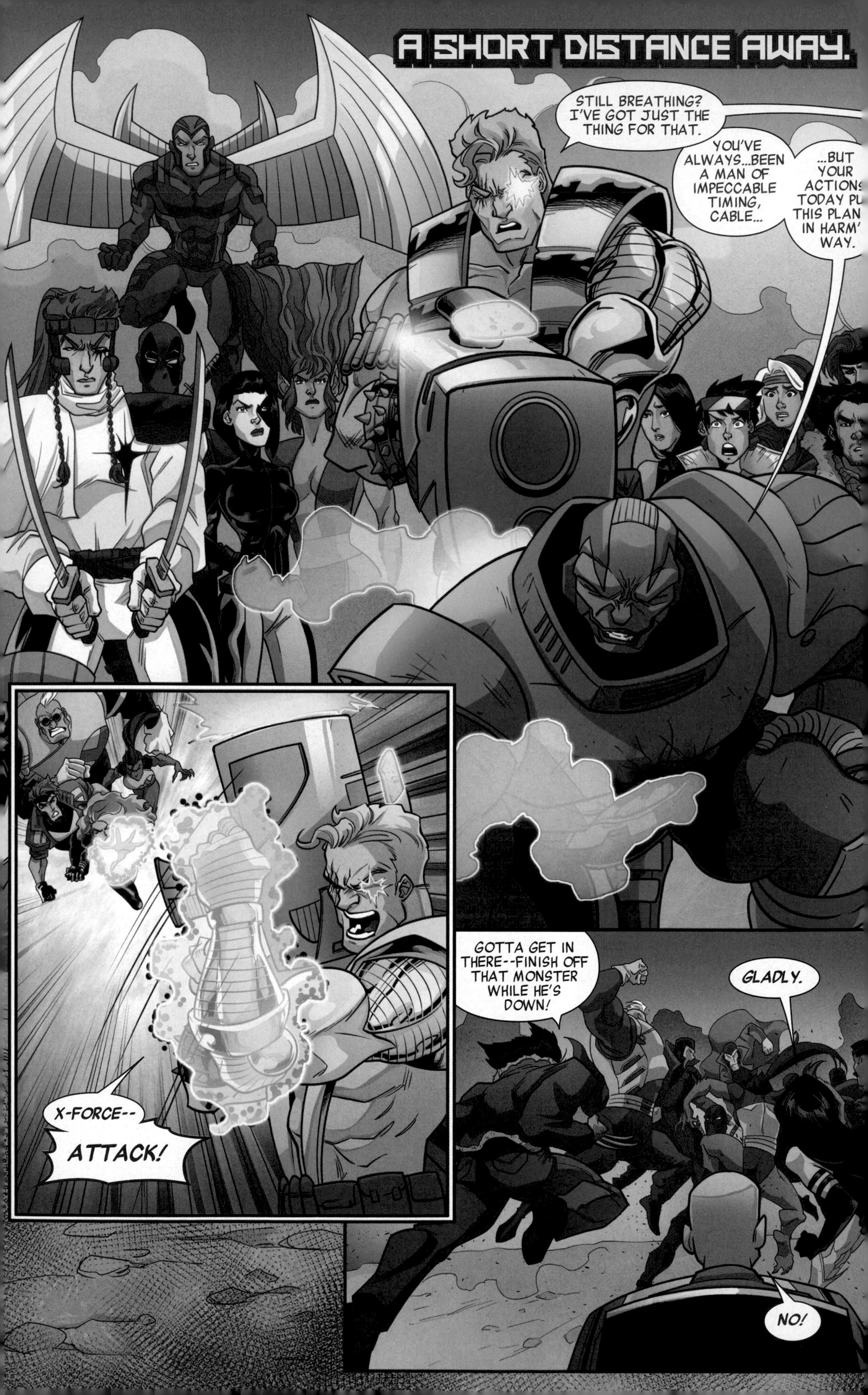
A SHORT DISTANCE AWAY.
STILL BREATHING? I'VE GOT JUST THE THING FOR THAT.
YOU'VE ALWAYS...BEEN A MAN OF IMPECCABLE TIMING, CABLE...
...BUT YOUR ACTIONS TODAY PU THIS PLAN IN HARM' WAY.
X-FORCE--
ATTACK!
GOTTA GET IN THERE--FINISH OFF THAT MONSTER WHILE HE'S DOWN!
GLADLY.
NO!

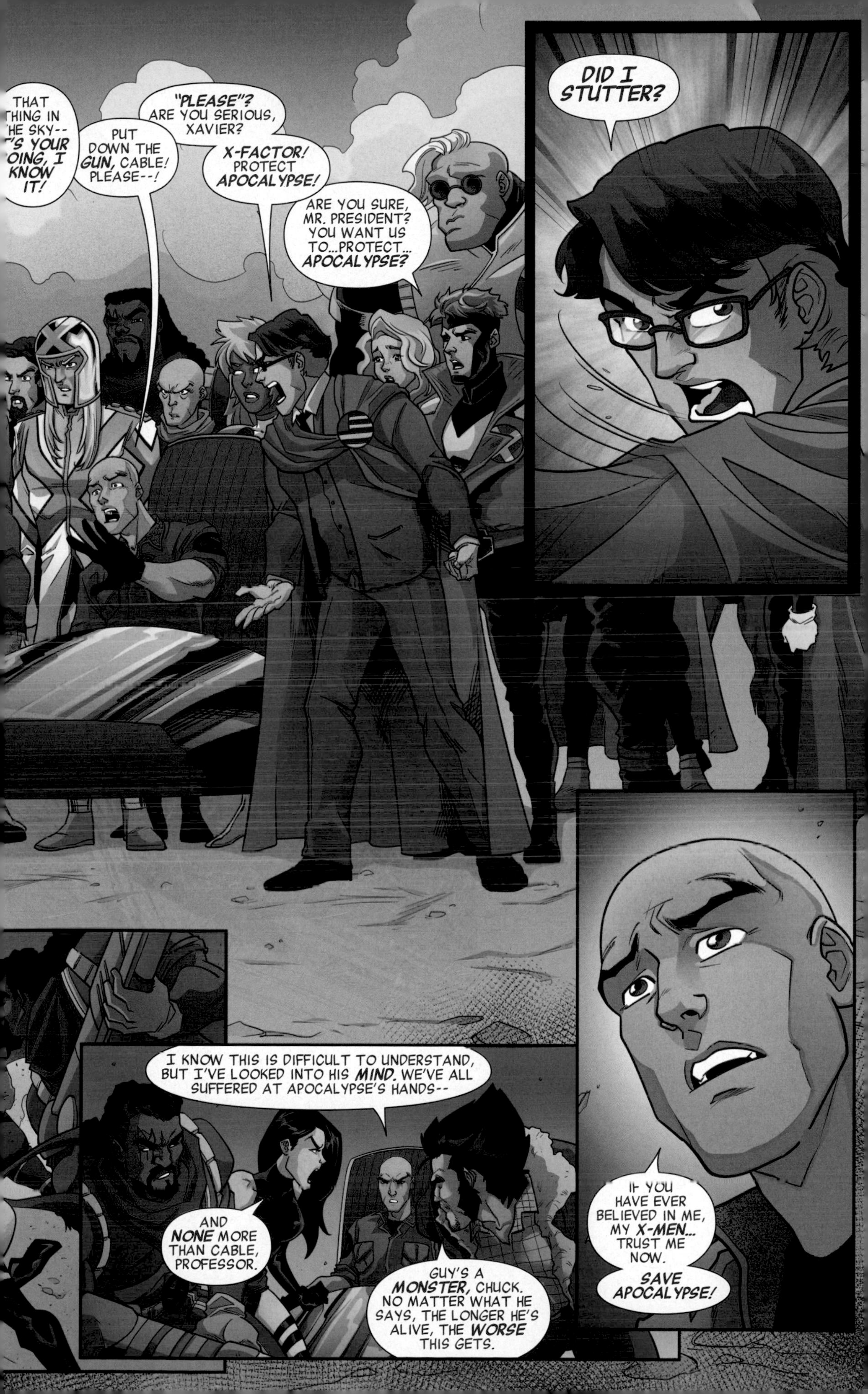
THAT THING IN THE SKY-- IT'S YOUR DOING, I KNOW IT!
PUT DOWN THE GUN, CABLE! PLEASE--!
"PLEASE"? ARE YOU SERIOUS, XAVIER?
X-FACTOR! PROTECT APOCALYPSE!
ARE YOU SURE, MR. PRESIDENT? YOU WANT US TO...PROTECT... APOCALYPSE?
DID I STUTTER?
I KNOW THIS IS DIFFICULT TO UNDERSTAND, BUT I'VE LOOKED INTO HIS MIND. WE'VE ALL SUFFERED AT APOCALYPSE'S HANDS--
AND NONE MORE THAN CABLE, PROFESSOR.
GUY'S A MONSTER, CHUCK. NO MATTER WHAT HE SAYS, THE LONGER HE'S ALIVE, THE WORSE THIS GETS.
IF YOU HAVE EVER BELIEVED IN ME, MY X-MEN... TRUST ME NOW.
SAVE APOCALYPSE!

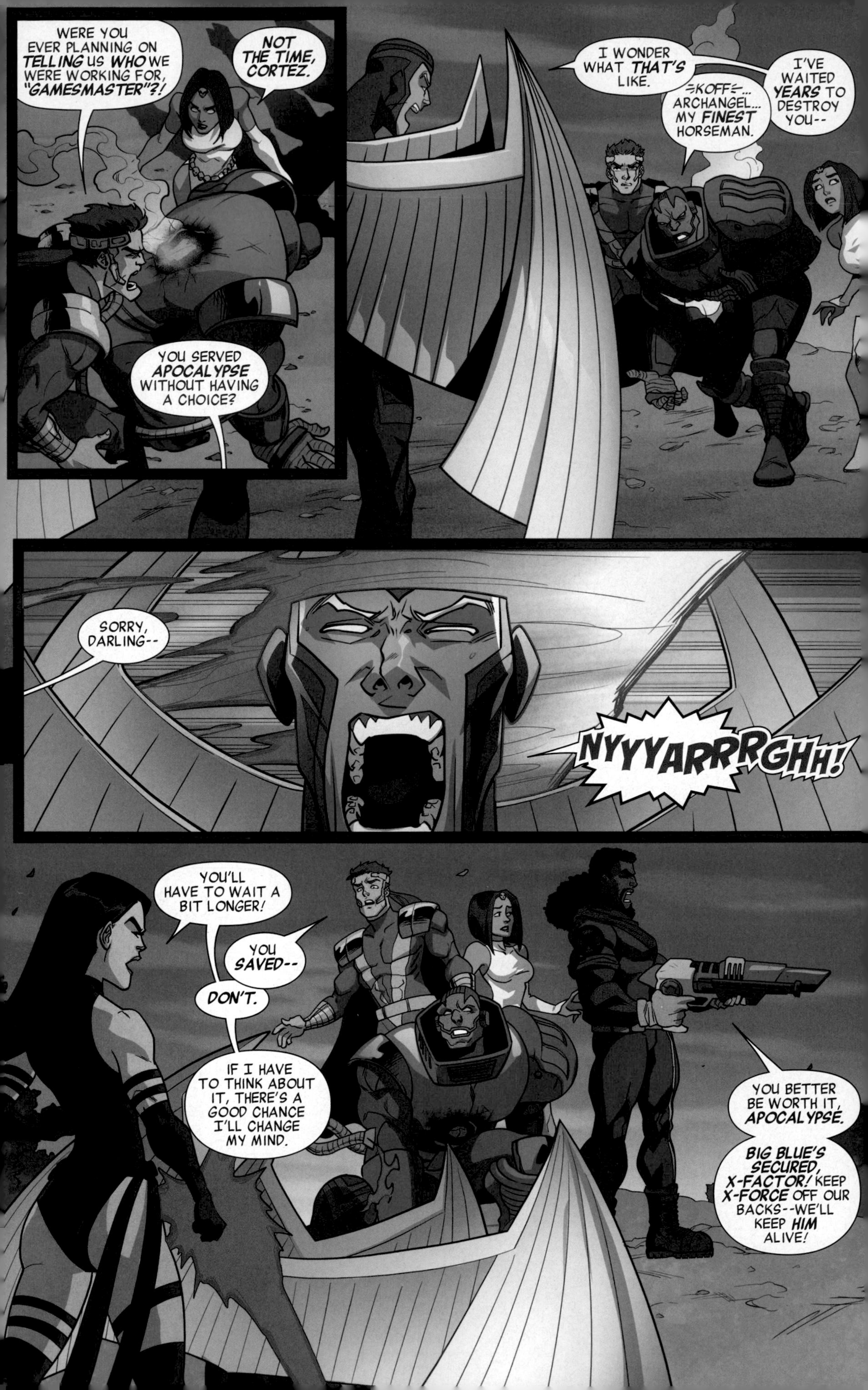
WERE YOU EVER PLANNING ON TELLING US WHO WE WERE WORKING FOR, "GAMESMASTER"?!
NOT THE TIME, CORTEZ.
YOU SERVED APOCALYPSE WITHOUT HAVING A CHOICE?
I WONDER WHAT THAT'S LIKE.
KOFF... ARCHANGEL... MY FINEST HORSEMAN.
I'VE WAITED YEARS TO DESTROY YOU--
SORRY, DARLING--
NYYYARRRGHH!
YOU'LL HAVE TO WAIT A BIT LONGER!
YOU SAVED--
DON'T.
IF I HAVE TO THINK ABOUT IT, THERE'S A GOOD CHANCE I'LL CHANGE MY MIND.
YOU BETTER BE WORTH IT, APOCALYPSE.
BIG BLUE'S SECURED, X-FACTOR! KEEP X-FORCE OFF OUR BACKS--WE'LL KEEP HIM ALIVE!

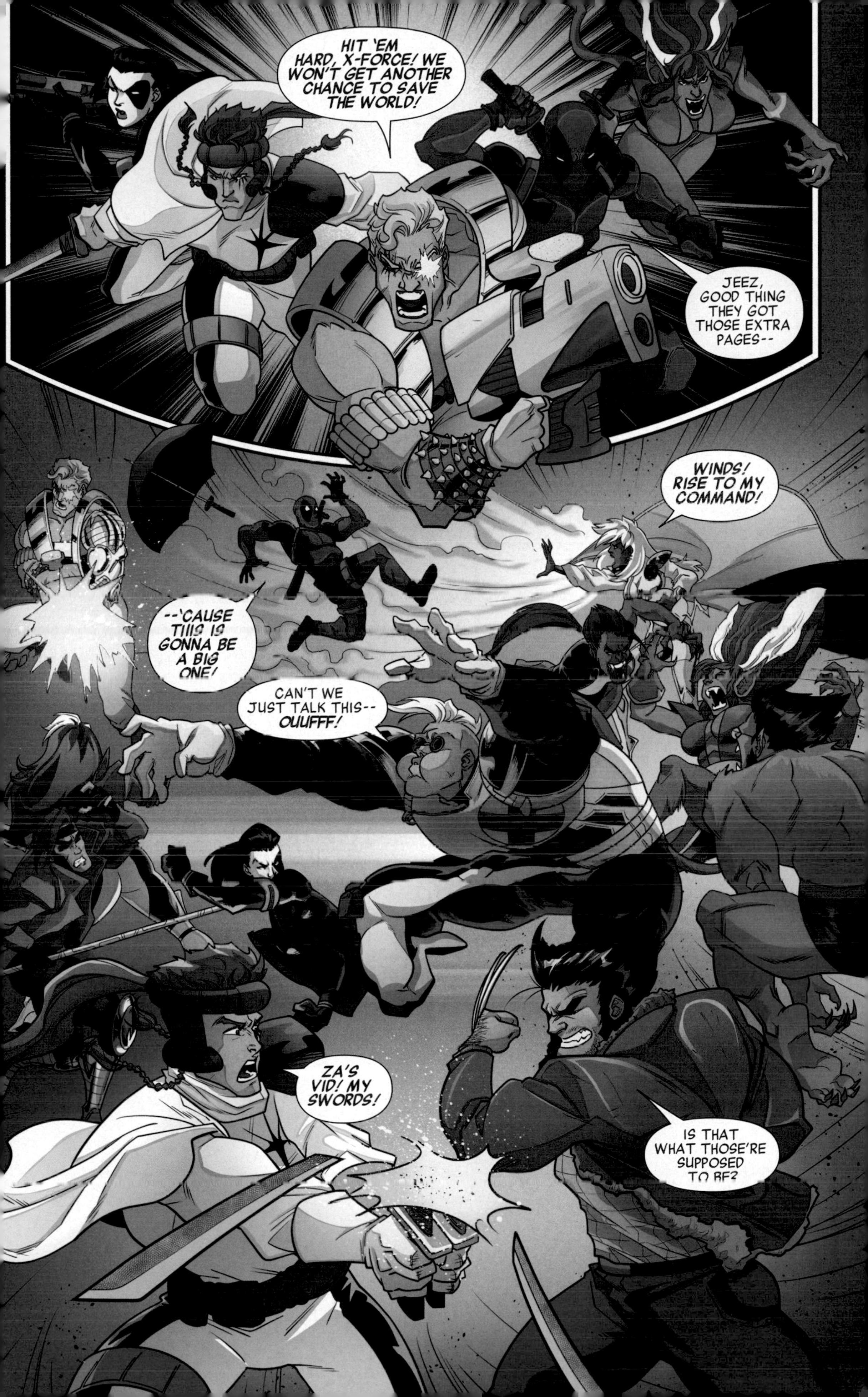
HIT 'EM HARD, X-FORCE! WE WON'T GET ANOTHER CHANCE TO SAVE THE WORLD!
JEEZ, GOOD THING THEY GOT THOSE EXTRA PAGES--
WINDS! RISE TO MY COMMAND!
--'CAUSE THIS IS GONNA BE A BIG ONE!
CAN'T WE JUST TALK THIS-- OUUFFF!
ZA'S VID! MY SWORDS!
IS THAT WHAT THOSE'RE SUPPOSED TO BE?

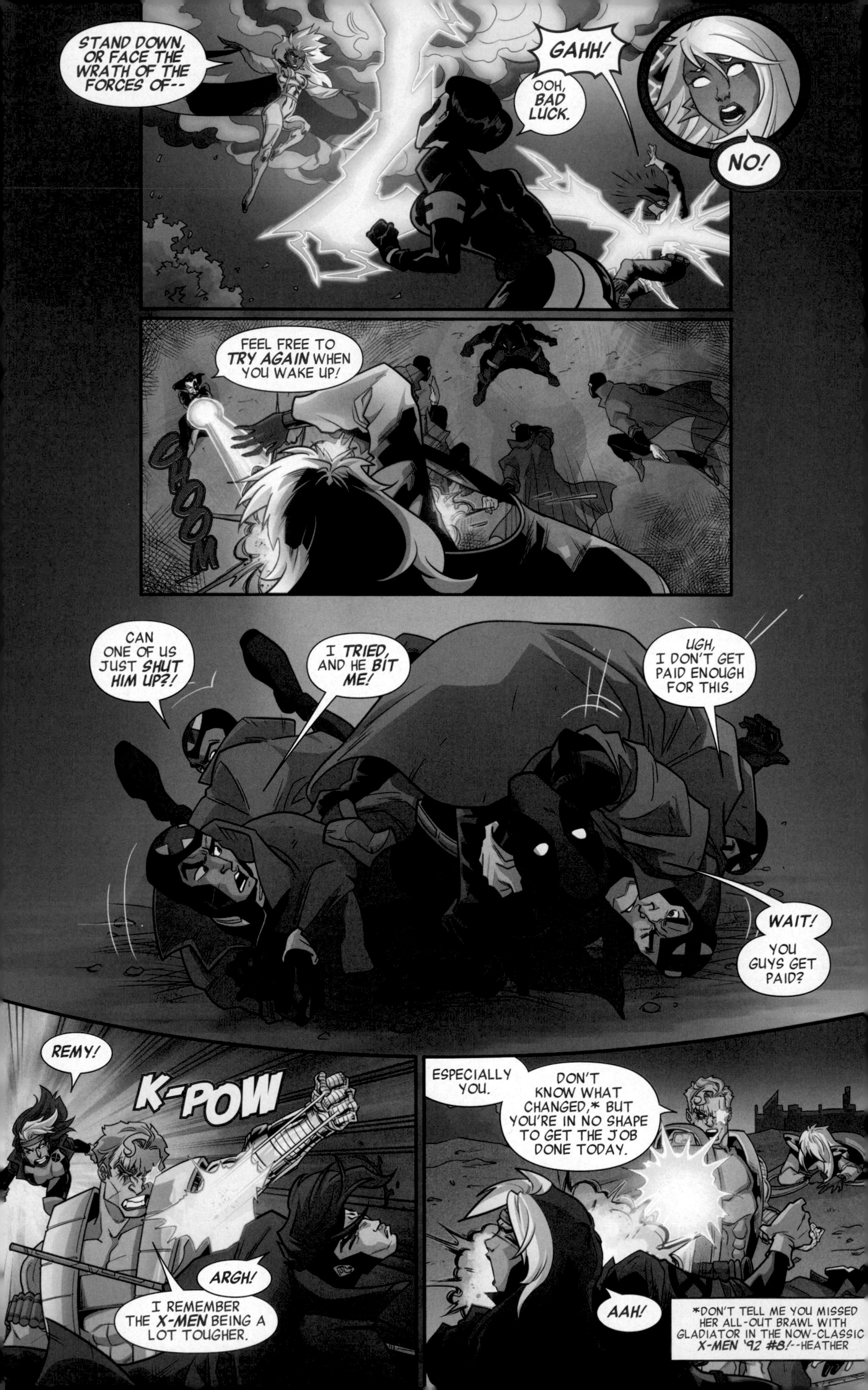
STAND DOWN, OR FACE THE WRATH OF THE FORCES OF--
GAHH!
OOH, BAD LUCK.
NO!
FEEL FREE TO TRY AGAIN WHEN YOU WAKE UP!
CHOOOM
CAN ONE OF US JUST SHUT HIM UP?!
I TRIED, AND HE BIT ME!
UGH, I DON'T GET PAID ENOUGH FOR THIS.
WAIT!
YOU GUYS GET PAID?
REMY!
K-POW
ARGH!
I REMEMBER THE X-MEN BEING A LOT TOUGHER.
ESPECIALLY YOU.
DON'T KNOW WHAT CHANGED,* BUT YOU'RE IN NO SHAPE TO GET THE JOB DONE TODAY.
AAH!
*DON'T TELL ME YOU MISSED HER ALL-OUT BRAWL WITH GLADIATOR IN THE NOW-CLASSIC X-MEN '92 #8!--HEATHER

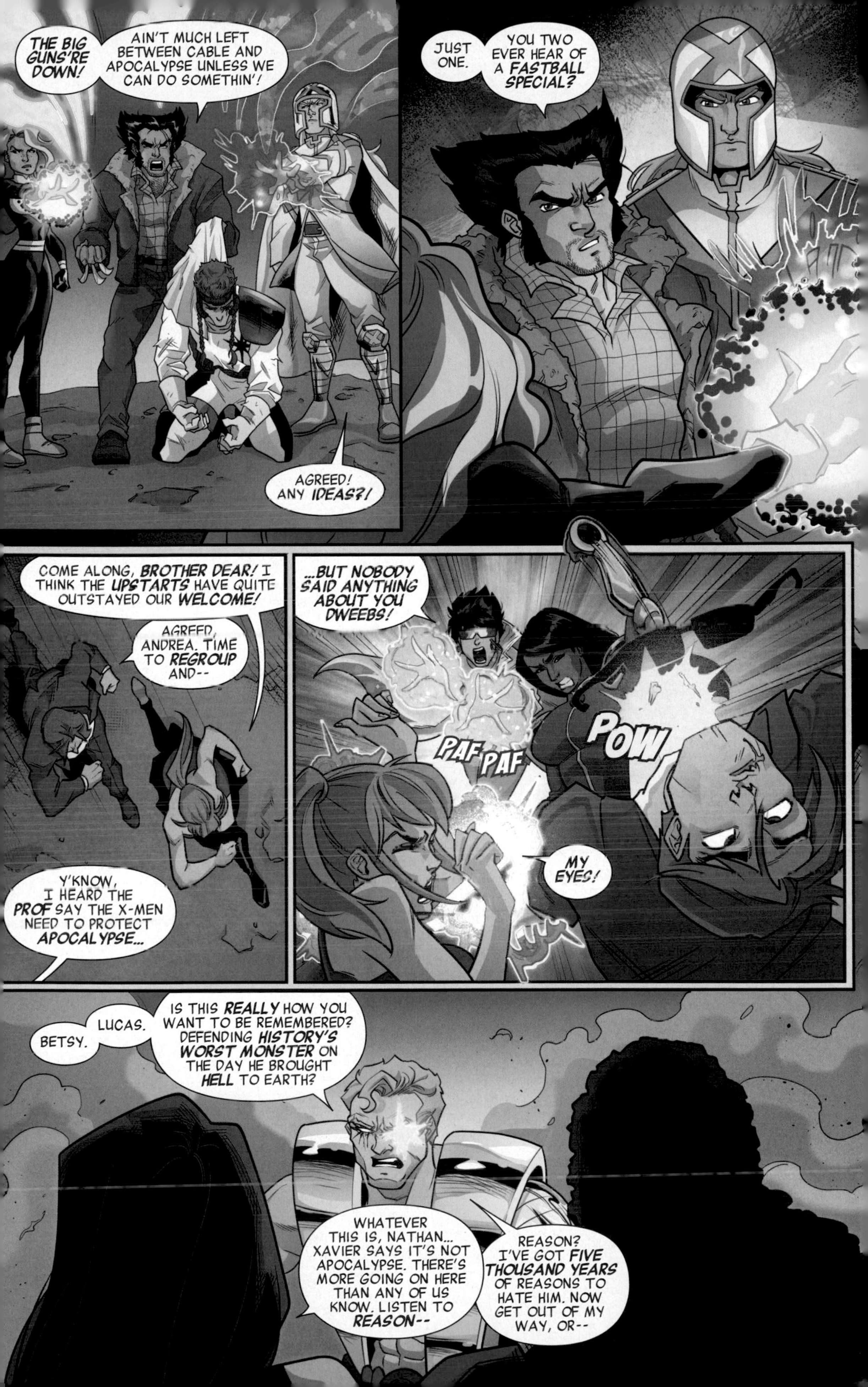
THE BIG GUNS'RE DOWN!
AIN'T MUCH LEFT BETWEEN CABLE AND APOCALYPSE UNLESS WE CAN DO SOMETHIN'!
AGREED! ANY IDEAS?!
JUST ONE.
YOU TWO EVER HEAR OF A FASTBALL SPECIAL?
COME ALONG, BROTHER DEAR! I THINK THE UPSTARTS HAVE QUITE OUTSTAYED OUR WELCOME!
AGREED, ANDREA. TIME TO REGROUP AND--
Y'KNOW, I HEARD THE PROF SAY THE X-MEN NEED TO PROTECT APOCALYPSE...
...BUT NOBODY SAID ANYTHING ABOUT YOU DWEEBS!
PAF PAF
POW
MY EYES!
BETSY.
LUCAS.
IS THIS REALLY HOW YOU WANT TO BE REMEMBERED? DEFENDING HISTORY'S WORST MONSTER ON THE DAY HE BROUGHT HELL TO EARTH?
WHATEVER THIS IS, NATHAN... XAVIER SAYS IT'S NOT APOCALYPSE. THERE'S MORE GOING ON HERE THAN ANY OF US KNOW. LISTEN TO REASON--
REASON? I'VE GOT FIVE THOUSAND YEARS OF REASONS TO HATE HIM. NOW GET OUT OF MY WAY, OR--

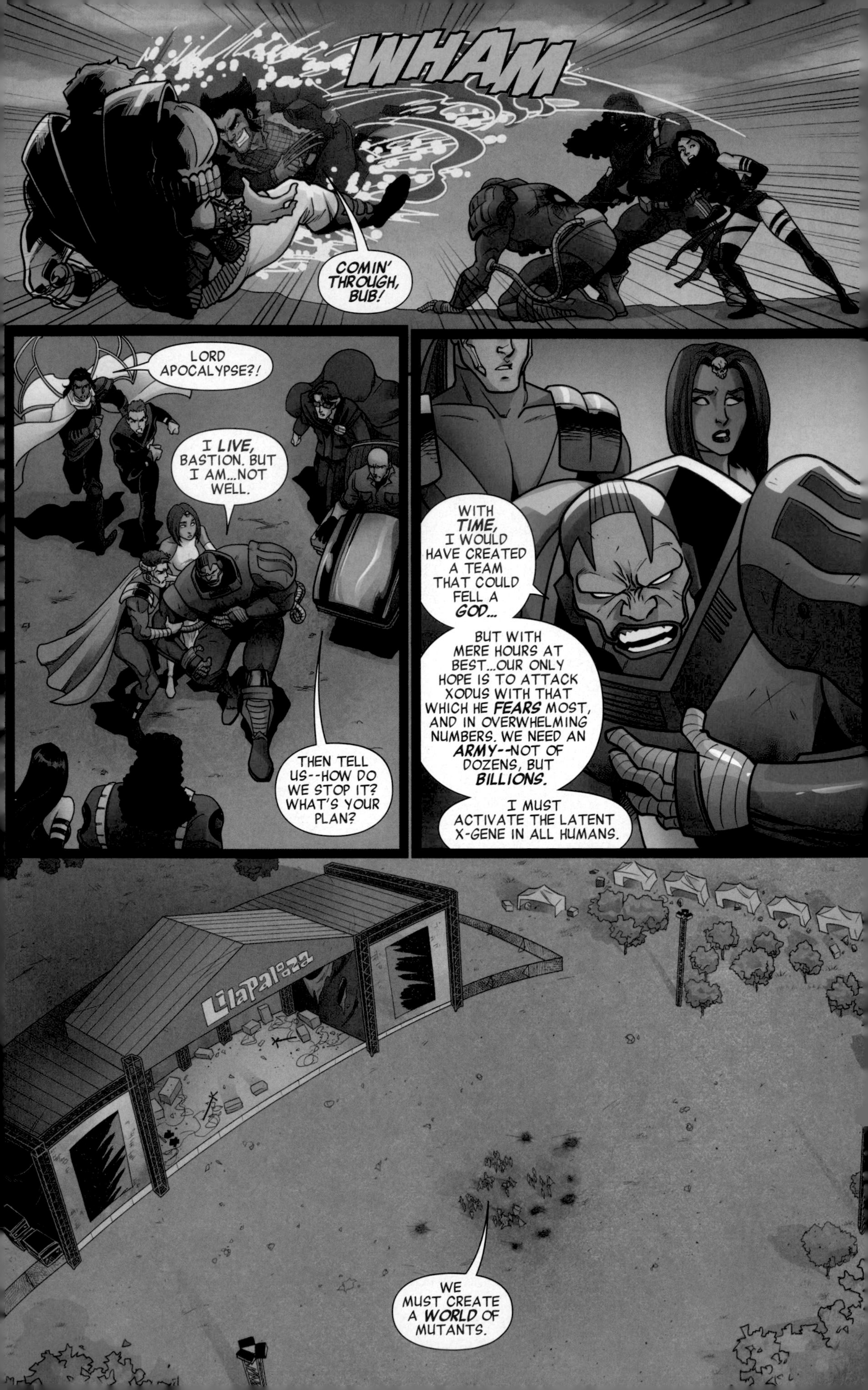
WHAM
COMIN' THROUGH, BUB!
LORD APOCALYPSE?!
I LIVE, BASTION. BUT I AM...NOT WELL.
THEN TELL US--HOW DO WE STOP IT? WHAT'S YOUR PLAN?
WITH TIME, I WOULD HAVE CREATED A TEAM THAT COULD FELL A GOD...
BUT WITH MERE HOURS AT BEST...OUR ONLY HOPE IS TO ATTACK XODUS WITH THAT WHICH HE FEARS MOST, AND IN OVERWHELMING NUMBERS. WE NEED AN ARMY--NOT OF DOZENS, BUT BILLIONS.
I MUST ACTIVATE THE LATENT X-GENE IN ALL HUMANS.
LILAPALOOZA
WE MUST CREATE A WORLD OF MUTANTS.

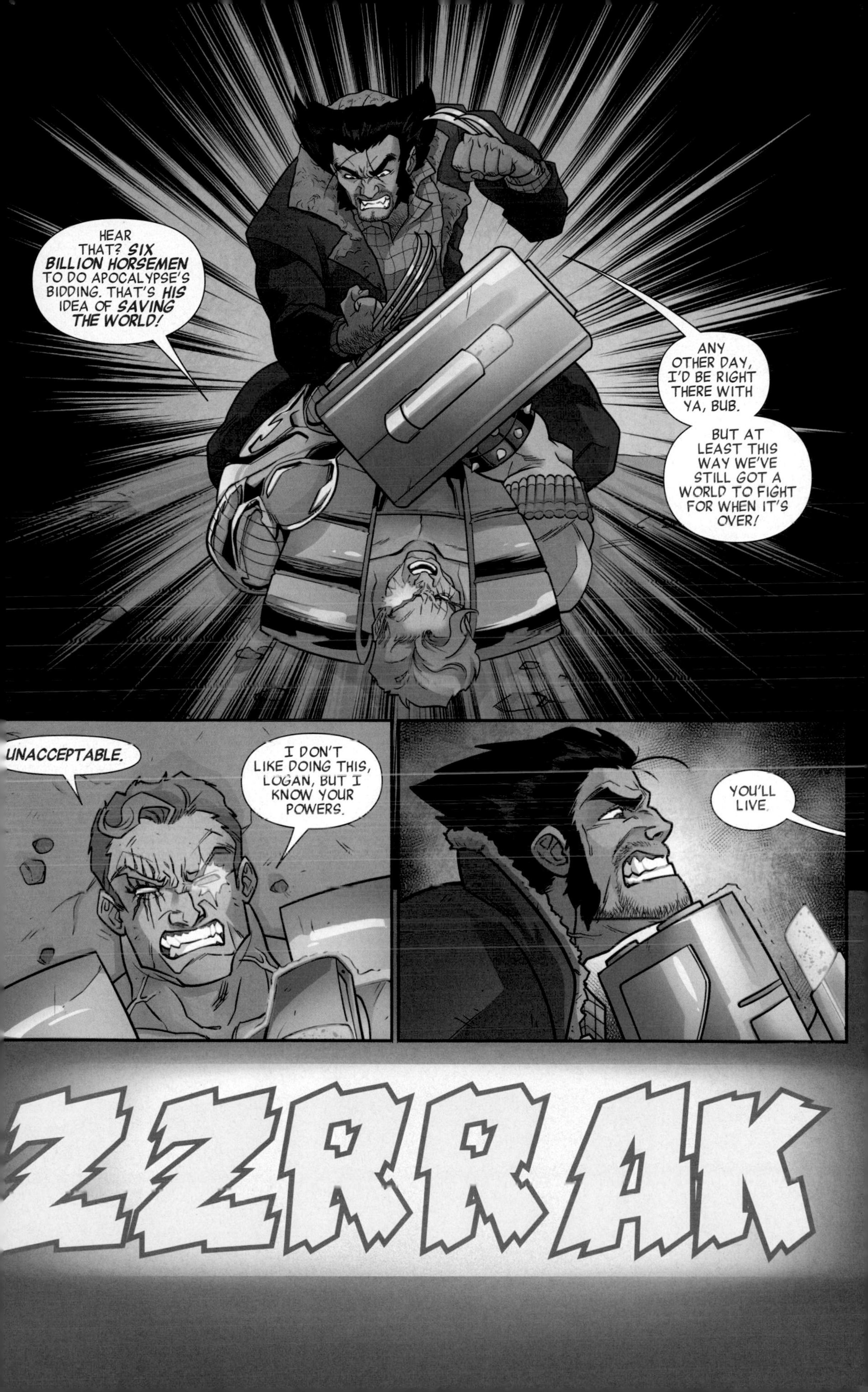

HEAR THAT? SIX BILLION HORSEMEN TO DO APOCALYPSE'S BIDDING. THAT'S HIS IDEA OF SAVING THE WORLD!
ANY OTHER DAY, I'D BE RIGHT THERE WITH YA, BUB.
BUT AT LEAST THIS WAY WE'VE STILL GOT A WORLD TO FIGHT FOR WHEN IT'S OVER!
UNACCEPTABLE.
I DON'T LIKE DOING THIS, LOGAN, BUT I KNOW YOUR POWERS.
YOU'LL LIVE.
ZZRRAK

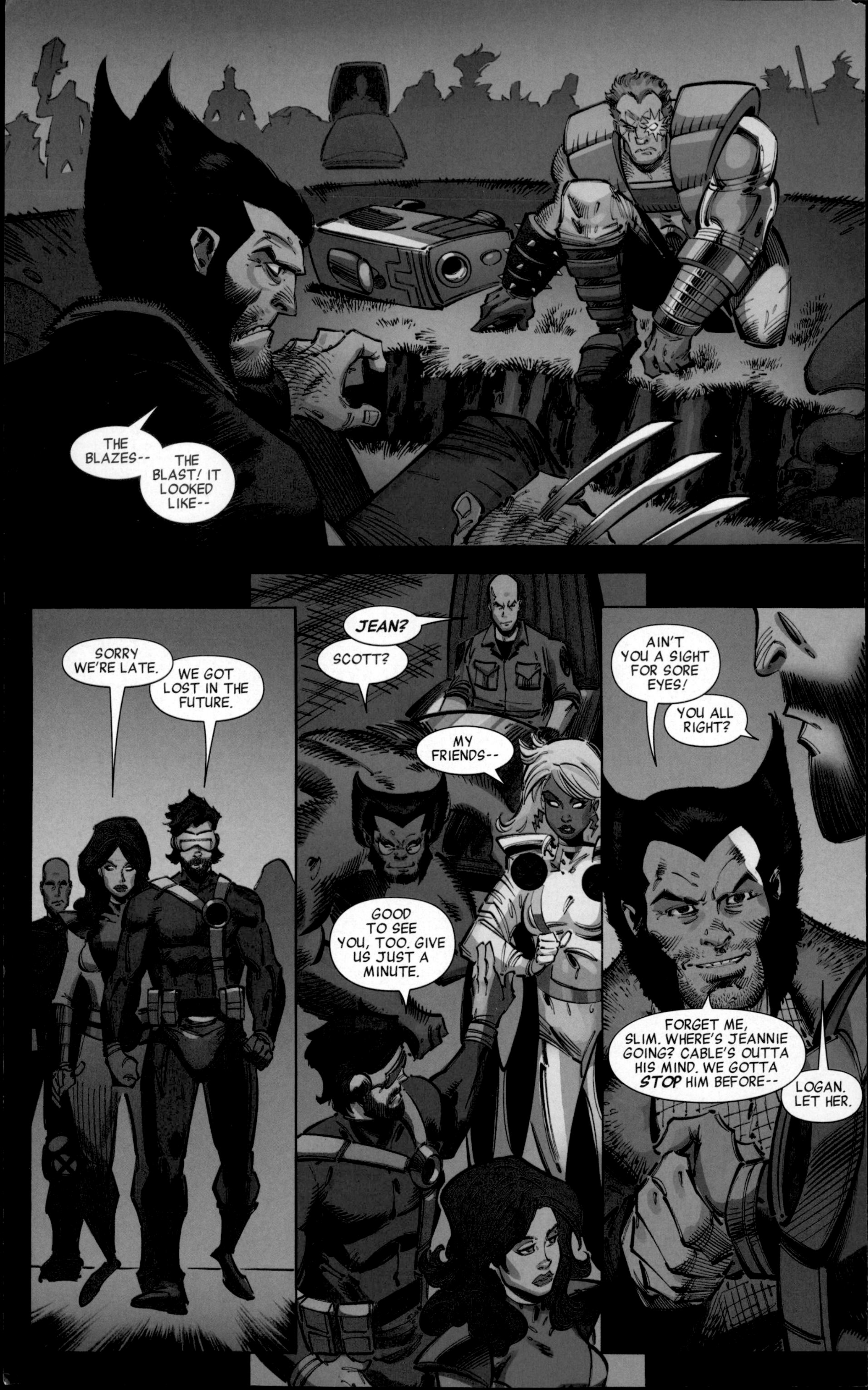
THE BLAZES--
THE BLAST! IT LOOKED LIKE--
SORRY WE'RE LATE.
WE GOT LOST IN THE FUTURE.
JEAN?
SCOTT?
MY FRIENDS--
GOOD TO SEE YOU, TOO. GIVE US JUST A MINUTE.
AIN'T YOU A SIGHT FOR SORE EYES!
YOU ALL RIGHT?
FORGET ME, SLIM. WHERE'S JEANNIE GOING? CABLE'S OUTTA HIS MIND. WE GOTTA STOP HIM BEFORE--
LOGAN. LET HER.

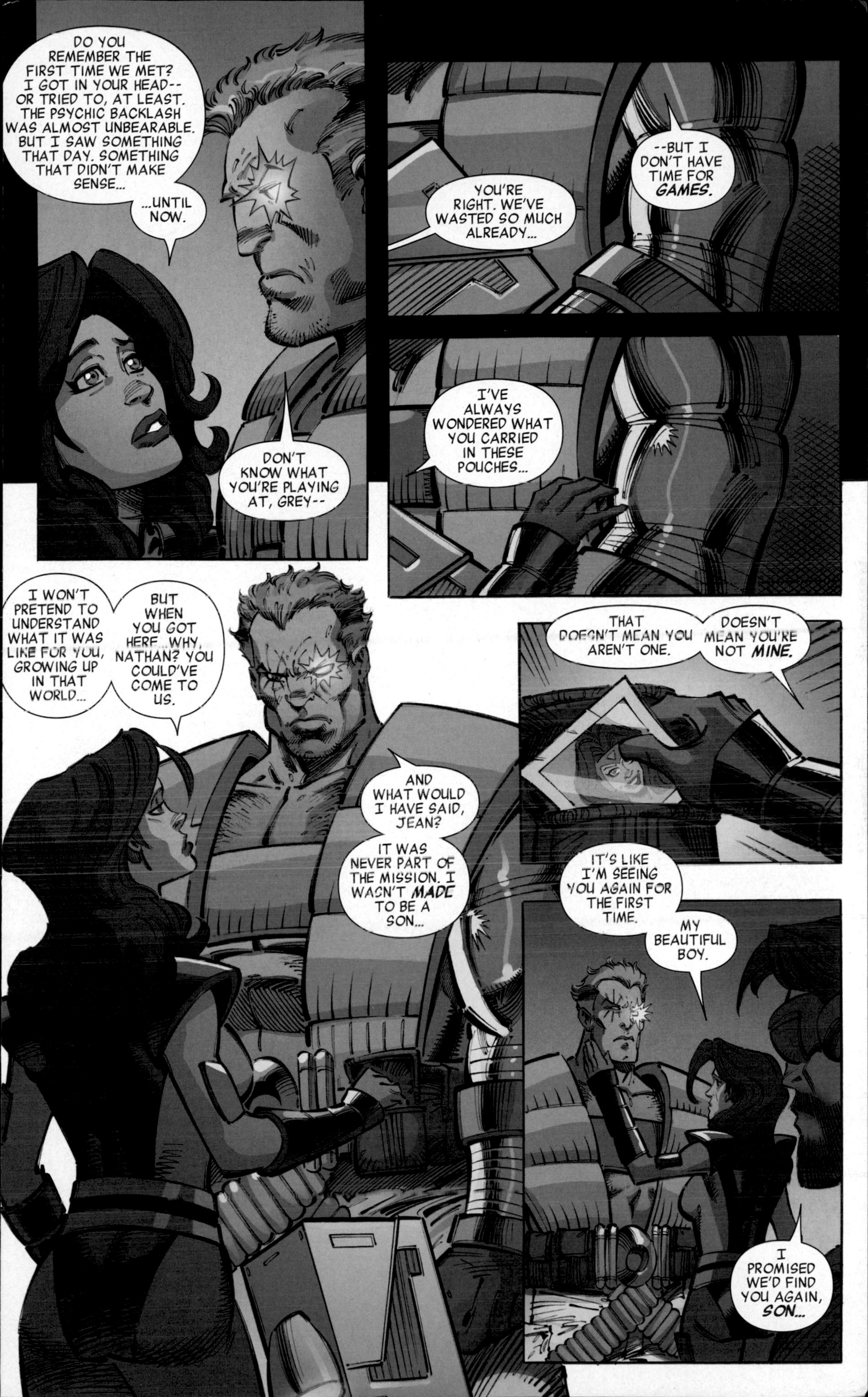
DO YOU REMEMBER THE FIRST TIME WE MET? I GOT IN YOUR HEAD-- OR TRIED TO, AT LEAST. THE PSYCHIC BACKLASH WAS ALMOST UNBEARABLE. BUT I SAW SOMETHING THAT DAY. SOMETHING THAT DIDN'T MAKE SENSE...
...UNTIL NOW.
DON'T KNOW WHAT YOU'RE PLAYING AT, GREY--
--BUT I DON'T HAVE TIME FOR GAMES.
YOU'RE RIGHT. WE'VE WASTED SO MUCH ALREADY...
I'VE ALWAYS WONDERED WHAT YOU CARRIED IN THESE POUCHES...
I WON'T PRETEND TO UNDERSTAND WHAT IT WAS LIKE FOR YOU, GROWING UP IN THAT WORLD...
BUT WHEN YOU GOT HERE...WHY, NATHAN? YOU COULD'VE COME TO US.
AND WHAT WOULD I HAVE SAID, JEAN?
IT WAS NEVER PART OF THE MISSION. I WASN'T MADE TO BE A SON...
THAT DOESN'T MEAN YOU AREN'T ONE.
DOESN'T MEAN YOU'RE NOT MINE.
IT'S LIKE I'M SEEING YOU AGAIN FOR THE FIRST TIME.
MY BEAUTIFUL BOY.
I PROMISED WE'D FIND YOU AGAIN, SON...

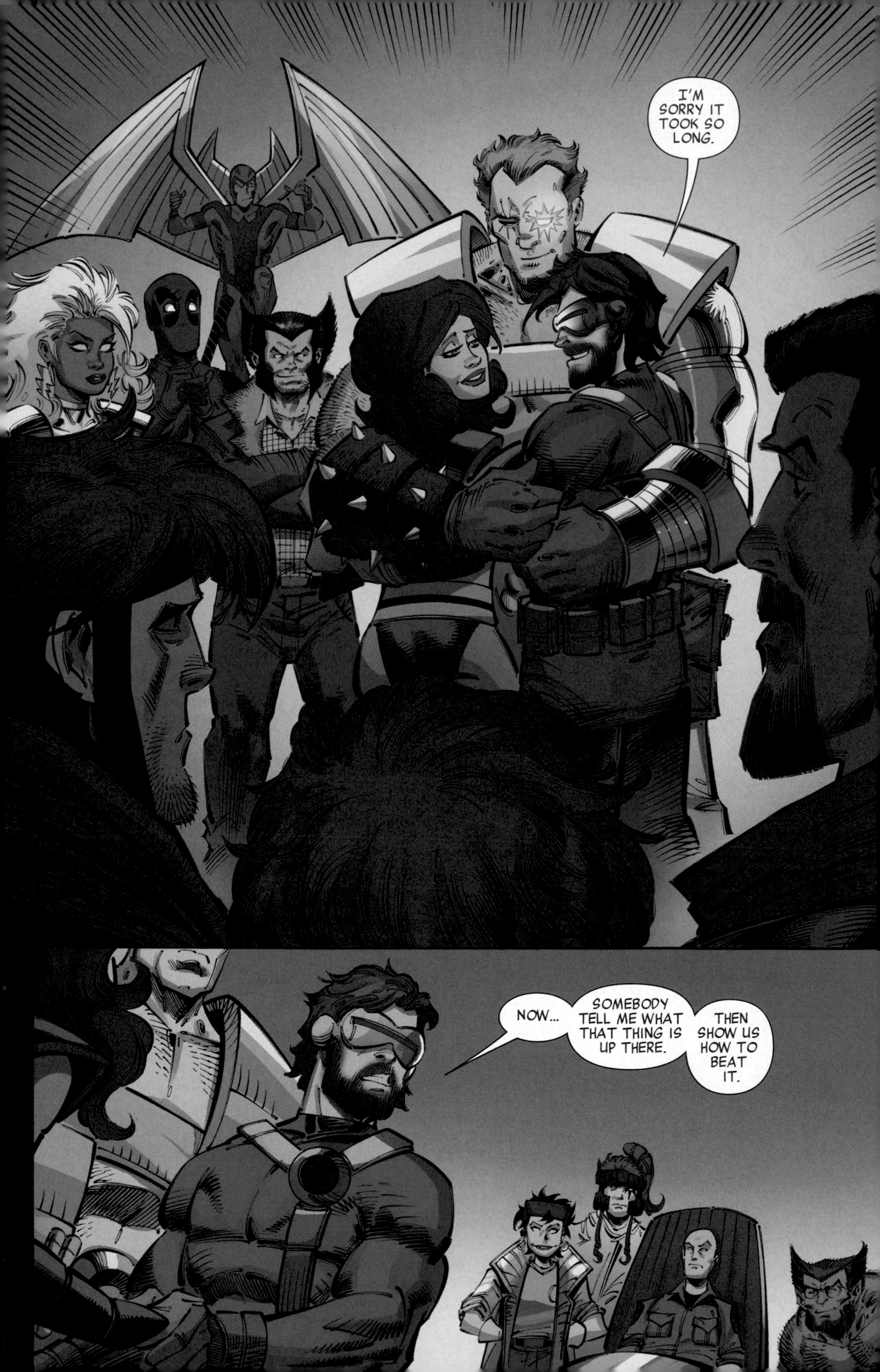
I'M SORRY IT TOOK SO LONG.
NOW...
SOMEBODY TELL ME WHAT THAT THING IS UP THERE.
THEN SHOW US HOW TO BEAT IT.

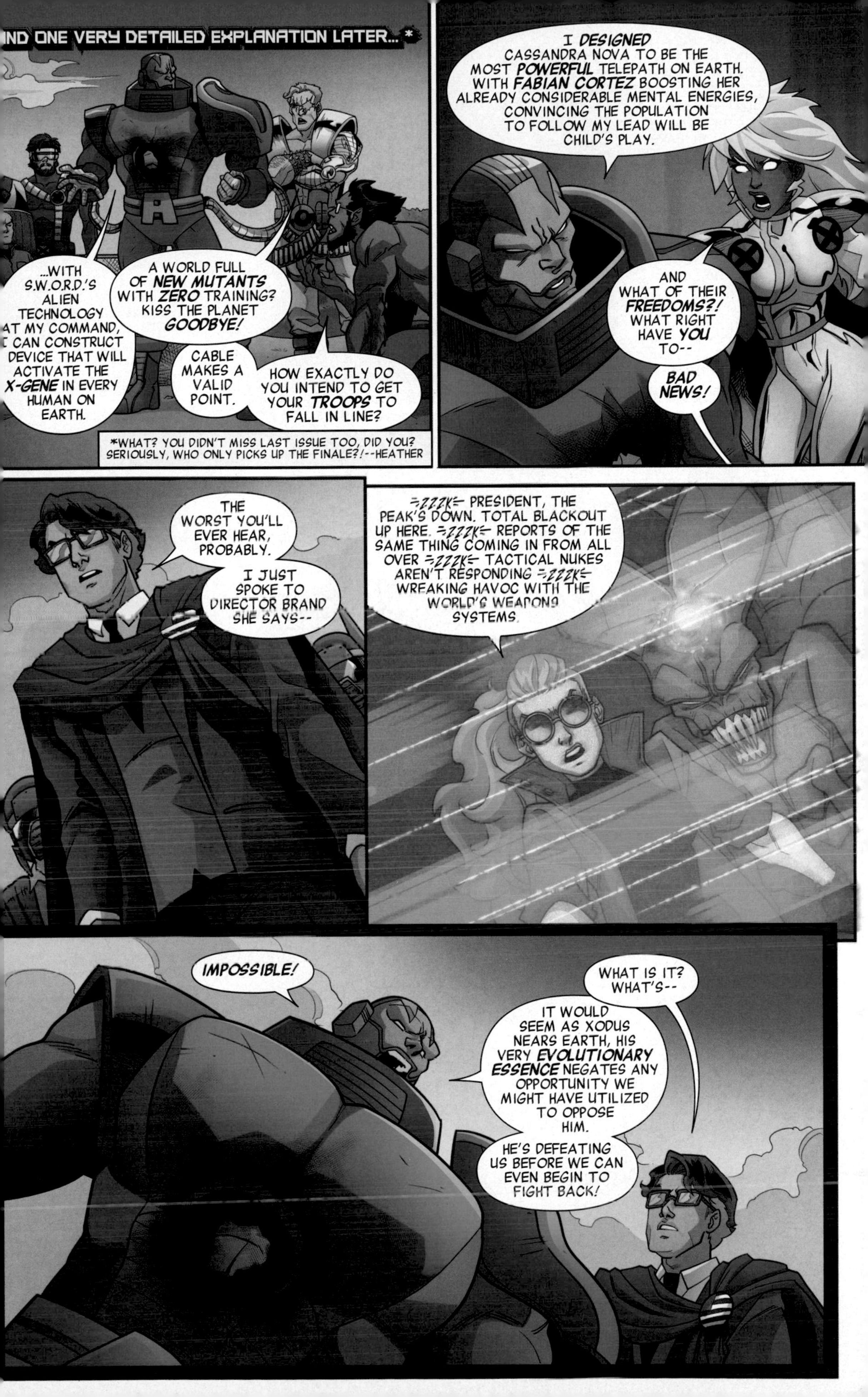

AND ONE VERY DETAILED EXPLANATION LATER... *
...WITH S.W.O.R.D.'S ALIEN TECHNOLOGY AT MY COMMAND, I CAN CONSTRUCT A DEVICE THAT WILL ACTIVATE THE X-GENE IN EVERY HUMAN ON EARTH.
A WORLD FULL OF NEW MUTANTS WITH ZERO TRAINING? KISS THE PLANET GOODBYE!
CABLE MAKES A VALID POINT.
HOW EXACTLY DO YOU INTEND TO GET YOUR TROOPS TO FALL IN LINE?
*WHAT? YOU DIDN'T MISS LAST ISSUE TOO, DID YOU? SERIOUSLY, WHO ONLY PICKS UP THE FINALE?!--HEATHER
I DESIGNED CASSANDRA NOVA TO BE THE MOST POWERFUL TELEPATH ON EARTH. WITH FABIAN CORTEZ BOOSTING HER ALREADY CONSIDERABLE MENTAL ENERGIES, CONVINCING THE POPULATION TO FOLLOW MY LEAD WILL BE CHILD'S PLAY.
AND WHAT OF THEIR FREEDOMS?! WHAT RIGHT HAVE YOU TO--
BAD NEWS!
THE WORST YOU'LL EVER HEAR, PROBABLY.
I JUST SPOKE TO DIRECTOR BRAND SHE SAYS--
=ZZZK= PRESIDENT, THE PEAK'S DOWN. TOTAL BLACKOUT UP HERE. =ZZZK= REPORTS OF THE SAME THING COMING IN FROM ALL OVER =ZZZK= TACTICAL NUKES AREN'T RESPONDING =ZZZK= WREAKING HAVOC WITH THE WORLD'S WEAPONS SYSTEMS.
IMPOSSIBLE!
WHAT IS IT? WHAT'S--
IT WOULD SEEM AS XODUS NEARS EARTH, HIS VERY EVOLUTIONARY ESSENCE NEGATES ANY OPPORTUNITY WE MIGHT HAVE UTILIZED TO OPPOSE HIM.
HE'S DEFEATING US BEFORE WE CAN EVEN BEGIN TO FIGHT BACK!

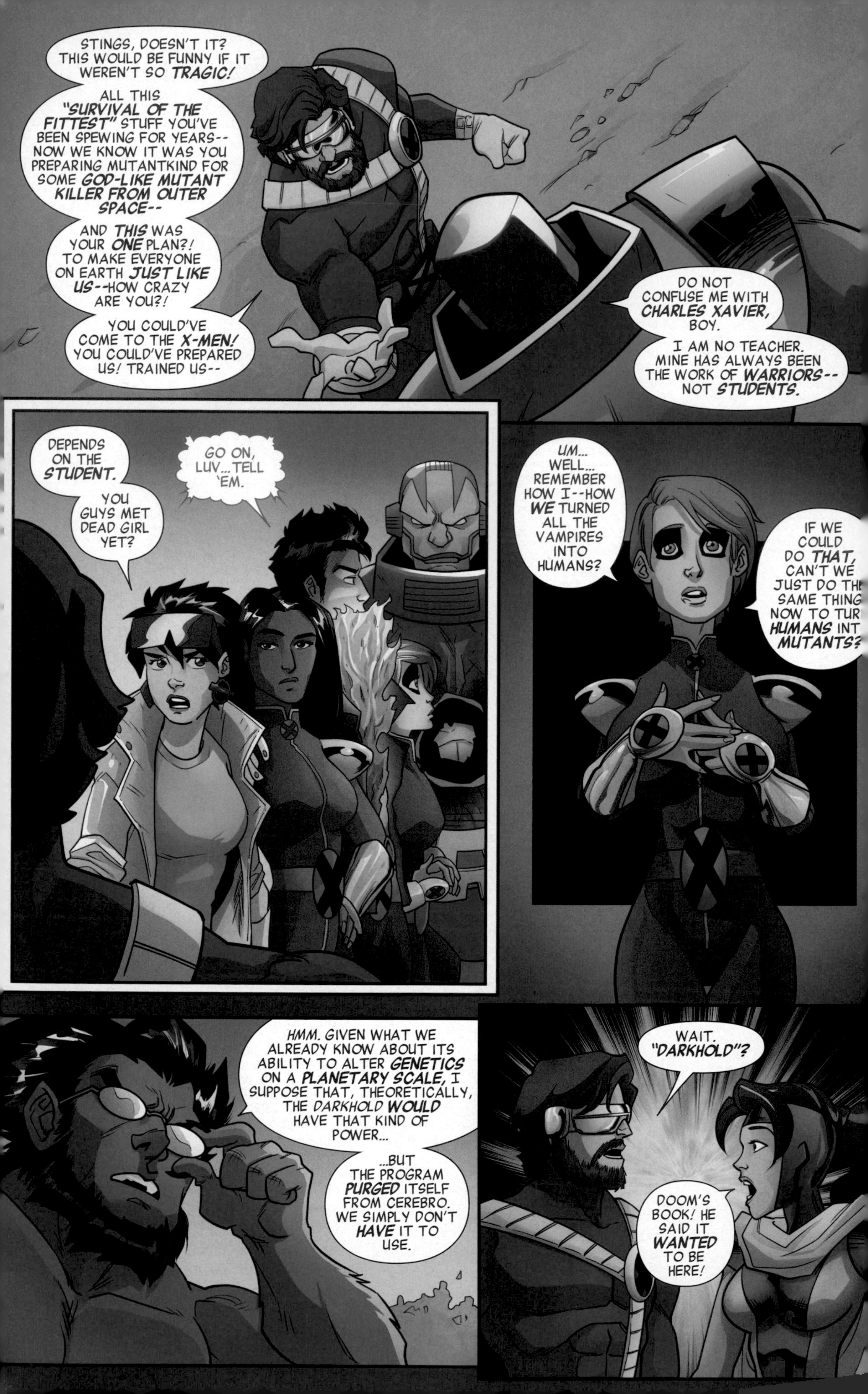

STINGS, DOESN'T IT? THIS WOULD BE FUNNY IF IT WEREN'T SO TRAGIC!
ALL THIS "SURVIVAL OF THE FITTEST" STUFF YOU'VE BEEN SPEWING FOR YEARS-- NOW WE KNOW IT WAS YOU PREPARING MUTANTKIND FOR SOME GOD-LIKE MUTANT KILLER FROM OUTER SPACE--
AND THIS WAS YOUR ONE PLAN?! TO MAKE EVERYONE ON EARTH JUST LIKE US--HOW CRAZY ARE YOU?!
YOU COULD'VE COME TO THE X-MEN! YOU COULD'VE PREPARED US! TRAINED US--
DO NOT CONFUSE ME WITH CHARLES XAVIER, BOY.
I AM NO TEACHER. MINE HAS ALWAYS BEEN THE WORK OF WARRIORS-- NOT STUDENTS.
DEPENDS ON THE STUDENT.
YOU GUYS MET DEAD GIRL YET?
GO ON, LUV...TELL 'EM.
UM... WELL... REMEMBER HOW I--HOW WE TURNED ALL THE VAMPIRES INTO HUMANS?
IF WE COULD DO THAT, CAN'T WE JUST DO THE SAME THING NOW TO TUR HUMANS INT MUTANTS?
HMM. GIVEN WHAT WE ALREADY KNOW ABOUT ITS ABILITY TO ALTER GENETICS ON A PLANETARY SCALE, I SUPPOSE THAT, THEORETICALLY, THE DARKHOLD WOULD HAVE THAT KIND OF POWER...
...BUT THE PROGRAM PURGED ITSELF FROM CEREBRO. WE SIMPLY DON'T HAVE IT TO USE.
WAIT. "DARKHOLD"?
DOOM'S BOOK! HE SAID IT WANTED TO BE HERE!

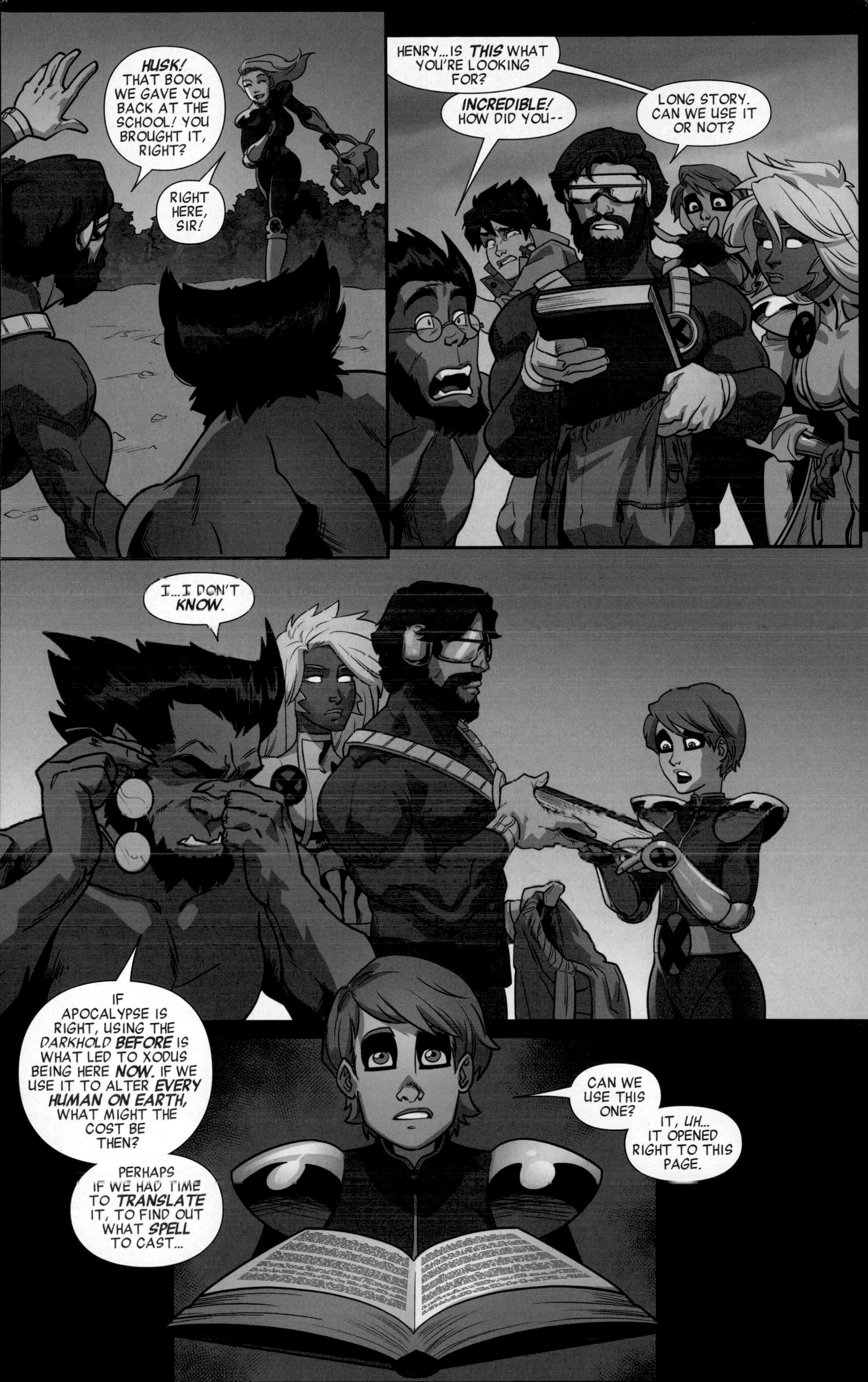
HUSK! THAT BOOK WE GAVE YOU BACK AT THE SCHOOL! YOU BROUGHT IT, RIGHT?
RIGHT HERE, SIR!
HENRY... IS THIS WHAT YOU'RE LOOKING FOR?
INCREDIBLE! HOW DID YOU--
LONG STORY. CAN WE USE IT OR NOT?
I... I DON'T KNOW.
IF APOCALYPSE IS RIGHT, USING THE DARKHOLD BEFORE IS WHAT LED TO XODUS BEING HERE NOW. IF WE USE IT TO ALTER EVERY HUMAN ON EARTH, WHAT MIGHT THE COST BE THEN?
PERHAPS IF WE HAD TIME TO TRANSLATE IT, TO FIND OUT WHAT SPELL TO CAST...
CAN WE USE THIS ONE?
IT, UH... IT OPENED RIGHT TO THIS PAGE.

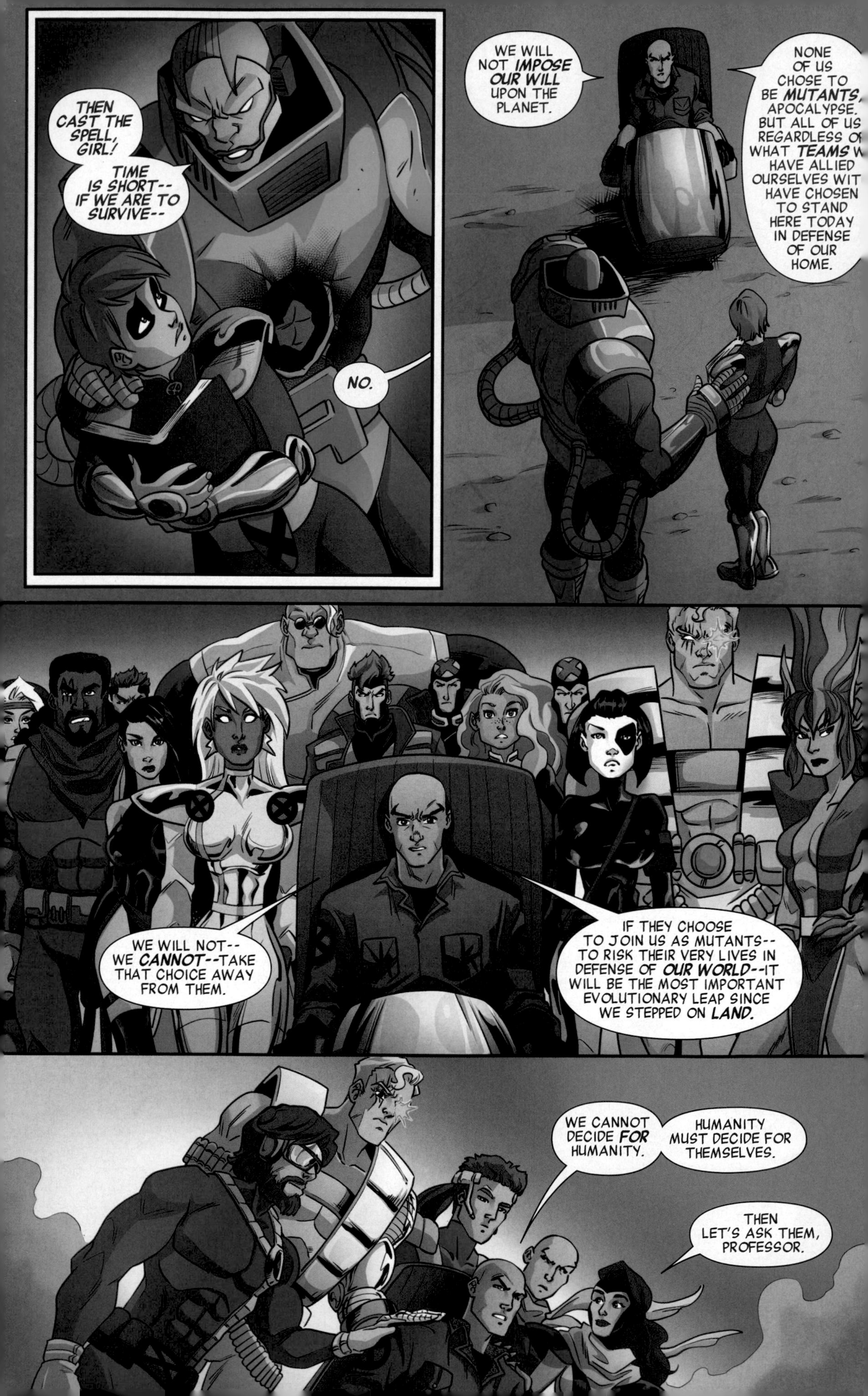

THEN CAST THE SPELL, GIRL!
TIME IS SHORT-- IF WE ARE TO SURVIVE--
NO.
WE WILL NOT IMPOSE OUR WILL UPON THE PLANET.
NONE OF US CHOSE TO BE MUTANTS, APOCALYPSE. BUT ALL OF US REGARDLESS OF WHAT TEAMS WE HAVE ALLIED OURSELVES WITH HAVE CHOSEN TO STAND HERE TODAY IN DEFENSE OF OUR HOME.
WE WILL NOT-- WE CANNOT--TAKE THAT CHOICE AWAY FROM THEM.
IF THEY CHOOSE TO JOIN US AS MUTANTS-- TO RISK THEIR VERY LIVES IN DEFENSE OF OUR WORLD--IT WILL BE THE MOST IMPORTANT EVOLUTIONARY LEAP SINCE WE STEPPED ON LAND.
WE CANNOT DECIDE FOR HUMANITY.
HUMANITY MUST DECIDE FOR THEMSELVES.
THEN LET'S ASK THEM, PROFESSOR.

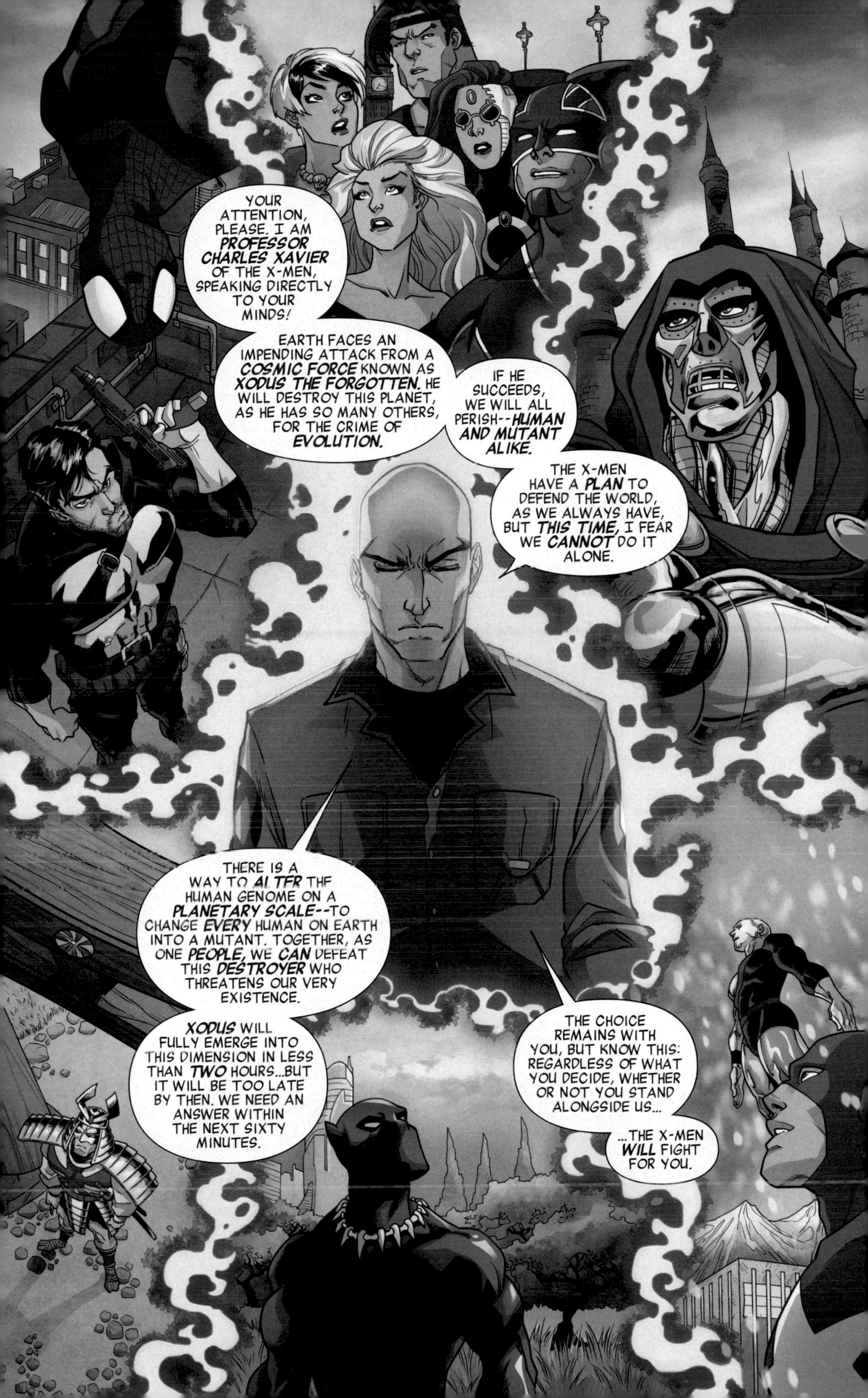
YOUR ATTENTION, PLEASE. I AM PROFESSOR CHARLES XAVIER OF THE X-MEN, SPEAKING DIRECTLY TO YOUR MINDS!
EARTH FACES AN IMPENDING ATTACK FROM A COSMIC FORCE KNOWN AS XODUS THE FORGOTTEN. HE WILL DESTROY THIS PLANET, AS HE HAS SO MANY OTHERS, FOR THE CRIME OF EVOLUTION.
IF HE SUCCEEDS, WE WILL ALL PERISH--HUMAN AND MUTANT ALIKE.
THE X-MEN HAVE A PLAN TO DEFEND THE WORLD, AS WE ALWAYS HAVE, BUT THIS TIME, I FEAR WE CANNOT DO IT ALONE.
THERE IS A WAY TO ALTER THE HUMAN GENOME ON A PLANETARY SCALE--TO CHANGE EVERY HUMAN ON EARTH INTO A MUTANT. TOGETHER, AS ONE PEOPLE, WE CAN DEFEAT THIS DESTROYER WHO THREATENS OUR VERY EXISTENCE.
XODUS WILL FULLY EMERGE INTO THIS DIMENSION IN LESS THAN TWO HOURS...BUT IT WILL BE TOO LATE BY THEN. WE NEED AN ANSWER WITHIN THE NEXT SIXTY MINUTES.
THE CHOICE REMAINS WITH YOU, BUT KNOW THIS: REGARDLESS OF WHAT YOU DECIDE, WHETHER OR NOT YOU STAND ALONGSIDE US...
...THE X-MEN WILL FIGHT FOR YOU.

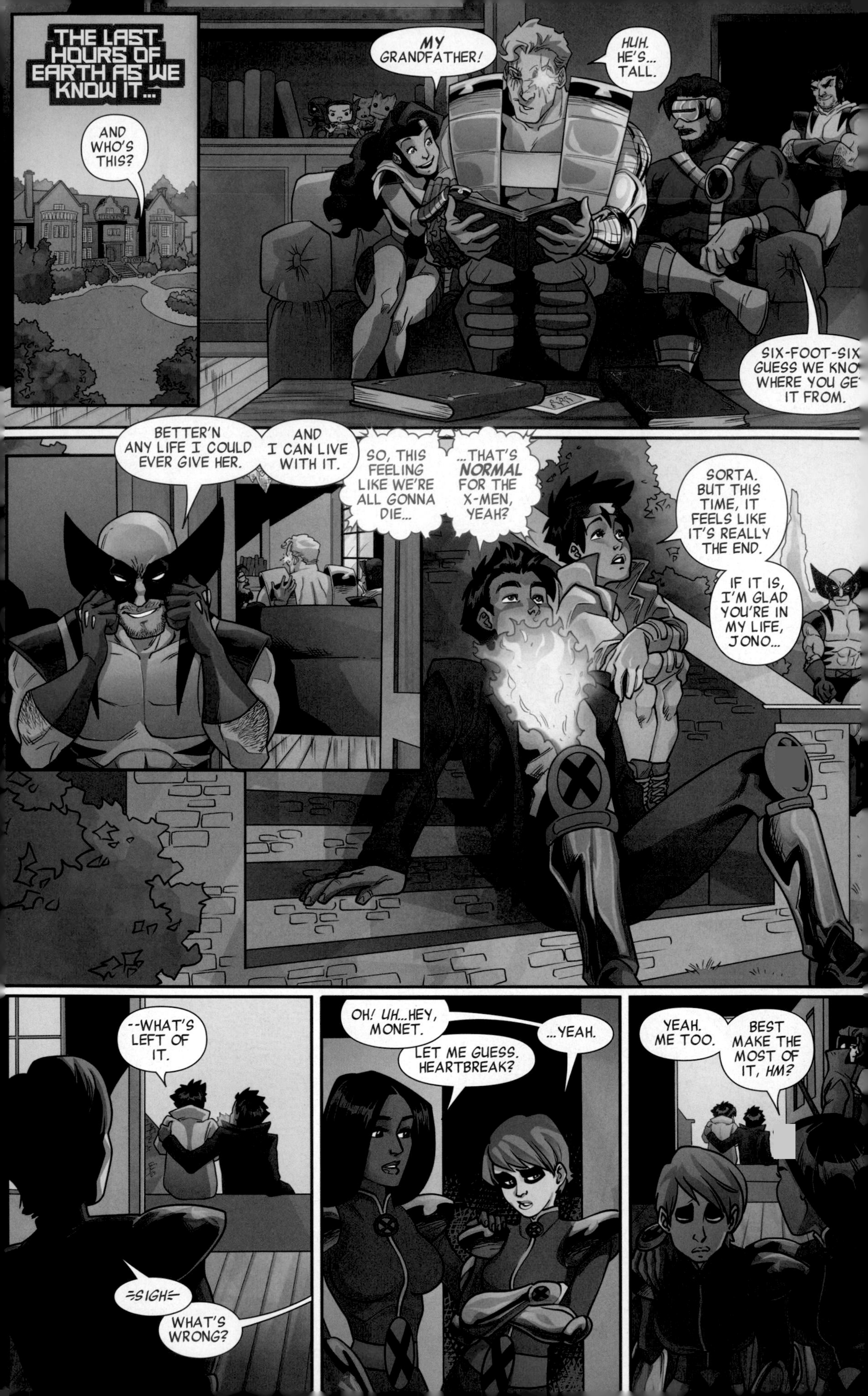
THE LAST HOURS OF EARTH AS WE KNOW IT...
AND WHO'S THIS?
MY GRANDFATHER!
HUH. HE'S... TALL.
SIX-FOOT-SIX. GUESS WE KNOW WHERE YOU GET IT FROM.
BETTER'N ANY LIFE I COULD EVER GIVE HER.
AND I CAN LIVE WITH IT.
SO, THIS FEELING LIKE WE'RE ALL GONNA DIE...
...THAT'S NORMAL FOR THE X-MEN, YEAH?
SORTA. BUT THIS TIME, IT FEELS LIKE IT'S REALLY THE END.
IF IT IS, I'M GLAD YOU'RE IN MY LIFE, JONO...
--WHAT'S LEFT OF IT.
SIGH
WHAT'S WRONG?
OH! UH...HEY, MONET.
LET ME GUESS. HEARTBREAK?
...YEAH.
YEAH. ME TOO.
BEST MAKE THE MOST OF IT, HM?

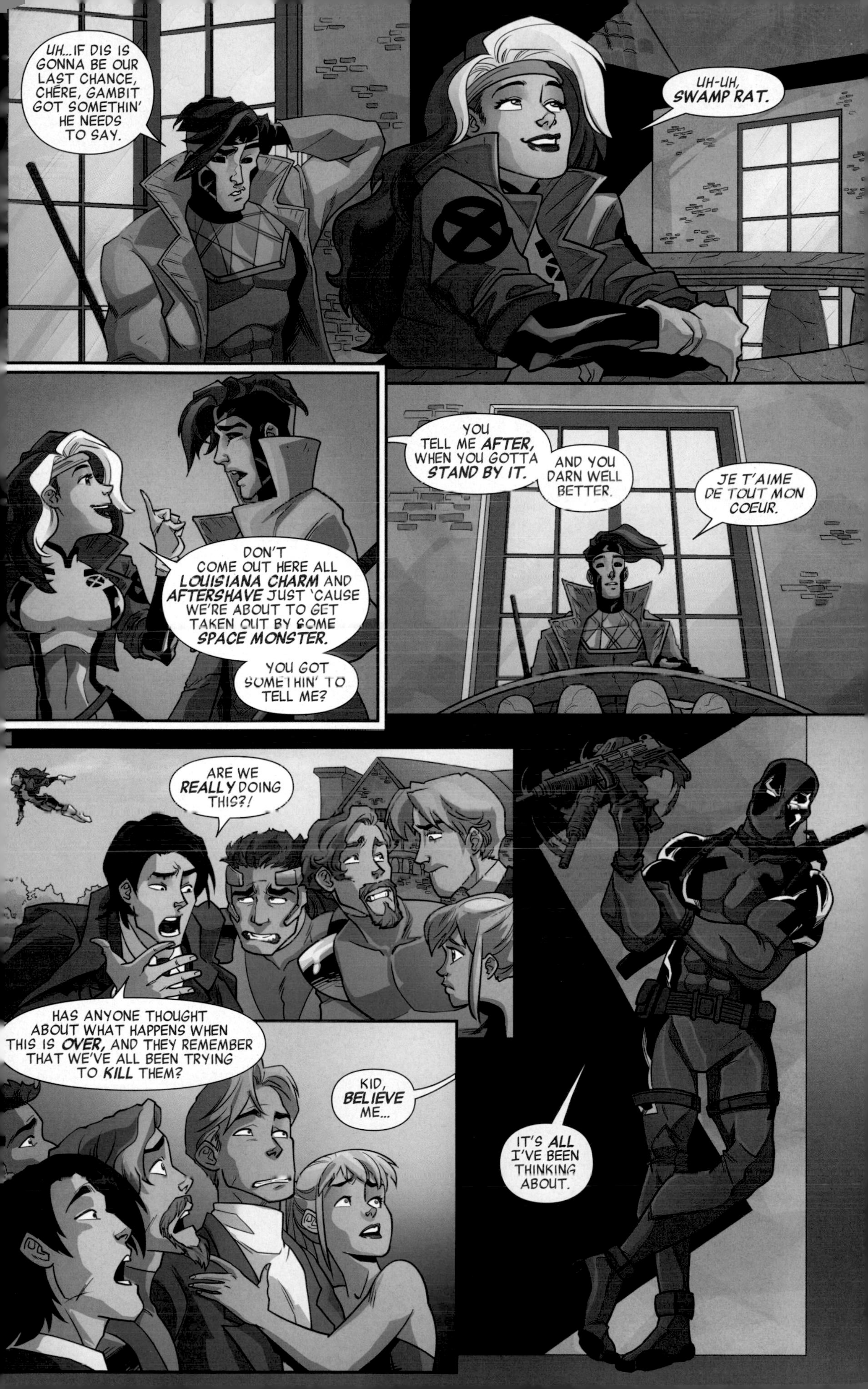
UH...IF DIS IS GONNA BE OUR LAST CHANCE, CHÉRE, GAMBIT GOT SOMETHIN' HE NEEDS TO SAY.
UH-UH, SWAMP RAT.
DON'T COME OUT HERE ALL LOUISIANA CHARM AND AFTERSHAVE JUST 'CAUSE WE'RE ABOUT TO GET TAKEN OUT BY SOME SPACE MONSTER.
YOU GOT SOMETHIN' TO TELL ME?
YOU TELL ME AFTER, WHEN YOU GOTTA STAND BY IT.
AND YOU DARN WELL BETTER.
JE T'AIME DE TOUT MON COEUR.
ARE WE REALLY DOING THIS?!
HAS ANYONE THOUGHT ABOUT WHAT HAPPENS WHEN THIS IS OVER, AND THEY REMEMBER THAT WE'VE ALL BEEN TRYING TO KILL THEM?
KID, BELIEVE ME...
IT'S ALL I'VE BEEN THINKING ABOUT.

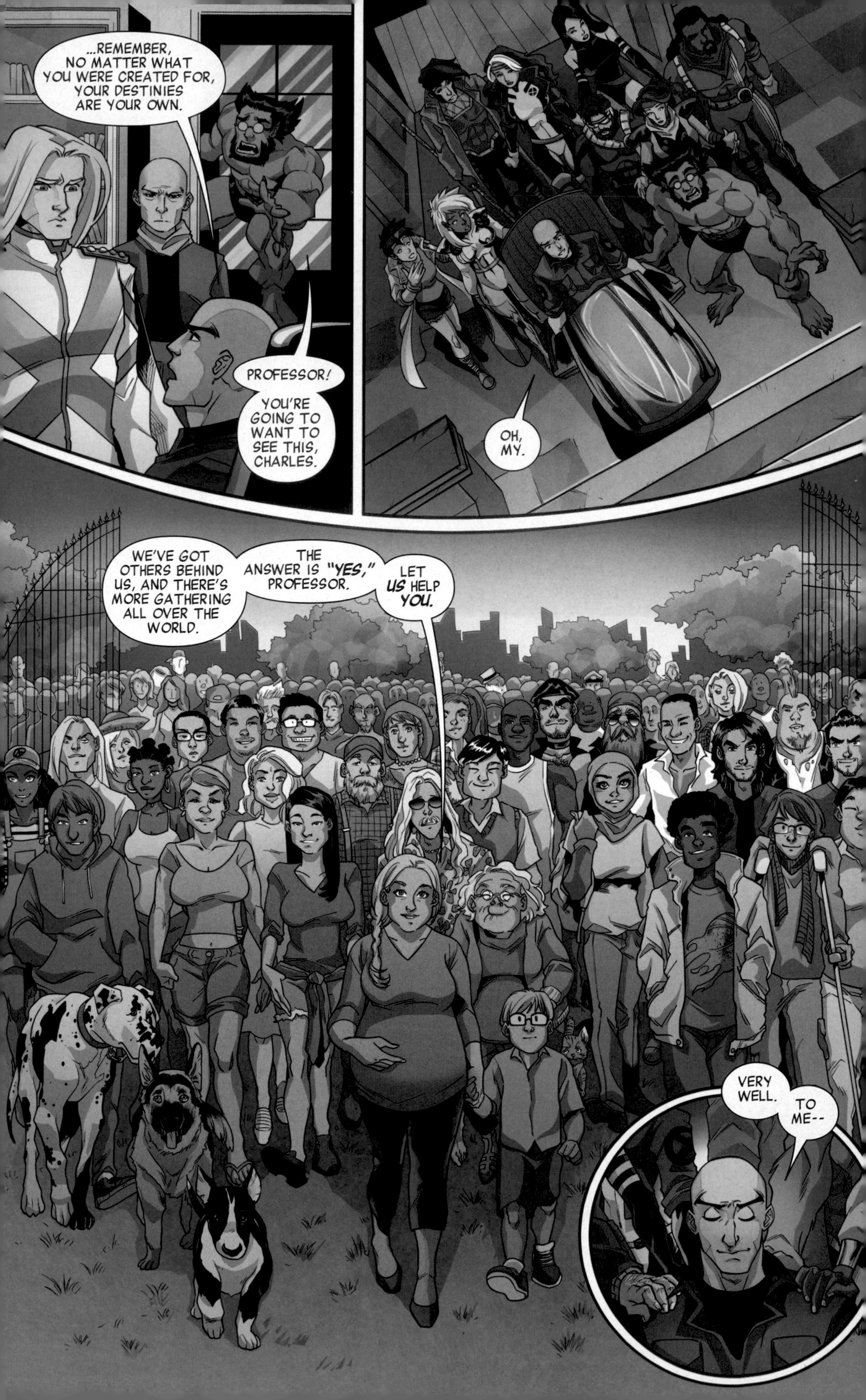
...REMEMBER, NO MATTER WHAT YOU WERE CREATED FOR, YOUR DESTINIES ARE YOUR OWN.
PROFESSOR!
YOU'RE GOING TO WANT TO SEE THIS, CHARLES.
OH, MY.
WE'VE GOT OTHERS BEHIND US, AND THERE'S MORE GATHERING ALL OVER THE WORLD.
THE ANSWER IS "YES," PROFESSOR.
LET US HELP YOU.
VERY WELL.
TO ME--

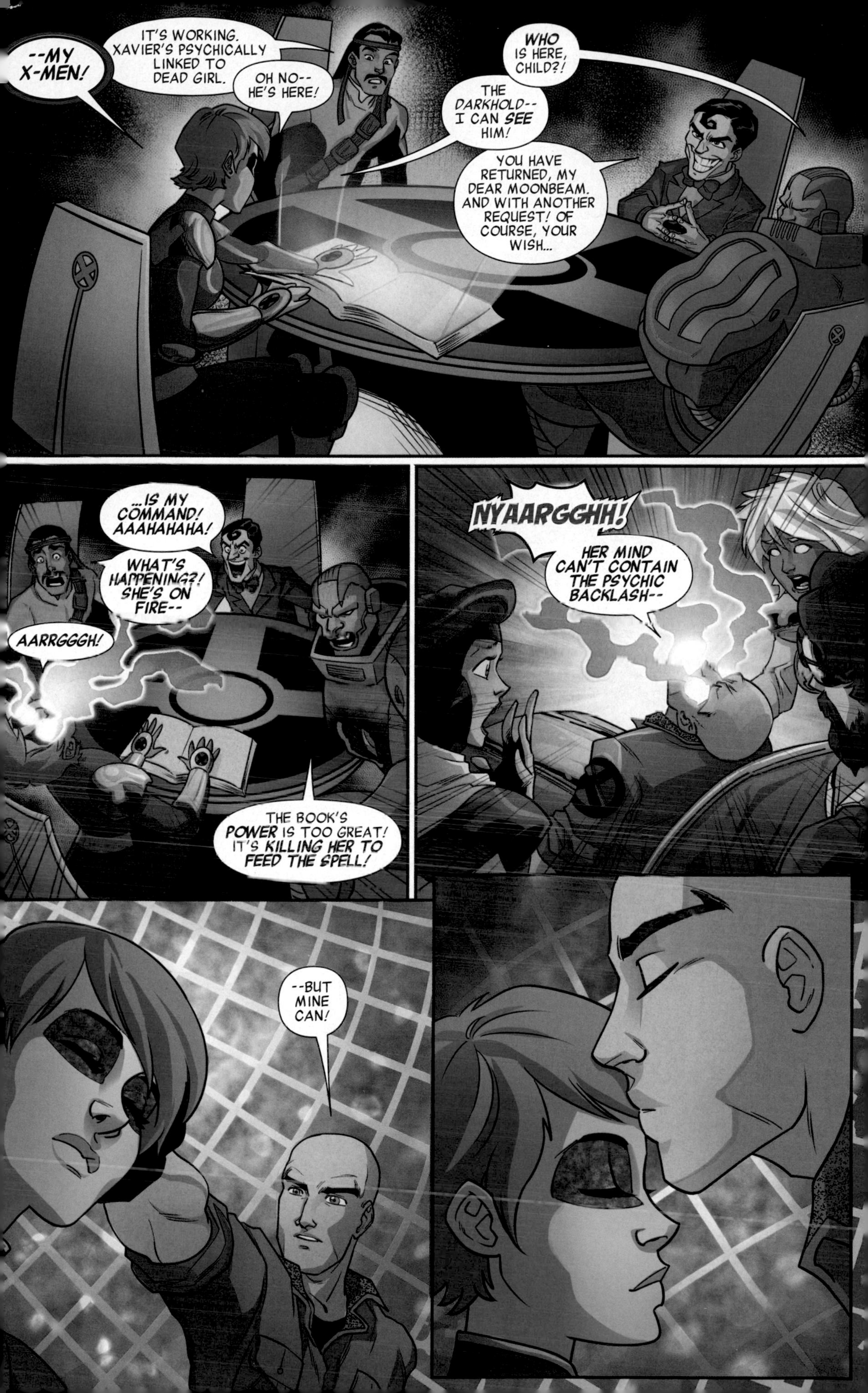
--MY X-MEN!
IT'S WORKING. XAVIER'S PSYCHICALLY LINKED TO DEAD GIRL.
OH NO-- HE'S HERE!
WHO IS HERE, CHILD?!
THE DARKHOLD-- I CAN SEE HIM!
YOU HAVE RETURNED, MY DEAR MOONBEAM. AND WITH ANOTHER REQUEST! OF COURSE, YOUR WISH...
...IS MY COMMAND! AAAHAHAHA!
WHAT'S HAPPENING?! SHE'S ON FIRE--
AARRGGGH!
THE BOOK'S POWER IS TOO GREAT! IT'S KILLING HER TO FEED THE SPELL!
NYAARGGHH!
HER MIND CAN'T CONTAIN THE PSYCHIC BACKLASH--
--BUT MINE CAN!

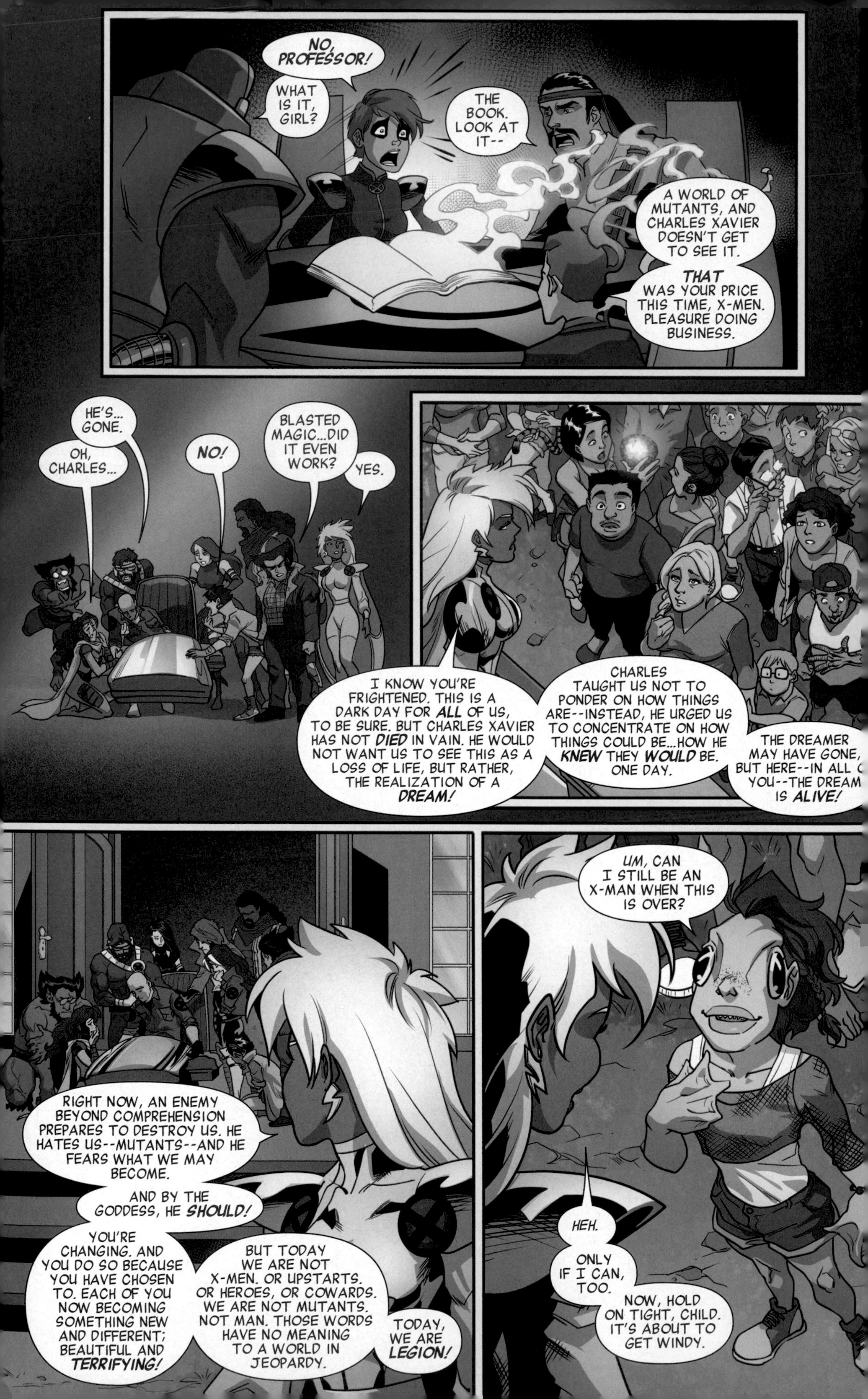
NO, PROFESSOR!
WHAT IS IT, GIRL?
THE BOOK. LOOK AT IT--
A WORLD OF MUTANTS, AND CHARLES XAVIER DOESN'T GET TO SEE IT.
THAT WAS YOUR PRICE THIS TIME, X-MEN. PLEASURE DOING BUSINESS.
HE'S... GONE.
OH, CHARLES...
NO!
BLASTED MAGIC...DID IT EVEN WORK?
YES.
I KNOW YOU'RE FRIGHTENED. THIS IS A DARK DAY FOR ALL OF US, TO BE SURE. BUT CHARLES XAVIER HAS NOT DIED IN VAIN. HE WOULD NOT WANT US TO SEE THIS AS A LOSS OF LIFE, BUT RATHER, THE REALIZATION OF A DREAM!
CHARLES TAUGHT US NOT TO PONDER ON HOW THINGS ARE--INSTEAD, HE URGED US TO CONCENTRATE ON HOW THINGS COULD BE...HOW HE KNEW THEY WOULD BE. ONE DAY.
THE DREAMER MAY HAVE GONE, BUT HERE--IN ALL O YOU--THE DREAM IS ALIVE!
RIGHT NOW, AN ENEMY BEYOND COMPREHENSION PREPARES TO DESTROY US. HE HATES US--MUTANTS--AND HE FEARS WHAT WE MAY BECOME.
AND BY THE GODDESS, HE SHOULD!
YOU'RE CHANGING. AND YOU DO SO BECAUSE YOU HAVE CHOSEN TO. EACH OF YOU NOW BECOMING SOMETHING NEW AND DIFFERENT; BEAUTIFUL AND TERRIFYING!
BUT TODAY WE ARE NOT X-MEN. OR UPSTARTS. OR HEROES, OR COWARDS. WE ARE NOT MUTANTS. NOT MAN. THOSE WORDS HAVE NO MEANING TO A WORLD IN JEOPARDY.
TODAY, WE ARE LEGION!
UM, CAN I STILL BE AN X-MAN WHEN THIS IS OVER?
HEH.
ONLY IF I CAN, TOO.
NOW, HOLD ON TIGHT, CHILD. IT'S ABOUT TO GET WINDY.

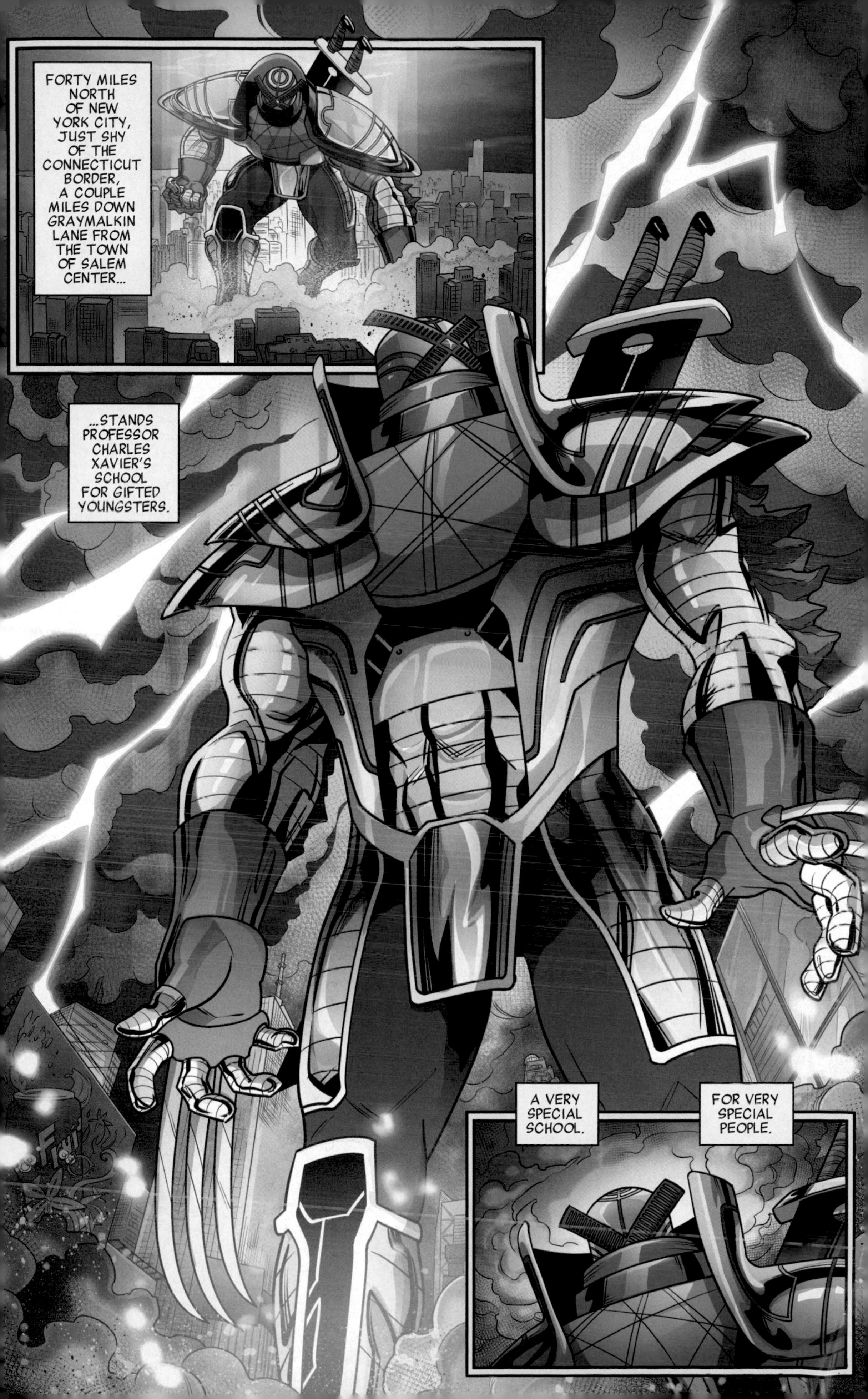
FORTY MILES NORTH OF NEW YORK CITY, JUST SHY OF THE CONNECTICUT BORDER, A COUPLE MILES DOWN GRAYMALKIN LANE FROM THE TOWN OF SALEM CENTER...
...STANDS PROFESSOR CHARLES XAVIER'S SCHOOL FOR GIFTED YOUNGSTERS.
A VERY SPECIAL SCHOOL.
FOR VERY SPECIAL PEOPLE.

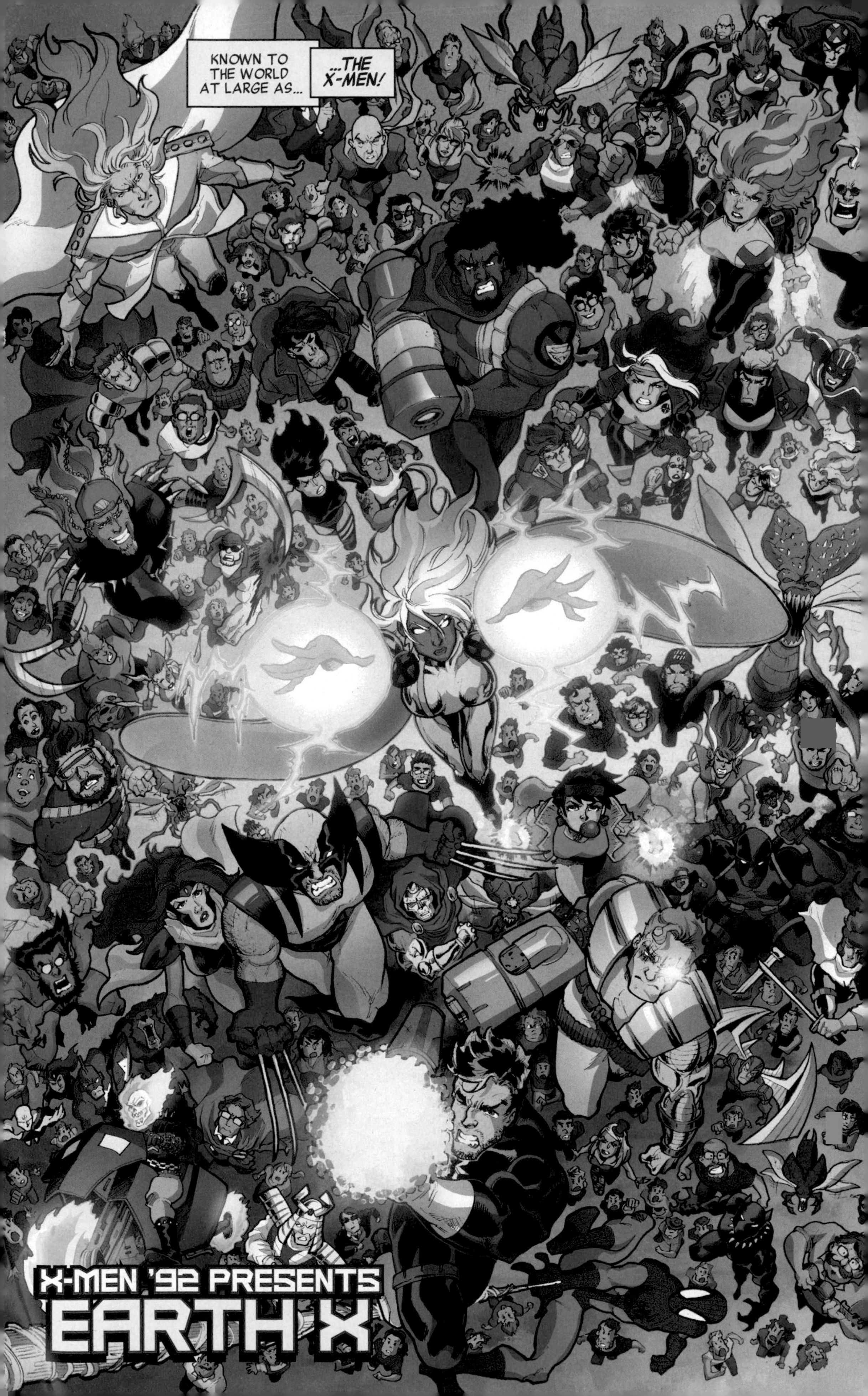

KNOWN TO THE WORLD AT LARGE AS...
...THE X-MEN!
X-MEN '92 PRESENTS
EARTH X